Praise for Black On ...
from across the advertising industry

"One of the earliest graduates of 4A's MAIP (Multicultural Advertising Intern Program), Mark shares his incredible journey through a storied advertising career. It's a reminder of the reason that MAIP was created nearly 50 years ago. Mark's experiences - shared through reflections via challenges and triumphs - highlight ways that we recognize the need to continue our work and support our 4,000+ community of MAIP alumni in the advertising and marketing industry."

4A's Foundation
American Association of Advertising Agencies

Despite the challenges, sometimes compromising colleagues and chaos of the 1970's world of advertising, Mark Robinson persevered and carved out a remarkable career as an African-American Ad Man, which is so adeptly demonstrated in his book **"Black on Madison Avenue."**

Through the pages of **"Black on Madison Avenue"** Mark tells the story of being the only one, maintaining one's moral compass, rising up the ranks and then moving on to one's own "shop" while also giving the reader an ad industry history coupled with a Black History Civil Rights lesson. An honest and inspiring read...

Constance Cannon Frazier
Principal, Cardinal Change Consulting
Former COO, American Advertising Federation

Finally, a book that advocates for diversity, equity and inclusion in advertising. Robinson makes the case for representation personal yet universal. As an educator, I will be assigning this book and am thrilled to have a resource written by an esteemed pro who embodies all that is good in the profession.

Robin Landa
Distinguished Professor, Michael Graves
College at Kean University

Mark Robinson has not written the typical Madison Avenue memoir -- thank goodness! **'Black on Madison Avenue'** is enlightening, written with tough love, the toughest love this side of a Marine drill sergeant. Mark is frank in his descriptions of the shortcomings of the advertising industry he has worked in for decades and offers concrete steps to take so that it no longer resembles what he calls a 'luminescent snowstorm.' Very much worth reading.

Stuart Elliott
Former Advertising Columnist, The New York Times

I've spent my professional career chronicling the African American experience in advertising. We've long needed more stories from that group of blacks who've driven the industry forward, and Mark Robinson has stepped into that gap and offered us his story. If you've any interest in advertising, business, race, client relationships, or just doing work, pick this book up.

Mark's book is filled with insight, surprises, and stories that will sometimes make you laugh out loud and other times shake your head in frustration. The time you spend with Mark won't be wasted, and you'll be glad you've added his book to your library.

JASON P. CHAMBERS, Ph.D.
Author, Associate Dean for DEI / Associate Professor, Advertising

Mark sharply illuminates the experiences of Black professionals in the advertising industry. Black creativity, excellence and innovation shine brightly. Entertaining, realistic, optimistic, and challenging, in all the right ways, **Black on Madison Avenue** *imparts timeless lessons that will leave you wanting more.*

Renetta E. McCann
Advertising Hall of Fame, Class of 2023

I bloody love this book.

Cindy Gallop
Former Chair, BBH / "The Michael Bay of Business"

Part autobiography, part history lesson, part cautionary tale. This unpredictable and vivid journey is a rare peek behind the Black curtain. It's densely packed with stories of an industry that at once accepted and rejected the author's talents for reasons most obvious to him and those who look like him and is, at its core, the story of all Black men and women who fell in love with an industry that rarely loved them back.

Danny Robinson
Chief Creative Officer, The Martin Agency

BLACK

ON

MADISON

AVENUE

MARK S. ROBINSON

Black On Madison Avenue

© 2023 by **Mark S. Robinson**

All rights reserved, including the right of reproduction, in whole or in part, in any form or by any means, electronic or mechanical, including photocopying, recording or any other information storage and retrieval system without the written permission of the author.

For additional information regarding bulk purchases, or author booking engagements, go to www.blackonmadisonavenue.com

FIRST EDITION

Alliance Books

ISBN:
Hardcover: 978-1-7366215-3-0
Paperback: 978-1-7366215-4-7
EPUB/Ebook: 978-1-7366215-5-4

Cover Design by 100Covers.com
Interior Design by FormattedBooks.com

Also by Mark Robinson

Place of Privilege
Young, Black and in an unexpected place of privilege
by Mark Robinson & Raymond Smaltz III

Dedication

To Laura

You are and always will be the miracle that heals my heart.

Author's Note

The stories I share in this book are based primarily on my own personal recollections and therefore the details of these stories are "as I remembered them" or in some cases "as I failed to remember them." After leaving one job or another, it was not my habit or practice to take files or documents with me. My memory is all I have. In the likelihood that I have gotten some details wrong, I say, "You're probably right and I apologize."

In a number of instances, I have omitted the names of individuals from the stories I share. This is an attempt to preserve and protect their privacy. If I mention a name in a story, it is meant to pay that person a sincere compliment and no insult, slander or libel is intended. In many cases, it would simply be impossible to tell the story without naming names.

This book is not intended to be gossip or a tell-all. It is simply a memoir of a life lived as an African American professional in the advertising agency business.

Contents

Preface

"Then go write it."

Everything began when I sent an email to Judann Pollack, the executive editor of Advertising Age, the industry's official journal. It was like a classic Rube Goldberg contraption set in motion, with each new step crazier than the one before. I had four short stories that I had written about various events from different stages of my advertising career. They were—at least, I hoped—interesting enough to share. I'm a Black man who has worked at Madison Avenue for over 40 years. I have stories that no one else can tell. That is not exaggeration or hype. It's just an unsettling reality, a sad and damning indictment of the advertising industry. So, I sent them to Judann and suggested that Ad Age feature one story per week for four weeks. I received an immediate response from Judann (Judy).

"Are these taken from a book? They feel like chapters from a book," she wrote in her email. She praised the stories and my writing but said that the magazine rarely ran series pieces. She suggested that I should consider merging some of the disparate story elements.

Eager to see my work in Ad Age (although I have been an Op Ed and letters contributor in the past), I took a stab at merging the stories. This was not easy, because there are significant narrative leaps (and time jumps) between stories, but I did my best to make it work. It didn't work. Judy wrote back to me, explaining that the piece was simply too long for the magazine. It also lacked context for the reader. What was the source of this story? Who was I? Why was I writing this?

Actually, there was a context or background to all of this. I had recently finished writing another book. A different book that had nothing to do with advertising, but as I was writing it, these other stories emerged with an energy and momentum all their own, like a voice that kept interrupting a prior conversation. I was able to set them to the side for as long as the practical demands of my first book required it. But once it was done, that voice insisted on having its say.

It seemed like a good idea initially, getting those four stories into the magazine. But it simply wasn't taking flight. And then Judy wrote me another email. "I'm wondering if you might be interested in doing the Ad Lib Podcast with me next week." Ad Lib was Judy's weekly podcast where she interviewed industry leaders and luminaries; the very important of the very big. Ad Lib was the kind of prestige exposure that PR professionals dream of getting for their clients. And it was being offered to me.

Of course, I said yes. I have never shied away from the opportunity to hear myself talk.

And so, when Judann introduced me to her podcast listeners, she said she would like me to share some of the stories from my book, "Black On Madison Avenue." But wait. I had not written that book. Not yet. "Black On Madison Avenue" was the title I had given to the set of four stories. There was no book. But we were on the air, and the last thing that I was going to do was correct her mid-interview. So, we just kept going, and I shared some of the stories. For an hour or so, we had a really terrific exchange.

Again, for the record, there was no book.

But as soon as the podcast hit the internet, I found myself having to explain to half the people I knew that this book did not exist. My wife, son, daughter, and brother all asked me how I could have written this book, and they didn't know. One of my closest friends was genuinely hurt that I hadn't told him about the book. Judy sent me an email saying listeners wanted to know where they could purchase the book. And all the while, I'm thinking that most writers would give their right arm for this kind of book launch publicity.

When I explained to everyone that there was no book, the response was universally the same; "Then go write it." So, here we are.

Black On Madison Avenue explains how—and why—I got into this business. And I will share some of the adventures I have had over the past 44 years. Yes, adventures. Have _you_ ever gotten into a shouting match with a Venezuelan Army general in the middle of a military coup? I have. But I also would like to give readers a sense of what it's like to be a Black professional in the advertising industry, because there really aren't that many of us. Not nearly as many as there should be. For an industry that professes to be the vanguard of creativity, popular culture and forward thinking, advertising is one of the most un-diverse white-collar professions in America.

In New York City, according to the 2020 U.S. Census, minorities (Blacks, Hispanics, Asians) represent roughly 66.5% of the adult work-force. At Madison Avenue ad agencies, however, based on data from the Bureau of Labor Statistics, minorities represent only 28.6% of all employees. **That's a gap of almost 38 points.**

If you were to count only white-collar agency jobs (_excluding secre-taries, mail room and office services from the group_), the percentage of ad agency minority employment drops to 27.1%. **That's a gap of 39.4 points.**

That seems fairly nasty, but how bad is it? According to the Bureau of Labor Statistics in Washington, **advertising agencies rank 336th out of 351 occupations for minority representation in management** (_i.e., VP and above_). Let's take a moment to allow that statistic to sink in. 336th out of 351 occupations. You truly have to wonder what ranked 337th, and does it involve wearing sheets?

I have been in the advertising agency business for 44 years. I have worked for several outstanding agencies on both the mainstream and multicultural side of the business. I have worked for some of the most respected, most sophisticated and most demanding packaged goods and service clients in the world, including Johnson & Johnson, Bristol Myers, Kraft Foods, Unilever, HBO, Coors Brewing Company, the U.S. Army and Diageo. I have helped to develop and launch seven new prod-uct brands, all successful, most leaders in their categories. Seven! (_How many people can match that record?_) I have started businesses, run ad agencies, run advertising training programs and lectured to both cor-porate and college audiences across the United States. And what does my experience buy me?

At mainstream agencies, it buys me absolutely nothing. As far as they are concerned I have been effectively out of the business since I left Grey Advertising in 1990. Working for a minority-owned advertising agency, no matter what your experience or credentials might be, does not mean squat to people who work for mainstream agencies. You might as well have been collecting unemployment checks or sitting in a hammock on the beach in the Caribbean. Mainstream agencies do not recognize the value of multicultural agencies or the work they do. A white advertising executive working for a relatively unknown Midwest agency with local and regional clients is more likely to be offered a senior management position at a New York ad agency than I am. That's why I started my own company. It became overwhelmingly apparent that my experience, my expertise and my accomplishments meant absolutely nothing to mainstream ad agencies and I could not rely upon them for meaningful employment.

It should come as no surprise to anyone that there are very few African American advertising professionals willing to come forward and speak on the record about their experiences at New York advertising agencies. We all have to pay the rent or the mortgage. We all have to feed ourselves—or more importantly—our children. We all have to survive in this business. It is hard enough for Black people to get a job in this business when you keep your mouth shut and go along. It is damn near impossible to remain gainfully employed when you speak up and start saying uncomfortable truths.

Since I work directly for my own clients, I do not rely upon any agency for my income. I am not hoping to be hired by an agency. But I have no illusion that being self-employed makes me somehow bulletproof. Speaking up and speaking out is likely to create enemies for me. I am likely to be attacked in ways that I cannot begin to anticipate or protect myself from. I may be doing irreparable damage to my livelihood. My hope always is to make enough new friends to balance out the new enemies.

Ultimately, however, my stake in this is not about risk or benefit. It's about self respect. I have given my entire adult professional life to this business. Advertising is not just what I do. It is a part of who I am. And if I wish to take some pride in what I do and who I am, I must take responsibility for addressing what's wrong with the advertising agency business and try to be a part of the solution.

Foreword

by Cindy Gallop

I moved to New York from London in 1998 to start up Bartle Bogle Hegarty's US office. In the twenty-five years since, I've given many interviews to our industry media. Especially in the early years of BBH New York, but regularly since, as reporters ask me about my career, one question recurs time and again, asked in various forms: "What for you was the biggest difference between the UK and US advertising industry?" "What most surprised you about the US ad industry versus the UK?"

My answer has always been the same.

The biggest surprise to me about the US ad industry, was that there were market divisions that did not exist in the UK. There was a thing called 'general market', and there were 'general market agencies', and then there were other population segments, and there were specific agencies for those segments—which is how I realized very quickly that 'general market' meant 'white'. While 'urban market'—another term I'd never come across before - was code for 'Black'. There were 'Hispanic agencies'. 'Asian-American agencies.'

My reaction was, "What on earth?!! EVERYBODY is 'general market'!" For years I've said that I find that division ridiculous. And Mark Robinson's excellent memoir proves the point.

I'm going to be frank: I love Mark's book. I love the way Mark celebrates everything those of us who are passionate about our industry, appreciate about it. And I love how Mark demonstrates how his talents, creativity and skills, combined with grit, perseverance and resilience overcame the shocking and shameful racism that he encountered at every turn. But at the same time, reading this book brought home to me how much our industry has excluded, and therefore suffered from the lack of, the exceptional diverse contributions that could have completely reinvented it. I couldn't stop thinking about that all the way through, however much I enjoyed Mark's highly entertaining stories (and there are many).

So I want everyone in our industry, and everyone who comes into our industry, to read this book—to understand what we've been missing out on, and to make sure we never miss out on it again.

Cindy Gallop
"The Michael Bay of Business"

CHAPTER ONE

Before We Were Consumers

From the very beginning, Black people were always in advertising. The only difference—the whole difference—was that the advertising was not created by us, and it was not created for us.

Advertisements in colonial America were most frequently announcements of goods on hand, but notably in this early period, goods on hand included notices of slave sales or appeals for the capture of escaped slaves. This persisted until the end of the Civil War. In fact, the popularity and diversity of slave ads during this time is quite remarkable. There were ads from slave brokers, much like modern day stockbrokers or real estate agents, selling groups of a dozen slaves or so, enabling buyers to select just what they needed. There were ads from entrepreneurs who had invested in the wholesale slave trade, announcing the presence of their ship in the harbor, newly arrived from Sierra Leone, with more than one hundred slaves on board. There were ads for estate sales of hapless farmers and plantation owners who may not have had any children to pass their property to. Slave advertising ran the gamut from five-line classified entries to full-page notices with elaborate typeface and illustrations.

Have you ever seen ads for merchants offering to pay top dollar to buy your used car? Well, in colonial and antebellum America, there were ads from slave brokers offering top dollar to buy your used Negroes. They will match any offer! And if you couldn't afford to buy a slave—maybe you were just starting out—there were plenty of ads featuring Negroes for rent. Who knew?

And based on the sheer abundance of advertising for runaway slaves, this was apparently a constant problem. I have seen hundreds of these ads. Most ads promised a $20 reward for the return of a runaway. (*That's about $500 in today's dollars.*) Even the rich, famous and powerful were not immune to the embarrassment and inconvenience of runaway slaves. According to an advertisement posted in a New Hampshire newspaper.

> "There is now living, in the borders of the town of Greenland,
> New Hampshire, a runaway slave of Gen. Washington, at
> present supported by the county of Rockingham."

Ona Judge was a servant of Martha Washington who ran away when she learned that she was about to be given as a wedding present to Mrs. Washington's granddaughter.

The advertising was not created by us, and it was not created for us, but we were always in advertising.

Well, that's not entirely true. I have seen some ads that were directed toward people of color. These were very different and were quite important in their own right. One of the advertisements that particularly caught my interest was an ad created and posted by a Boston abolitionist group in April of 1851. This ad was a response to the Fugitive Slave Act, a new law passed by the United States Congress six months earlier on September 18, 1850. The Fugitive Slave Act was part of the Great Compromise of 1850. The act required that slaves be returned to their owners, even if they were in a free state. The act also made the federal government responsible for finding and returning escaped slaves. Here is some of what the Boston ad said:

CAUTION!!

COLORED PEOPLE OF BOSTON, ONE & ALL, You are hereby respectfully CAUTIONED and advised to avoid conversing with the Watchmen and Police Officers of Boston. For the recent ORDER OF THE

MAYOR & ALDERMEN, they are empowered to act
as KIDNAPPERS and Slave Catchers...

As a matter of context, it is helpful to understand that in the colonial and antebellum south, local police forces were created specifically as "slave patrols" with the principal function of tracking and capturing all those runaway slaves featured in the runaway ads. In the north, local police forces were primarily private, for-profit operations designed to protect the private property of merchants and the wealthy. Throughout history, local police forces in both the south and the north have been used—either directly or indirectly—as instruments of racism and white supremacy. But that is getting us a bit off-topic.

After the Civil War and the passage of the Thirteenth Amendment, advertising the buying, renting, selling or recapturing of enslaved people went away completely. Advertising went in "a different direction."

As a bi-product of the industrial revolution and the mass-production and distribution of goods, the post-reconstruction era of the 1870s and 1880s saw the birth of modern advertising in America, the promotion of branded consumer products. N.W. Ayer and J. Walter Thompson were two of the earliest advertising agencies and produced some of the earliest national ads. Prior to 1900 (and for a while thereafter), advertising was dominated by just three industries; food products, soap and cleaning products, and tobacco products. And in all three industries, Blacks were an integral part of the advertising message.

Blacks in America were not a customer base for the products of these companies. Heck. That was not considered even for a second. The very idea was ridiculous. The majority of Black people still alive at that time had been born into enslavement and servitude. Emancipation was not that long ago. So why then did these great big companies and their national brands choose—again and again—to use Black people in their advertising? The simple answer is that Black people were a highly entertaining—and reliable—way for companies to sell their products to white American households.

One of the biggest and earliest advertising mascots were the Gold Dust Twins; a (racist caricature) drawing of two Black toddlers, naked, bald heads and wearing jungle tutus that read "Gold Dust". Gold Dust Soap Powder was an all-purpose soap product marketed by Lever and was a leading brand of soap powder in America (and internationally marketed by Unilever) for over 60 years. The Gold Dust Twins were featured on the front of the package and in hundreds of ads that showed them washing dishes, doing laundry, and generally solving the problems of the American housewife. In their day, the Gold Dust Twins were bigger, more popular, and more recognizable than the Olsen Twins.

This was not random or arbitrary imagery. This was not gratuitous. This was marketing science. The association of mascot and product carried a potent and effective strategic message to the consumer. Households with class and sophistication had Negro servants that washed the dishes and did the laundry and all the rest of the unpleasant chores. The fancy homes. But you too could escape all of that household drudgery! Simply buy Gold Dust Soap Powder and everything practically cleans itself! The advertising was a huge success.

The ironic truth behind the marketing science of this era was that Black people did everything. And they did it better.

And this implicit marketing principle was never more in play than it was in the kitchen. Advertisers recognized that a sure way to communicate good taste and high-quality food was by using a Black spokesperson. (*Buy our product and your food will taste as good as if you had a Negro in the kitchen cooking it for you!*) A Negro in your food ad was the equivalent of the Good Housekeeping Seal of Approval. And the absolute gold standard for brand spokespersons was Aunt Jemima. For more than a century, Aunt Jemima was a guarantee of a delicious breakfast. No other brand icon has been as popular, as powerful and as effective for so long.

In a 1995 article in the journal Southern Cultures, Maurice Manring wrote:

> *Peering out from every supermarket's shelves, between Pop Tarts and maple syrup, is a smiling riddle. Aunt Jemima brand pancake mix has been part of the American life for more than a century now, an overwhelmingly popular*

choice of consumers. The woman on the box has under-gone numerous makeovers, but she remains the same in important ways, a symbol of some unspoken relationship among Black servant women, the kitchen, and good food. This symbol remains too strong a merchandising tool for its owners, the Quaker Oats Company, to give up.

Jemima wasn't the only aunt in America's kitchen, however. There was Aunt Sally's Baking Powder, Aunt Dinah's Molasses, and an uncountable number of Black mammies whose faces adorned American products at the turn of the century. And of course, there were the uncles too; Uncle Ben's Converted Rice, Uncle Tom's Smoking Tobacco, Uncle Remus' Syrup. (In fact, Uncle Tom's Smoking Tobacco is a product that is <u>still</u> on the market in Great Britain and available via Amazon.) Calling Black people "aunt" and "uncle" was both a product of southern culture and a manipulative element of southern revisionist history. The term suggested that Black people were always part of the extended family in one sense or the other. "*They are not our servants. They are just like family to us.*"

A convenient illusion. A collective lie.

But they were servants. And their status as servants implicitly elevated the status of white consumers, because it meant that you were classy enough and important enough to have someone serve you. In advertising that graced American newspapers, magazines, and billboards from the 1890s to the 1950s, showing a Black person in an ad was an effective way of communicating superior quality and sophistication. Butlers and porters and maids would serve these products to people who only enjoyed the very best in life. These were not ads by obscure or long-forgotten obsolete brands. These were the brands that consumers continue to use and enjoy today. Hines Root Beer. Jell-O. Maxwell House Coffee. Budweiser. And dozens, dozens more. It is fair to say that American advertising would not have been the same without us.

CHAPTER TWO

The Pepsi Revolution and My Family in Ads

It is not hyperbole to say that in the late 1940s Pepsi single-handedly changed the course of advertising and marketing history forever. It sounds like typical advertising puffery, but it's not. It is also extremely likely that almost no one in the advertising business today (unless you work for Pepsi) knows this story.

In the 1930s, Pepsi was just one of a multitude of small-time cola brands competing against the Coca-Cola goliath. At the time, Pepsi was owned by the Loft Candy Company. Loft was interested in the brand mainly so it could be sold from the soda fountains of their candy stores. However, while all of the other cola brands were selling their 6-ounce bottles for a nickel, Pepsi charged the same nickel for a 12-ounce bottle. (Because Loft cared more about their fountain sales.) During the Great Depression, that was a monumental difference, especially among the poorest households and African Americans. This king-size value made enough of a difference in Pepsi's success that in 1938 Pepsi was spun off as its own independent company.

But that's still not the revolutionary story that I'm talking about. It's only the preamble.

In 1938, Walter S. Mack Jr., a politically connected, progressive Republican, New York businessman, became the first president of the newly independent Pepsi Company. One of the first things Mack did was successfully sue Coke for the right to call Pepsi a "cola." And the Pepsi-Cola Company was born. Mack referred to himself as "an unrepentant capitalist and liberal" who enjoyed bucking the status quo. He told his board of directors that Pepsi had survived the Great Depression due to the brand's popularity among loyal Negro customers who appreciated the value of the 12-ounce bottles. He intended to treat Negro customers as a consumer segment that was important to the company's future growth.

Walter Mack and Pepsi intended to treat Black people as consumers, important consumers. No other American corporation of any size or significance had ever contemplated such a thing. It was literally unimaginable.

Mack began to set the program in motion in 1941; however, the onset of World War II pushed their marketing plans back. Even during the war, Walter Mack looked for ways to grow his company, especially among American Negroes. Because the U.S. Army only operated segregated canteens, (Canteens were club venues in cities across the country that provided off-duty servicemen with nights of dancing, entertainment, free food and nonalcoholic drinks, and even opportunities to hobnob with celebrities.) Pepsi opened three of its own fully integrated canteens that served thousands of Black and White servicemen during and after the war.

In 1947, Walter Mack hired Edward Boyd, a National Urban League staff member and placed him in charge of the brand-new program. Boyd hired a dozen African American salesmen who traveled the country tirelessly through the late 1940s and early 1950s, spreading the new gospel of Pepsi at Black churches, social clubs, schools, athletic events, barber shops, etc. Pepsi's all-Black sales team endured taunts, insults, and threats from co-workers, competitors and the local KKK.

It was the simultaneous invention of multicultural marketing and grassroots marketing.

The very first in-store display—which later became a newspaper and magazine ad—featured an attractive, young Black mother holding a six-pack of Pepsi while her son reached for one. In the background is the daughter and dad in a pressed white shirt and tie. A decidedly "normal" middle-class American family image. By the way, the young boy in the ad was Ron Brown, who would grow up to become the U.S. Commerce Secretary in the Clinton Administration. This was the very first national ad to treat African Americans as attractive, desirable consumers. This was revolutionary.

The American marketplace has never been the same since. Pepsi kicked ass and became an international soft drink giant and a peer and true rival to Coca-Cola. Other American corporations in every product category began to market their products to Black consumers.

In 1956, **Vince Cullers**, an art director at Ebony (the largest and most successful Black magazine in the country), launched America's first Black advertising agency in Chicago, formalizing a new segment of the industry. One of the agency's first ad campaigns was for Johnson Products, a Chicago-based Black hair care company. The agency's first national ad campaign was for Kent Cigarettes. Tobacco companies were always happy to sell their products to Black consumers; at the time, those consumers were happy to oblige. Today, African Americans have a lower incidence of smoking than the general population in spite of the relentless targeted advertising.

When he was a young man, my dad was a professional photographer. He did a lot of fashion photography, capturing beautiful Black women models in stylish dresses and big fancy hats. Back then, you never saw these models in the mainstream fashion magazines, but the newsstands in Harlem and Chicago and other cities around the country were filled with Negro publications (Ebony, Jet, Sepia, Tan, Hue, Color, Jive) that featured and celebrated Black beauty and style. These were the kinds of pictures my father took. And, I'm told, he was very good at it. My mom, before she began her career in business, was a fashion model. And from time to time, they worked together.

Years ago, while rummaging through my parents' basement, I found what is known in the retail marketing business as a riser card. It's a cardboard display piece that's roughly three feet tall and two feet wide and has an advertising image promoting a product for sale in the store.

It draws the customer to purchase the product. Beer and soda brands use them all the time. That very first Pepsi ad I mentioned was on a riser card. This particular card was for Ballantine Beer and featured five beautiful African American models enjoying the beer. Ballantine, which has been around since 1840, was at its height in the 1940s and 1950s. By then, it was twice the size of Anheuser Busch and was one of the largest privately held corporations in America.

The ad, which may have been shot by my dad (I'm not sure) included my mom, Rita Robinson, as one of the models. One of the very early ads to feature Black models for a major national brand, featured my mom. My beautiful, amazing mom. Another model who was in the ad was a friend of hers, Audrey Smaltz. Audrey later left modeling not long afterward to become a fashion runway mogul and CEO of The Ground Crew, one of the biggest fashion-show stage management companies in the business.

Modeling was only a temporary phase in my mom's career as well. She enjoyed it for a few years, but her dreams were focused on the corporate world, going to an office and doing important things. And, in addition to raising a family, that's exactly what she did. But in 1966, when my mom was a rising young professional at Time Incorporated, the parent company of Time Magazine, Life, and Sports Illustrated; she received a phone call from someone from her former modeling days. They were creating an ad campaign for a "bigtime national brand" that would be targeted to Black consumers. The campaign would feature real people; attractive young, Black professionals, and authentic aspirational figures enjoying the product in their everyday life. They asked my mom if she would be interested. The product was Coca-Cola.

"Enjoying the product in their everyday life" meant shooting the ad in our home. So, one day an entire production crew showed up and took over our house. It was like a tornado had arrived and just hovered over our house. The concept of the ad was that my mom was a successful businesswoman and a successful mom, and of course, Coca-Cola made it all possible. The ad was shot right in our living room, sitting on the floor in front of our fireplace. Mom (while holding a bottle of Coke) was playing chess with my older brother Michael, while I sat observing the game. I was nine years old at the time, and I must say that I think I was absolutely adorable. We looked like the perfect, upwardly mobile Negro family, which was exactly the point. I have another older brother, David, who was not in the ad layout, so I have no idea where he was that day. I think maybe my dad took him to the movies as a consolation.

Here is the headline and copy from the ad:

Rita Robinson: She leads the two-career life.

With Coke to help her all the way. A successful publishing executive at Time, Inc., she's also a devoted wife and mother of three boys. Both careers require equal time. And yet, Mrs. Robinson manages with ease. Of course, she always has plenty of Coca-Cola on hand to help keep her going.

The ad ran in Ebony and a whole bunch of other Black publications in 1966. So, I was in the ad business even before the age of ten. And apparently, it stuck with me.

CHAPTER THREE

Afraid of the dark

"For 13 months, I was the Jackie Robinson of television," wrote Nat King Cole in a revealing 1958 article for Ebony magazine entitled "**Why I quit my TV show**." "After a trail-blazing year that shattered all the old bug-a-boos about Negroes on TV, I found myself standing there with the bat on my shoulder. But the men who dictate what Americans see and hear didn't want to play ball."

That was more than sixty years ago. So it is understandable that many people might not know all that much about the legendary singer, Nat King Cole. I'm happy to fill in a few blanks.

Nat King Cole began his professional career in the 1930s as the pianist and leader of the King Cole Trio. One night, a club owner told Nat, "The vocalist didn't show tonight, so you gotta sing."

Nat protested, "But I don't sing. I'm a piano player."

The club owner insisted, "You want to get paid, tonight, you sing." And thus, launched one of the most "unforgettable" voices in jazz.

In 1937, Nat wrote and sold his first song, "Straighten up and fly right", which became a huge hit and a staple of nightclubs in the late 1930s and 1940s. In 1942, Nat King Cole signed with Capitol Records, a fledgling new label at the time. Nat's two-decade run of chart-topping hits turned Capitol Records into a recording empire and an iconic Hollywood landmark known as "The house that Nat built."

Nat's songs included "Unforgettable", "Smile", "Mona Lisa", "Route 66", "Nature Boy", and "When I Fall In Love". It would simply take too long to list all of his big hits.

According to Billboard, from 1938—1965, Nat released more than 100 Top Ten singles and two dozen Top Ten albums. That's more than Michael Jackson and Whitney Houston combined. No one has matched his record. Nat King Cole is in the Grammy Hall of Fame, the Songwriters Hall of Fame, and the Rock and Roll Hall of Fame. Only Lennon and McCartney can make that claim. And since his death in 1965, over 100 more Nat King Cole albums have been released. Five were gold records; another five were platinum. Only Elvis can make that claim.

In 1956, Nat Cole was one of the most successful entertainers in the world. Of ANY color. His gentle, romantic style of singing endeared him to millions, and his record sales were phenomenal. There was every reason to believe that a TV show starring Nat King Cole would be a huge hit. Nat saw the potential for something more than just entertainment success. "It could be a turning point," he said, "so that Negroes may be featured regularly on television."

But this was 1956, and Civil Rights was very much an active battleground. Many, especially in the media establishment, did not feel America was ready for Negroes to host their own TV programs, no matter who that Negro was. Nat originally signed a contract with CBS, but the network got cold feet, and the deal fell through. Later in the year, NBC stepped forward, and on November 5, 1956, The Nat King Cole Show was on the air.

The show featured some of the biggest performers of the time, including Ella Fitzgerald, Peggy Lee, Sammy Davis Jr., Tony Bennett, Count Basie, and Harry Belafonte. The orchestra was conducted by Nelson Riddle. It was the best entertainment on TV. There was just one small problem. This was a network TV show that did not have a single national advertiser. Not one single advertising agency was willing to buy national airtime on the show for any of their clients. National airtime meant that the ads would run in southern markets, and advertisers were afraid of white southern boycotts of their products. A representative of Max Factor cosmetics, a potential sponsor for the program, claimed that a Negro couldn't sell lipstick for them. Cole was angered by the comment. "What do they think we use?" he asked. "Chalk? Congo paint?"

The result was that NBC was forced to create a patchwork of local sponsors in just a handful of key markets. Rheingold Beer advertised in New York. Gallo Wines and Colgate Toothpaste in Los Angeles. And Coca-Cola in Houston. It was not uncommon for the show to air without any commercials. Advertising sponsorship is the lifeblood of television, but the Nat King Cole Show was getting none of it. The show was never able to turn a profit. Despite the losses they suffered, NBC kept the show on the air for a second season. Nat even used his own money to underwrite expenses. Finally, after 64 weeks, Nat King Cole made the decision to cancel the show.

In the Ebony magazine article that served as a postmortem on the show, Cole praised NBC for its good faith efforts. "The network supported this show from the beginning," he said. "From Mr. Sarnoff on down, they tried to sell it to agencies. They could have dropped it after the first thirteen weeks."

Nat King Cole placed the blame squarely on the advertising industry. "Madison Avenue," Cole said, "is afraid of the dark."

But the advertising agencies of Madison Avenue were not at all happy being called out publicly as racist, nor were their clients. Nat Cole's remarks in a national magazine were a cold slap in the face by an uppity Negro. The men of Madison Avenue, the men in the grey flannel suits, were the kingmakers, the tastemakers. They would see to it that they had the last word in this feud. And they were quite capable of showing their venal, petty, and vengeful side to do it.

The late 1950s and early 1960s were the heyday of celebrity endorsement advertising. Everyone from John Wayne to Jack Webb and Lucille Ball were making lots of extra bucks plugging products. Celebrity endorsers and the products they shilled were so inextricably intertwined that you had TV shows like the Bob Hope Texaco Star Theater. All the big celebrities were cashing in.

Except for Nat King Cole. On Madison Avenue, Nat's name wasn't even whispered. Despite out-shining and out-selling virtually every other performer, Nat Cole could not get the time of day from any advertising agency. Madison Avenue got the last word, after all.

CHAPTER FOUR

Kidnapping Jim Jordan

Sometime during my junior year at Amherst College, I attended a talk being given by Jim Jordan, an Amherst alum. It was a Career Weekend event and several alumni had come back to campus to give talks on their chosen profession. Jim Jordan, who had graduated from Amherst in 1952, was a famous—and great—advertising executive straight out of the Mad Men era. And just like Don Draper, Jim Jordan wrote some of the best advertising lines of his time. Advertising headlines like: "Schaefer is the one beer to have when you're having more than one," "Us Tareyton smokers would rather fight than switch," "Delta is ready when you are," "Quaker Oatmeal, it's the right thing to do" and "Wisk beats ring around the collar."

Jim Jordan loved advertising and loved what he did. As I sat there in the Red Room in Converse Hall (a small amphitheater with walls lined in red carpeting), listening to him speak, his passion and his joy burst from every word he said. He was hypnotic. And he said something I will never forget (because I have repeated it over and over to others). He said, "*No other profession on this planet enables you to combine boundless, breakthrough and occasionally brilliant creativity with commerce, consequences, competition, collaboration, community service, immediacy and the potential for immortality. **Nothing else even comes close.**"*

All I knew was, from that moment on, I wanted to do what he did. I wanted to be in advertising. After his speech, Jim Jordan was supposed to join students for a luncheon in the faculty dining hall in Merrill Science Center at the opposite end of campus (I have no idea why they put the faculty dining hall inside Merrill Science Center), but I casually walked up to the podium, put my hand on Jim Jordan's arm and said, "Mr. Jordan, I was so inspired by everything that you said, and I would love the chance to talk to you one on one. Could I buy you lunch in town?" He said yes, and we walked off campus together to one of the local restaurants in town. I spirited him away for myself. Apparently, there were dozens of students and a college administration handler over at Merrill Science Center, wondering what the hell happened.

About a month later, I was having lunch in Valentine Dining Hall (the Annex, of course, where all of Amherst's Black students ate their meals) and sitting next to a classmate, Jimmi Williams, as he struggled to fill out a stack of paperwork. It looked like a college application, but since we were already in college, I knew that couldn't be it.

"What are you doing, Jimmi?"

"Man, I don't know." Jimmi shook his head. James "Jimmi" Williams III was a tall, skinny, dark-skinned brother from Greensboro, North Carolina, who spoke with an almost falsetto high-pitched voice and a buttery Carolina accent. Jimmi's easy-going demeanor and ever-present smile belied his true calling as a fiery and passionate leader and activist among the Black students at Amherst. There wasn't a person of color on that campus at that time who didn't admire and look up to Jimmi. The school administration knew that when Jimmi spoke, he spoke for all of us. And there was more than one occasion during my time at Amherst where that solidarity was put to the test. Jimmi was also one of the most likable students on campus. "I had no idea this application would be this hard to fill out." He said. "I'm about to throw in the towel."

"What's it for?"

"It's for an internship program this summer working in advertising. It's a special minority internship program." And then he pushed the pile of papers away. "You want it?"

The internship program was called MAIP (Minority Advertising Internship Program), and it was created and sponsored by the 4A's (American Association of Advertising Agencies), the advertising industry's trade association. Founded in 1973, MAIP was a 10-week paid internship at prestigious advertising agencies for aspiring, diverse entry-level advertising professionals. Selected candidates receive real-world work experience, networking opportunities within the industry, and a valuable professional credential to better position themselves in the marketplace. Simultaneously, the program offers advertising agencies the opportunity to meet and engage with interested young minority would-be ad professionals.

Since 1973, the 4A's has conducted the Minority Advertising Internship Program to encourage African-American, Asian-American, Hispanic-American, and Native-American college students to consider advertising as a career. The program offers Ad agencies a cost-effective way to identify, observe and recruit highly qualified student talent.

In the first few years, 10-12 qualified undergraduate and graduate students were selected. Because of its success, the size of the program grew steadily each year. For the past decade, 120 students were selected each year. Since its inception, MAIP has graduated more than 4,000 interns.

When major advertising agencies invariably bemoan that they cannot find minority talent to hire to make their organizations more diverse, the 4A's and MAIP reliably respond, "Here we are."

But at that particular moment, back in the spring of 1977, I did not know any of this and I genuinely struggled to be cool and not show my excitement to Jimmi. "Sure, I'll take a look at it." And started to gather up the papers.

"Better you than me, my brother. Better you than me."

Part of playing it cool was not even bothering to look at the papers while we sat and ate lunch. I "strolled" over to Robert Frost Library to find a quiet and private place to review the application. Of course, as soon as I looked at the papers, I realized that I couldn't use them because Jimmi had already filled in his name and personal information, although not much else. So, now I ran over to the Career Counseling Office in Converse Hall to pick up a fresh blank copy of the application. Peggy, the assistant to Henry Littlefield, Amherst's career counseling dean, was sitting at her desk when I explained what I needed. She calmly pulled open a file cabinet drawer and withdrew a manila folder. She quickly scanned the paperwork to be sure it was the right application before handing it to me.

"Sorry, sweetheart, but I think you're screwed."

"What? What do you mean?" My adrenaline had already started pumping on the run over to Converse Hall. Now I was practically twitching.

"Did you look at the first page?" She said, pointing to the top of the page. "The deadline for submission is tomorrow. In New York. What are you going to do? Fill it out tonight and drive it there?" She flashed a wicked smile. "Why the heck didn't you get this done sooner?"

"Peggy..." I said, desperation in my voice. "I just found out about this a half hour ago. What am I going to do?" Fortunately, Peggy and I knew each other fairly well and she liked me. I was not pre-med or pre-law. I was business focused, and I was in and out of the Career office all the time.

But here's the problem. Assuming that I could work through the night to complete the lengthy application, which included multiple essay questions that I would need to write, I still had to deliver the completed paperwork to New York City by tomorrow. And this was 1977. There was no email. The internet did not exist. Fax machines weren't invented yet. Even Federal Express was not a mainstream operation at the time. And the idea of jumping on a bus to New York City to hand deliver an internship application did not seem like a realistic idea.

Peggy looked at me and sighed. She brushed her hand in my direction and shooed me. "Look. Go away and let me see what I can do. Come back in an hour and I'll let you know."

I did as I was instructed and returned promptly in an hour, probably in 55 minutes.

"Okay, I spoke to them. Here's the deal." Peggy pointed a finger at me. "If you get your application finished by tomorrow and you get the envelope postmarked tomorrow, they will accept the application whenever it shows up next week." She smiled. "You're gonna owe me big time for this."

"I will be back tomorrow with my application and a big bouquet of roses for your desk." And that is how I was accepted into MAIP, the Minority Advertising Internship Program, in the summer of 1977 and got my start in advertising.

◆ ◆ ◆

THE SUMMER OF '77

I did my internship in advertising that summer between junior and senior year at an agency called Cunningham & Walsh. They were a big player in the advertising industry at the time, however, a decade later they would be swallowed up by another industry giant, NW Ayer (who, 15 years later, would meet a similar fate). The experience was everything I wanted it to be, even the tedious grunt work that interns always have to do. I was fortunate to have bosses and teachers that were invested in me, they were gratified by my enthusiasm, and they rewarded it with bigger, more interesting assignments.

The internship placed me in the media department at Cunningham. I think the application asked me if I had a preference, but I honestly did not know enough about the organizational structure of advertising agencies to understand where I might fit in best. So instead, I wrote that it was my desire to learn about ALL of the agency's departments. (Suck up. Yes, I know.)

I have a lot of great memories from that summer. It seems that summers are always more tightly packed than the rest of the year. More things happen in the summer, and a lot of things were happening in the world around me. 1977 was the "Summer of Sam." A lot of people are probably too young to understand the reference or to know what that meant to people living in New York City, but it was a grim, dangerous, harrowing time. A mentally deranged man named David Berkowitz was trolling the city at night and killing people—usually couples—with his .44 magnum revolver. In letters he sent taunting the NYPD, he called himself "Son of Sam." Sam, it turns out, was his neighbor's dog, who spoke to him and told him to kill. That summer, every New Yorker walked the city streets looking over their shoulder, doing their best to suppress—or at least manage—their paranoia.

1977 was the summer of Star Wars, which I probably saw three times that summer. One of my fellow MAIP interns had a great tee shirt that said, "Let the Wookie win." This was also the summer of the July 13th New York City blackout. Unlike the blackouts of 1965 and 2003, which affected the whole northeastern region, this one exclusively affected New York City. And unlike the other two blackouts, this Blackout resulted in mass looting, vandalism and civil unrest. New Yorkers who were fed up with the privations of the city's economic depression and sustained racial inequality exploded in an angry, long-deferred catharsis that set over 1,000 fires and looted over 1,600 stores and businesses. It was a dark time (sorry, pun intended) for New York.

All of the MAIP interns were staying in a dormitory at NYU for the summer, in the middle of Greenwich Village. At the time that the lights went out, I was having pizza with a couple of other interns at the Orchidia, a Ukrainian restaurant on East 9th Street. The lights went out and the owners lit candles and started giving away the food for free, so we stuck around. My most vivid memory of that night was of two NYPD patrolmen who rushed into the restaurant. I don't know what kind of mayhem was going on outside at that moment, but the two officers had a look of panic on their faces. They announced that they were going to stay here and advised everyone to do the same. They told everyone to stay calm, but it was obvious to all of us that we were a lot calmer than the two of them. Somehow, we all made it through the night.

At the summer's conclusion, I was eager to return to school for my senior year. I felt the wind at my back and the sun in my face. I felt like I could see my future laid out in front of me. Most people begin adulthood wholly uncertain what they want to do with their life, uncertain and overwhelmed with anxiety about what the right path and right choice should be. For many people, that uncertainty lingers and looms like a shadow behind them for many, many years. For some, it can sap the joy from whatever choices and actions they take in life.

But not for me.

Perhaps I was just a simpleton who never asked myself the hard questions. (This remains a possibility.) Perhaps I just never examined my life all that carefully and critically. And if I had, I might be there alongside all the others. Maybe. But I don't think so. Instead, I feel that I was blessed to know what felt right for me. In my gut and in my heart, I knew that advertising was the right career choice for me.

My friend Sheldon Levy was a graduate of the very first year of MAIP in 1973, four years ahead of me. Sheldon led a long and distinguished career in advertising as a TV producer and head of broadcast production at Saatchi and was recognized for his many achievements.

In 2019, Sheldon passed away after a long illness. The 4A's did not keep very good records during the early years of the MAIP program; however, according to the records we have, with Sheldon's passing, I am now the oldest living MAIP alum still working in the advertising industry.

CHAPTER FIVE

Saying "No Thank You"

In the spring of my senior year at Amherst College, while struggling to complete my thesis work by the submission deadline, I began looking beyond Amherst in my search for a permanent job. Through contacts made the previous summer during my 4A's MAIP internship, I lined up a series of job interviews with various advertising agencies in New York City. I scheduled the interviews during Spring Break, when I would be able to get away from campus and make the trip to the city. In addition to the 3 or 4 contacts that I had lined up, I had an interview scheduled at Dancer Fitzgerald Sample through a more inside connection.

William Vickery was a senior vice president at the agency who was an alum of Amherst College. Vickery and I did not know each other, but we were fellow members of the Amherst family. Our shared bond to this extraordinary place of privilege meant I was automatically entitled to call upon him for special consideration. That was—and is—simply how things worked. That was one of the principal benefits of existing in a place like Amherst. Having that simple connection opened doors that don't open for everyone else. Having a diploma from an elite place of privilege meant two things. First, it meant you possessed a credential that only a tiny fraction of a percentage could claim, a credential of intelligence, ability and status that was genuinely enviable. Second, it meant there was a small, elite army of powerful and extremely accomplished people in the world who would take your phone call and respond to your request the way that any friend might.

21

It was the unspoken understanding and expectation that these people would tip the playing field—maybe just a little bit—in your favor. And as a young African American man, I was starting out with the playing field tipped against me. So any help tipping that playing field back in my favor was sought, appreciated, and definitely needed.

I obtained Bill Vickery's contact information from the Amherst Alumni Office, and Mr. Vickery (who had graduated 20 years earlier) was happy to be of service to a fellow member of the Amherst family. Bill arranged for me to meet with the Personnel Director at Dancer Fitzgerald Sample. That was all I asked of him, and it was as easy as one phone call. The rest would be up to me. I have decided not to share the Personnel Director's actual name for this story. The reason will quickly become obvious. I later learned that she was more commonly known as the "Dragon Lady."

When I met with the director in her office, she greeted me by saying, "You have a resume?" I readily handed a copy to her, which she set to the side of her desk without reading. She then started the conversation by saying, "Mr. Vickery asked me to meet with you."

I already knew this, of course. But I think this was her way of letting me know that this meeting was not her idea, but simply a courtesy to one of her executives.

"I'm told you are very bright. Is that so?"

There aren't many good ways to answer that question. "I'm flattered by the compliment. I work hard and I believe that I have a strong aptitude for advertising account management."

Advertising account management is not the creative guys. It's not the copywriters or the art directors. Account guys don't create ads. They manage the business. They are business people. They manage the money. They manage the client relationship, and they manage the staff, the agency team assigned to a particular account. And—if you are really good at what you do—account guys manage the advertising strategy (at least they did back then). They understand the client's business well enough to chart the direction of the advertising. They are the orchestra conductors.

"I see." The director said dryly. "And what has drawn you to desire a career in advertising?"

I told her about meeting advertising icon Jim Jordan. I told her about my 4A's internship the prior summer, about the things I learned and my experiences. Occasionally she would steal a glance at my resume from the corner of her eye.

"I can see you are very bright." She said without smiling. "So, I should be very honest with you. We don't hire Negroes in account management at Dancer Fitzgerald Sample. Those are important positions and that would make our clients uncomfortable. I think you will find that is true at any major agency. They might not tell you the truth. I will tell you the truth. If you would like to consider a trainee position in our media department, I would be happy to set up those interviews right now."

There was a pause. I was taking this all in. She was assessing how well I was taking this all in.

"What would you like to do?"

I stood up. "Thank you. I appreciate your honesty. I am not interested in a position in the media department, so Dancer would not be an agency that I could work for."

She did not get up. "Well, you will find the same thing at any place you interview."

I smiled, or at least I did my best to put one on my face. "Then I will just have to keep interviewing until someone offers me the right job."

If I had not attended Dalton and Amherst, that interview with Dancer's personnel director would have gone very differently. If I had attended public school and gone to a public college, the interview probably never would have happened in the first place. I wouldn't have had the contacts or connections. I wouldn't have known someone like Bill Vickery. I might never even have been exposed to advertising as a career choice. The advertising industry did not have any outreach programs to minority students. If you didn't already know about the MAIP internship, you would never know the opportunity existed. And even if I did know about advertising as a possible profession, if I had not attended Dalton and Amherst, I probably would have had much lower expectations for my job search and interview, and I probably would have been very willing to settle for less than my stated objective. I would have gladly accepted her offer to interview for the media department.

There is nothing wrong with the media department and I do not wish to disparage media people or the creative department or the production department or the research department. They simply were not the choice I had made. They weren't what I wanted to do. And Dalton and Amherst taught me to respect my own choices, to be confident in my own abilities. My parents taught me to respect authority, but Dalton and Amherst taught me never to be intimidated by it. Dalton and Amherst taught me to never, ever be a pushover.

Upon reflection, what I did that day was fairly revolutionary. I turned down a job opportunity because it wasn't good enough. I turned down the opportunity for a well-paying, fairly prestigious white-collar job because it wasn't good enough. I doubt that anyone in my family had ever done that before. Ever. And I come from a fairly privileged family. The freedom—and the power—as a young Black man to be able to say to a white person in authority, "*No thank you.* I will go out and I will get something better for myself," was mind-blowing. It was revolutionary. I am sure that the personnel director at DFS thought that I had lost my mind.

In fairness to Dancer's personnel director, she was simply being coldly candid about the unspoken reality of the advertising agency business. It was and still is—quite literally—one of the whitest white-collar professions in America. That is a sad fact backed up by data from the Bureau of Labor Statistics. If I thought that Dalton and Amherst were overwhelmingly white, I was about to step onto the luminescent snowstorm of Madison Avenue. It seems that throughout my life I have been a diverse presence in very un-diverse worlds. I'm not the first (and fortunately, I'm not the last), but I am part of that "early wave" that begins to create change. It's not a role that I specifically or intentionally sought out, but I am proud of it nonetheless. It is rewarding to know that some things are different because I was there.

Advertising agencies are like private clubs. To get a job in advertising, especially a job in account management, which was the "face of the agency", you had to have a lot of the right things. You had to come from the right families, which did not include most ethnic groups, but especially did not include Blacks. You had to graduate from the right schools, and that included membership in the right fraternities and social clubs. You had to have the right look, which was usually tall, slender and Nordic. If you only had one of these things, you probably had to settle for a job at a second-tier agency, or a job in another department. If you had two of these things, your chances were good that you would get a good job at a good agency. And if you had three of these things, Madison Avenue was your buffet. You could pick and choose what you liked. This was your personal moveable feast.

As for me, I had to find my way in with just the "right schools" on my pedigree.

◆ ◆ ◆

"MY LAST OFFICIAL ACT"

One of the agencies that responded to my request for an interview was SSC&B. In the 1970s, a lot of advertising agencies had begun changing their names to acronyms. Originally, the partnerships that founded agencies were usually two people, an easy enough name for a company. Easy to say, easy to remember. But as time went on, new partners were added and eventually, many of these ad agency names began to sound like Wall Street law firms. Acronyms were punchier, more modern-sounding and they solved major over-crowding on letterhead and business cards. And so, Sullivan, Stauffer, Colwell & Bayles became SSC&B.

What made SSC&B especially desirable was that they had one of the few fully developed management training programs in the industry. Several big agencies claimed to have training programs, but in reality, they were little more than underpaid gopher jobs with no structured learning process. A lot of those training programs were simply, "Let's hire a bunch of eager-beavers and see who shines after six months." SSC&B, on the other hand, had a formal curriculum, scheduled seminars and speakers, and assigned project work. Graduate business schools like Thunderbird and Wharton regularly fed their best into SSC&B's training program. SSC&B would be one of the best places to start in the advertising business.

When I came in for my interview at SSC&B, I met with Bill Timm, the Personnel Director, just as I had at Dancer Fitzgerald Sample. But Bill could not have been more different from Dancer's director. Bill Timm was in his early sixties, a round, soft-edged man who displayed ease and self-assurance balanced with genuine humility. He was warm and welcoming and made me feel like he wanted to spend as much time with me as he could. In fact, he said to me, "Is it okay if we take up your whole day today? Do you have other appointments?"

I told him that I was hoping to spend many years at SSC&B, and so spending the day there was simply getting off to a good start.

He had arranged for me to be interviewed by five different people within the agency. This is customary only after the agency has made a preliminary decision that they are interested in you. I was pumped up that this was happening on my initial visit. Of course, I only remember one of the five people that I met with, because she was the most important. Bill Timm said I would meet with Mary Ayers, the agency's only woman executive vice president, and something of a legend in the industry.

Mary Ayres played an important part in the history of women in advertising. She was one of the first women to work on the business side—in account management—rather than in the creative department, and she was one of the first women to be made vice-president of a major agency. It was Mary's idea to take Noxema, an old drug store skin cream used for healing sunburns, and transform it into a beauty product to be used to wash and cleanse the face. Mary was also the strategic brains behind the meteoric rise of Cover Girl cosmetics in the 1960s.

But Ms. Ayers was retiring. In fact, that day at SSC&B was her very last day before leaving. It was a day she would spend signing a few important papers, reminiscing with colleagues and later there would be a big farewell party. When I was shown to her office, a grand corner office space on the 42nd floor, with baby blue carpeting so thick it made you feel taller, one side of the room was stacked with boxes, all labeled for their contents and their destination. But there was still a comfortable space for the two of us on her couch. Our conversation was casual, easy-going and unhurried and we wandered through many different topics. After forty minutes, I said that I must be taking up too much of her last official afternoon and I should be on my way. I told her that it meant a great deal to me that she would take the time on her very last day to spend some of it with me and that I was grateful for the gift of her time.

At the end of the day, I returned to Bill Timm's office because he wanted to know how I felt the interviews went and so I could find out if there would be any "next steps" in the process.

"I think that you impressed a few people," he said. "I thought that you might."

I told him that I was the one who was impressed by everyone I met, and I thanked him for arranging for me to meet Mary Ayers.

"Mary sent me a note." Bill smiled. "Would you like to read it?"

"Absolutely," I said, hopeful that she had given me a positive review. Bill Timm handed the piece of paper to me. It was an official typed memorandum on SSC&B stationery. This is what it said.

Bill,

You knew just the perfect thing for me to do on my last day. Meeting this charming and intelligent young man has given me one more reason to believe that our agency's future is bright and strong. We need him and more people like him.

As my last official act as an officer of this agency, I am directing you to make an offer of employment to Mark Robinson and vigorously persuade him to accept our offer.

Mary

And that's how I got my first job in advertising.

CHAPTER SIX

Groundhog Day and the Shine Man

When I first started working at SSC&B, I was on cloud nine. I worked for one of the best advertising agencies in New York. True, it wasn't actually ON Madison Avenue. It was on Second Avenue and 47th Street in a slick new skyscraper called Dag Hammarskjold Plaza, just a block from the United Nations. Thirteen countries had their consulates or missions in our building. Dag Hammarskjold Plaza was a 49-story black steel colossus that was the tallest building in the neighborhood. The agency occupied eight floors in the building, from 35 to 42, and my office was on the 40th floor. Yes, I had an inside office with no windows, but when I was in my boss' office I could gaze out the window in sheer marvel.

I wore three-piece suits; the best I could afford, which wasn't very much on a management trainee's salary, but I felt like a million bucks. I had a secretary that I shared with just two other people, and she called me "Mr. Robinson." I was one of the few management trainees hired with just an undergraduate degree. Most of my peers had MBA's; half were from Thunderbird, one of the best graduate business programs in the country. However, unlike most of them, I had actual agency experience because I had been a part of the 4A's MAIP (Minority Advertising Internship Program) fellowship the summer before. I knew first-hand the pace, the expectations, the daily duties and the roles of the people

I worked with every day. I knew, not from studying it, but from doing it. And it actually made a pretty big difference that was noticed by my bosses and by my peers. The MAIP program had been an effective training and preparation tool.

On the 40th and 41st floors of Dag Hammarskjold Plaza, where account management resided, we had certain 'norms' for the way things were. Not rules, really, just expectations of demeanor. Cultural norms. For example, all of the men (about 10% of the department was women) in account management wore suits and ties all the time. There was no such thing as 'business casual', not on Fridays, not in the summer. Nope. If you were walking about on your own floor, it was perfectly acceptable to leave your suit jacket behind. But if you were going to a meeting on another floor, if you were going to see someone in any of the other departments, you wore your jacket. It was your uniform. It was an outward symbol of your status within the company.

So perhaps I could be forgiven for feeling just a bit like a junior master of the universe. In fact, just a few weeks after I started work, the agency scheduled me for a photo shoot for the annual SSC&B recruitment brochure. I'd only been there a few weeks and already I was good enough to attract other talent. Of course, the real reason I was being photographed for the brochure was the agency's naked desire to show off its "diversity." Up until that point, the faces in the agency recruitment brochure were primarily white, male and cisgender. They even had a fairly standard look. SSC&B did not have a single other Black face in the company that wasn't pushing a mail cart or sitting at a typewriter. That became pretty apparent (to me and to almost everyone else) when I continued to be featured four years in a row, while other faces changed annually. I reached the point where I openly joked with Human Resources that they wouldn't have to photograph me every year if they would just hire another Black person. Apparently, it was easier for them to just keep using me.

This little game of Groundhog Day was very much an apt metaphor for the way that advertising agencies approached the challenges of progressive change, whether it was for diversity or sexism or simply understanding new media and marketing practices. Agencies would rather keep doing what they have been doing while everything else around them changes. And the only time that agencies make any effort to change is when clients take their dollars and put them someplace else because some other resource has figured out how to give the clients what they want.

There were many things that soon relieved me of any misplaced arrogance or inflated sense of myself, including daily micro-aggressions that occasionally progressed from mosquito bites to mosquito infestations. But the moment that mattered most and did the most to remind me of who I was and the community of people to which I belonged was a quiet moment of simple, innocent eye contact.

The account management executives at SSC&B were accustomed to various services that could be provided from the convenience of one's own office. One of these was the shoeshine man. He would stroll the halls of the 40th and 41st floors and knock gently on your office door or quietly poke his head inside. If you wanted a shoeshine, you gestured for him to come inside, and he would shine your shoes while you worked or talked on the telephone. When he was done, you looked down at your shoes, paid the man and he went on his way to the next office.

Working in an office, there was never much opportunity for my shoes to get dirty. And my apartment was only three blocks from the office, so it was probably a month that went by before I requested my first shoeshine. That day I was in my office, working at my desk. My door was open and the shoe-shine man, a Black gentleman in his 60s (I'm guessing), tapped gently on my open door and looked inside. I said, "Sure" and waved him in. I sat in my desk chair and he got down on one knee and began working on my shoes. I looked down at him on his knees before me and he looked up at me, making eye contact, a gesture of friendliness.

In an instant, my stomach tied up in knots. I have had lots of shoeshines before, in places like airports and Grand Central Station. But those were different. Those felt completely different. Suddenly, I felt like the absolute worst kind of person. He could see the awkwardness and discomfort in my eyes. He kept shining for a few more beats, then spoke.

"You're new to this place. This is your first shine."

"Uh huh," was all I could say.

Without pausing from his work, he looked up at me and smiled. "I'll bet your folks are pretty proud of you being here. I've never seen one of us sitting behind one of these desks."

"Thank you." I couldn't think of anything to say.

He continued to work until he was finished, and my shoes sparkled better than new. "Well, sir, I'm happy to meet you. Whenever you need a shine, you just let me know. I'll be around."

I paid him and tipped him, feeling that I did not have as much cash in my wallet to tip as much as I wanted. The following week he came around and gently tapped on my office door. I wasn't sure that I wanted another shoeshine, but I did not wish to reject his services. This was how he made his living and I wanted to respect his work and respect him. But I did not want to be like all the other executives in that office. That was simply not okay for me.

"Would it be okay if I just gave you my shoes, instead of you getting down on the floor?"

He looked at me quizzically. "You want me to shine them standing up?"

"No, no." I waved my hand. "I thought maybe you could sit down," I said, gesturing to one of my chairs. "And we could talk while you worked."

"Okay" he shrugged and sat down. "What you want to talk about?"

So, we talked—that day and many times after that—mostly me asking him his observations about the other executives in the office, sometimes about his life outside of work, occasionally just office gossip.

From that point forward, I tried to remind myself regularly that I am not an advertising man who happens to be Black. I am a Black man who happens to be in advertising. And I have more in common with the man who shined my shoes than with the other executives on the 40th floor. His name was Jacob, but I may have been the only executive who knew his name. I may have been the only executive who cared that he had a name.

The collective opinion of many of the secretaries in the office was that most of the junior executives at the agency were full of themselves. Full of themselves and full of crap. For the most part, these secretaries were right. A lot of the junior executives would use their pecking order position above the secretaries as a way of making themselves feel important, feel superior. The account executives and assistant account executives would constantly complain about the unreliability or incompetence of the secretaries. And in the days before the existence of computers and word processing software, multiple document revisions were commonplace, often simply because an AE did not review their work beforehand. They did not care. It was the secretary's problem. They had more important things to worry about.

Generally speaking, the secretaries were very loyal and dedicated to the bosses who saw them as hard-working co-workers and who treated them with decency and respect. These secretaries understood that the nature of the ad agency business was manic and high-pressured. Most of them liked the feeling of being part of that world, part of that excitement and high-level achievement and they did whatever was needed of them. But they hated the junior executives, the brats who looked down their noses at working-class women, and talked about them in sexist, even misogynistic terms, like a bad taste in their mouths.

I could see the whole power performance dynamic on display, and I could see its toxic effects. I had no appetite for it. I don't think that I was (or am) any more humble than any of the other junior executives at the agency. I have always had a pretty high opinion of myself. I have never lacked self-confidence. But I know what it's like to be the means by which others feel superior. I know what it's like for others to feed their egos by making me feel "less than." And I know what it's like for others to have a fully formed perception of me based solely on their preconceived notion of me.

The fact that I was the only Black executive at the agency does not mean that I have any greater sense of humanity than my peers and co-workers. No. I don't believe so. But I do believe that—as a Black man—my life experiences have probably fed and encouraged a greater sense of empathy, a greater ability to appreciate and understand what someone else is feeling, and why they are feeling it. I think these differences have been part of my professional strengths. I think they are part of what makes me a better marketer, and what has made me a better boss.

To be clear, however, the insights and advantages that my life experiences bring to my professional experiences don't have to be beyond the reach of others. These are learned skills and knowledge. Others certainly could learn them as well. If advertising agencies became more diverse and more inclusive, the people who work there would routinely be exposed to different people, different cultures, different perspectives and different life experiences. That exposure and interaction would be an almost inescapable growth experience. The path to becoming more enlightened people would have the fortunate by-product of making them better marketers as well.

◆

As a management trainee, I had almost no interaction with the management supervisor of my group. My boss was the account executive. Her boss was the account supervisor. And her boss was the management supervisor, a tall, lean (almost wiry) man with short-cropped blonde hair and grey eyes. I know it is unfair to make this association to him, but whenever I think of him I see an image of a Nazi SS officer from some WWII movie. He had that same brittle severity.

When I first started, I had been in several meetings where he was present. It is agency protocol to drag the trainee along to meetings to observe and to take notes, although people rarely asked me for my notes. You try to look like you belong there, without being too noticeable. In these meetings, the management supervisor never spoke directly to me, and I certainly did not speak to him. As a trainee, my job was to listen and observe, not to speak. But after two or perhaps three months on the job, he called me to his office for a conversation. I came prepared to receive an assignment.

"So, how's it going so far?" He looked at me, squinting slightly. "You've been here, what, two-three months? You like it?"

"Absolutely," I responded. "I think I'm learning quite a bit."

"Well, that's the whole point," he said brusquely. "We spend quite a lot of money training you. I hope you're learning something."

After another moment or two, the conversation took a different turn. "So, how did you get this job anyhow? You know, my cousin has been trying to get a job at an agency with no luck. He's interviewed a bunch of places, but nothing happens. He even interviewed here. …Nothing." He shook his head.

"Where does he work now?" I asked, just to participate somehow in the conversation.

"The phone company." (Back then, there was only one company that could be called "the phone company.") And then he looked at me. "But if *you* can be trained to do this job, so can he. Why not, right? Of course, you have affirmative action on your side, so you have a leg up on the competition."

I tilted my head slightly to the side, aware that my mouth was about to open. Somehow, I managed to keep it closed. After a moment or two of silence, I pretended that I could hear someone in the hallway looking for me, so I stood up. "I'll do my best to keep learning." And I walked out.

That was probably the only one-on-one conversation we had in the six months that I worked in his group.

CHAPTER SEVEN

Drinking Tea and Only Cute Babies

After six months in the Management Training Program, I graduated to assistant account executive and then, in what seemed like the blink of an eye, I was promoted to full account executive. This was no longer the bottom of the pecking order, but still pretty close to bottom. All the same, it felt pretty good.

I was in a new group now, working on the Lipton Tea account. It was a big account with a big problem. Lipton Tea had a 70% share of market in a product category that was rapidly declining. Lipton "owned" a market that was dying in their hands. There wasn't much point in growing market share any further because the only people in America drinking tea were little old ladies, librarians, and British expats. Soft drinks were king, and coffee was growing rapidly. The big push in Lipton's new products group was something called "coffeetee", some dreadful tasting concoction that was half coffee and half tea. The client was convinced it was going to be a big hit.

At the same time, Lipton's R&D unit was developing a new line of teas. Back then, the world of teas was divided into three groups; 1) black teas; regular and decaf, the standard no-frills tea that everyone knew; 2) gourmet teas, such as Earl Grey and Darjeeling, 3) herbal teas, such as chamomile or mint. That might seem like a lot of choices, but for a typical "middle market" tea drinker (such as myself), that still left a great deal of unmet need. Black teas were okay, but could get pretty boring after awhile. Gourmet teas were interesting, but they were quite expensive and were usually sold loose in fancy tins rather than in tea bags. I always ended up with tea leaves stuck in my teeth. And the herbal teas just had no appeal. They lacked a caffeine kick and always tasted weak and watery.

Where could a tea lover get a full-bodied cup of tea with interesting flavor that didn't require a trip to a fancy specialty tea shop?

That's what the R&D unit at Lipton was working on, a line of "flavored teas" like raspberry, peach, blackberry and vanilla. They had research that suggested that products like these would appeal to existing tea drinkers (thereby driving up frequency and volume of consumption) and—more importantly—appeal to younger non-tea drinkers, bringing new people into the category. As a tea drinker myself (I absolutely hate the taste of coffee), I thought this was a brilliant idea. Why didn't anyone come up with this sooner?

My agency colleagues on the account, however, saw this as just another wild idea that would quickly crash and burn. They were putting all of their chips on coming up with a new television ad campaign for Lipton Tea using Don Meredith. And so, as the only tea drinker on the Lipton Tea account, I asked if I could focus my time on the new product development work.

I always felt that they said yes just a little too easily, that they were quite happy to have me split off from the rest of the group to work alone. There was a cozy social relationship among the rest of the group, of which I was never part. In the office, they would talk about their personal lives or the things that they did together after work. I was rarely ever included.

In any case, I spent my time working with and getting to know Noble Fleming, whom most people called "Toby." Mr. Fleming, a gentleman more than twice my age, was the head of the Royal Estates Tea Company. They select and purchase all tea for Lipton. In addition to being the head of the company, Toby was an internationally recognized "tea master", perhaps the best tea taster in the world. Lipton had even done an ad campaign around Toby at one time. And in the Lipton R&D labs, Toby and I spent our afternoons tasting tea and spitting into large, chrome-plated cuspidors (gross!). I learned all about the many types and grades of tea and the proper way to evaluate them. I am now something of an unofficial expert on teas. While most men receive neckties on Father's Day, my son gives me exotic teas.

The end result of our labors was the launch of Lipton Flavored Teas, supported by an ad campaign that looked more like soft drink advertising and featured an attractive young actress (Joanna Cameron) from the TV series Isis (kind of a Wonder Woman knock-off). The success of the launch cannot be overstated. Lipton Flavored Teas were the first teas other than the standard ordinary black tea to be carried on major supermarket shelves. And the product flew off those shelves like they were giving it away. The number of Americans drinking tea increased, especially among younger drinkers. The frequency of tea consumption increased. Lipton revenue increased. They had launched a very profitable new product that single-handedly revitalized and transformed the industry. From then on, the space dedicated to tea on supermarket shelves doubled, eventually including herbal brands and specialty brands.

And because none of my agency colleagues were terribly interested in working on the project, my role in the launch success was even more conspicuous to the client. It was tea-time and I got my promotion to account supervisor.

◆ ◆ ◆

CUTE BABIES & FUSSY CLIENTS

In the latter part of my tenure at SSC&B, I worked on the Johnson & Johnson Baby Products account. By then, I had already worked on the launch of three separate, highly successful new product introductions and this had become something of a specialty for me. I loved it. New products fit perfectly with my own entrepreneurial spirit. I loved the idea of making something from nothing, of starting with nothing except imagination, good research and perspiration. And so, on J&J Baby Products, I worked on a project that was extremely unpopular with the company's senior management, Johnson's Baby Cornstarch Powder.

When the project managers initially took the idea to senior management—as the story goes—they were practically brow beaten in the conference room. Johnson's Baby Powder was far and away one of the company's most successful and lucrative products. And it was made from talc. The whole world loves Johnson's Baby Powder. And it has one of the most recognizable fragrances of any product. It is synonymous with babies. A senior executive told the managers, "We own talc mines. We don't own corn fields. Why in God's name would we want to make this product?"

But here's the thing. Talc is a rock. It is ground to an incredibly fine, incredibly soft, smooth powder, but it is still a rock. When a mother sprinkles it all over her baby, it does not absorb any moisture; it just forms a stone barrier. And the way some moms sprinkle that stuff, it is likely that the baby is actually inhaling a whole lot of rock into their lungs. Medical researchers were just beginning to recognize this. Pediatricians were just beginning to hear about this. And the Johnson & Johnson project managers realized that these whispers and murmurs by a small handful in the medical profession would—sooner or later—turn into a public outcry.

The new product was made from corn. It was abundant. It was cheaper to manufacture. It was capable of absorbing 115 times its own weight in moisture. And most importantly, it was completely digestible or absorbable by the body without adverse effects. The only significant downside was that the launch of this new product would almost certainly trigger the eventual demise of the company's biggest cash cow. It was a tremendous risk.

The company decided to take the risk. They launched Johnson's Baby Cornstarch Powder (a name that doesn't exactly roll off the tongue) and got out in front of public awareness of the dangers of talc powders. They didn't stop making the talc product, and the advertising never denigrated talc or addressed the issue head-on, but every year the new product grew, and the old product got smaller and smaller. Eventually, they began calling the new product "Johnson's Baby Powder with Cornstarch." It probably worked out better than they ever imagined.

Our agency produced a lot of ads for the new Cornstarch Powder, a lot of TV shoots and print shoots. A lot of babies. But in all the ads with all the babies, not one baby was ever a Black baby. Not one. I am fairly certain that this did not bother anyone except me. I am fairly certain that the observation did not even occur to anyone except me. No one noticed. No one cared.

But one day, as I sat in a casting session with one of the agency's art directors, watching baby after baby get powdered as part of their audition, I turned to the art director and asked him a simple question. "Joe, how come we never have any Black babies in any of our ads?"

Joe was a middle-aged Italian guy, a real New Yorker and a veteran of the advertising business. He had a voice that sounded like he gargled with gravel. We had a solid, friendly relationship, so he was not at all defensive about my question. On the contrary, his answer suggested that he saw this as an opportunity for me to learn, a teachable moment.

"Mark, you gotta understand," he put down his cigarette and leaned toward me, as if speaking in confidence. "This is Johnson & Johnson, a very uptight client. Those guys are perfectionists. They only want cute babies in their ads. I mean really cute babies."

I'm sure that I could not conceal the stunned expression on my face, but Joe did not seem to notice. He picked up his cigarette and went back to watching babies getting powdered.

CHAPTER EIGHT

Zsa Zsa's Revenge

In 1980, I began my next major account assignment at SSC&B:LINTAS on the Los Angeles, California-based Carnation Pet Food account. It was an important and high-profile piece of new business that agency management fought hard to win. SSC&B had promised the Carnation executives that they would be getting all of the resources, experience and creative fire-power of a top tier New York ad agency, and that is what Carnation wanted. But it wasn't enough. The client said that their brand teams were accustomed to working with an agency that was just ten minutes down Wilshire Boulevard, an agency that could drop what they're doing and run right over for a meeting, an agency that would spend time outside of the office getting to know their people. That kind of "personal touch" was important to them. They challenged us to make it work.

Whatever it took, we promised that we would deliver. SSC&B promised that we would service their business as if we were just down the street. No matter what. And so, for the next three-plus years, I spent three days a week in Los Angeles, every week, 50 weeks a year. That left about one and a half days each week in the New York office. It was an absolutely insane schedule. You constantly felt like the juggler on the Ed Sullivan Show (remember the Ed Sullivan Show?) who was spinning six plates on six different sticks. I kept the plates spinning while trying to keep the clients happy and trying also to have a personal life. Central to the advertising agency's culture was the expectation that your personal life and your family life was a poor second place behind your commitment to the job.

What I learned, and what became a useful and valuable life lesson, was that if you do something often enough, you find that you can do almost anything. The impossible soon becomes routine.

One of the first—and biggest—routines was the plane flights. American Airlines had an early afternoon non-stop 747 jumbo jet flight that arrived at LAX by late afternoon, giving you plenty of time to pick up your car, get to your hotel, check in, and relax before dinner. (*This was in the early 1980s, when—if you were fast on your feet—you could arrive at the airport 15-20 minutes before your flight and still make the plane.*) And with a few rare exceptions, I took the same flight every week for three years. I quickly graduated to American's top frequent flyer status and flew first-class every time. Invariably, one of the other first-class passengers—one of the white passengers—would try as politely as possible to point out to me that I had inadvertently sat down in first-class and that the coach seats were further back. Or they would nonchalantly ask, "What's your seat number?"

Occasionally, if the mood struck me, the person sitting next to me would awkwardly attempt to ask if I was in the correct seat, and I would turn to them and announce that this was going to be my Rosa Parks moment. I was fed up and I refused to move to the back of the plane. Totally aghast, my seatmate would press the call button, summoning the flight attendant. But when the flight attendant arrived, what my seatmate heard was the warm, familiar greeting of, "Good afternoon, Mr. Robinson. Can I bring you some champagne?"

The flight crew—who were always the same because I always took the same flight—were like my extended family. I knew them as well as my own agency staff. And when the time finally came, after three-plus years on the Carnation account, I told them that next week would be my final flight, the flight crew found a way to close off the upper deck of the 747 and throw a private party for me with dancing and non-stop champagne. Even the captain joined in. We hugged. Some of us cried. And we promised to stay in touch. We were still saying long goodbyes after the plane had landed at JFK. Passengers exiting the plane craned their necks, attempting to look up the spiral staircase to see what was all the commotion upstairs.

The hotel was another steady routine, but we wound up shifting to new hotel routines a few times during my tenure. Our first steady hotel was the Beverly Hilton, a major Beverly Hills landmark at the intersection of Wilshire and Santa Monica Boulevards and site of a few different award shows and the Motion Picture Academy's Governors' Ball. We stayed at the Beverly Hilton for probably nine months. But then, one night, as we were drinking in the hotel bar (which was a very covert and barely lit space off the hotel lobby), my new boss, a very, very intoxicated Ian McGregor, exclaimed loudly (very loudly), "Wait a minute. Wait. Do you mean to tell me there are hookers in this bar? Real hookers? Where? Point them out. Show me the hookers."

To the four of us who were sitting and drinking with Ian, this was absolutely hysterical. Ian was our new boss making his first trip to the coast and his barely understandable accent was one-third thick Scottish Highland, one-third Rhodesian, and one-third Johnnie Walker. Unfortunately, however, this did not go over well for the rest of the bar. Not with the other patrons at the bar. Not with the hookers. Not with the hotel's management. Nothing was said. There was never a fuss. But suddenly our agency travel department was unable to make any reservations for the following week. We found a new hotel.

Our next hotel was Le Parc; a small boutique, all-suite hotel tucked away on a quiet residential street in West Hollywood. Now that we knew our way around town and LA was our "home away from home", Le Parc was much better suited to our needs and our lifestyle. While the Beverly Hilton was a gigantic palace that attracted both tourists and Hollywood industry types, Le Parc was tiny by comparison and did not attract any of the "see or be seen" crowd. However, the hotel was a favorite among a number of rock musicians and bands. If you were having lunch in the hotel's only restaurant, you were likely to see Billy Joel having breakfast. Or you might run into Duran Duran by the rooftop swimming pool.

One day as I was exiting the hotel parking garage in my rental car, another vehicle was arriving and attempting to enter. If we had both been driving Hondas we might have been able to navigate the hotel's narrow driveway without colliding into each other. (Of course, if we had both been driving Hondas, we would not have been in West Hollywood.) But I was driving a big convertible and the other car was a stretch limousine. Oddly enough, I did more damage to the limo than he did to me.

As the limo driver and I began exchanging information, about a half dozen passengers started popping out of the back of the limo. It was the Australian rock band, Men At Work. They were incredibly good-natured and offered to have drinks together later that evening. They shrugged off the car's damage by saying, "We wouldn't be much of a rock band if we brought back the limo in the same condition we got it, would we?"

I made new friends.

Of course, my time on the Carnation account was not all hanging out and goofing off. We actually got quite a bit of work done. Carnation had three main divisions; Dairy Products (the stuff most people associated with Carnation), Contadina Pastas and Sauces, and Pet Foods (for cats and dogs). Carnation's Pet Food division had done quite a lot of fun and memorable advertising. Even today, decades after the company discontinued the advertising; people still remember the "Real Beef" branding iron mnemonic on the top of Mighty Dog's distinctive little dog food cans. And my favorite commercial for Friskies Buffet was the marching band parade of real parakeets strutting past a cat who could not be distracted from his bowl of Friskies Buffet.

A lot of silliness that made quite a lot of money.

In 1981, Carnation was preparing to launch Fancy Feast. It would be a major new ultra-premium cat food brand, a real game-changer creating a new segment in the pet food category. The Fancy Feast can would be half the size of a regular cat food can, but at twice the price. It was an identical business model to Mighty Dog and employed much the same consumer-pet psychology, going after the market segment that wanted only the very best for their beloved pet. The product would be hugely profitable. It could stack twice as many units on the same square footage of supermarket shelf and make twice the revenue on each can. A lot of client and agency resources went into the development of this new brand and a lot of money was riding on its success.

The agency had developed a launch campaign that featured a beautiful, luxurious white Persian cat with an ultra-pampered woman's voice.

The voice we had chosen was a famous—perhaps infamous—female movie star whose career had built an image of an ultra-pampered princess. A diva in the most classic sense. She was also someone who was instantly recognizable by her voice, so she was a perfect choice for the voice-over role. We chose Zsa Zsa Gabor.

On the day of the voice-over recording session, Zsa Zsa came into the studio, and everyone immediately noticed that something was clearly amiss. Zsa Zsa was definitely off her game and her voice was faint and scratchy, not the royal velvet we were counting on. There was speculation whispered among the agency team that perhaps Ms. Gabor was badly hung over, but her agent explained that she had the flu. We forged ahead and completed the recording session, but after trying countless takes, we knew we were not going to get what we needed. Of course, the producer insisted we could "fix it in the mix" (a catch-all phrase for post-production manipulation of whatever you had filmed or recorded), but we never got that far. Once the client heard the recording, we were told to go back and do it over. And this time get it right!

So, we called the agent and explained that we would need to bring Zsa Zsa back in for another session. He said, "Sure. But she just left for Europe. She'll be back in about six weeks."

Wait, what? No. We couldn't wait six weeks. We had a launch schedule. We had to be in market. It would be an absolute disaster if the client started shipping products to grocery stores without supporting advertising.

"Sorry," the agent explained. "There's nothing I can do."

The entire agency team was in full panic mode.

One of us suggested that we simply fly to Europe and record her there. But her agent insisted that he did not know her whereabouts and had no ability to track her down. He wasn't even sure what country she was in. Maybe the south of France, maybe Italy. Maybe Majorca.

And then . . . I came up with this brilliant idea. Our actress had a sister who looked and sounded just like her. In fact, their careers more or less paralleled each other. Why not record the sister?

So that's what we did. We went out and hired Eva Gabor. The former star of the TV show Green Acres was actually doing quite a bit of voice over work for several animated Disney films at the time. She sounded great. The client loved the new recordings. Everyone was happy and we finished the commercials and got them on the air in time for the launch. And the launch? It was a huge success. Huge.

Happy ending, right? Not so fast.

Some time afterward, Zsa Zsa returned from her extended European vacation. She saw—and heard—the commercial on TV. Perhaps no one else could tell the difference, but she could. Zsa Zsa knew it wasn't her voice. She knew it was her sister.

But here is the critical piece of information that the rest of us didn't know. The two sisters were personal and professional rivals. They hated each other. Despised each other. Zsa Zsa's attorneys immediately filed a $4 million lawsuit against Carnation, against the agency and me personally. (Why me??) Zsa Zsa claimed that by substituting a "sound-alike" performer we had deprived her of legitimate income, subjecting her to public embarrassment and that our example would encourage other advertisers to do the same.

This was my first exposure to this kind of high-stakes litigation. And while the higher-ups at Carnation and at SSC&B and all the lawyers were all strategizing and figuring out what to do, no one was communicating anything to me. I was far down the company ladder, which meant I was expendable, and no one would bat an eye.

For the next several months, I was convinced I would be fired and personally on the hook for a multi-million dollar legal judgement. And during those months, I aged about a decade. Fortunately, during those months, sales of Fancy Feast skyrocketed. The product was doing so well the client asked us to cut back on the ad schedule. That meant that Carnation was flush with cash and in a generally good mood. That also meant—fortunately for me—that Carnation was in the mood to settle the suit and put it behind them, so that's what they did. Everyone was able to walk away from the table satisfied that things worked out for the best. I was able to breathe normally again.

And our new cat food brand got bigger and bigger.

CHAPTER NINE

Chopsticks

After Carnation, I went to work on the Lever Brothers account. Lever was an extremely important account to the agency. Unilever, Lever's international network, single-handedly made it possible for SSC&B to become a major global advertising powerhouse, with business operations in 30+ countries. In fact, our agency's name, SSC&B:LINTAS, came from "Lever International Advertising Services." Being assigned to a Lever account was an overt signal that you were important to the agency. You were being groomed for bigger things. I was going to work on the All Detergent account for Lever, and it was just about as exciting as it sounds. At least I learned how and why laundry detergent works, even if that was the only thing that I learned from the experience.

And at least I could be grateful for the fact that Lever no longer manufactured or sold Gold Dust Soap Powder, discontinued sometime in the 1950s, as pickaninny brand mascots began to fall out of favor.

My new boss was a woman named Claire. She had been at the agency less than a year and had not been someone that I had any opportunity to get to know before we began working together. I had no idea what she was told about me before she met me, but apparently—whatever it was—it did not please her. The negative energy during our first encounter broadcast off of her like steam off hot, wet pavement. Our initial conversation was filled with things she said that I would "need to learn" in order to keep up on the business. And if I did not keep up, no one was going to carry me.

Okay.

My impression of Claire was rather blank. She was not remarkable either in any positive or negative way. Just plain. She had an impressive business school pedigree, (although I can't recall from where), and wielded it like a truncheon against anyone who was not sufficiently impressed by her. My boss on Carnation was a terrific person and a valuable mentor. I quickly realized—and accepted—that my new boss on Lever would be none of those things.

After our first meeting, Claire said, "Let's go out to lunch tomorrow and get to know each other better."

"That would be great." I smiled. "I look forward to it."

The next day, I met her in the lobby of our office building, Dag Hammarskjold Plaza, and we strolled together up 48th Street toward Fifth Avenue. After a few blocks, we arrived at Hatsuhana, a Japanese restaurant just in the block from Madison Avenue, and stopped at the front door.

"Is this alright? I felt like having sushi." She looked at me with an oddly curved smile. I'm not sure what response or reaction she was expecting. Perhaps she thought I might recoil at the idea of such an exotic cuisine. Perhaps she thought I might prefer a barbecue rib joint or something from the Colonel.

"Whatever you like, I'm fine with."

In the early 1980s, Japanese culture in America was ascendant. Japanese car companies had begun to dominate the American automobile market. Japanese electronics products in cameras, televisions, and audio were over-taking and, in many cases, literally wiping out their American competition. Japanese real estate investors had actually purchased Rockefeller Center. In August of 1982, the New York Times ran a front-page story entitled, "Culture of Japan Blossoming in America." If you were in business in America, especially in New York City, you were probably captivated by the World of the Rising Sun. And there was no better way to show that you were ultra-sophisticated and genuinely worldly, than to show that you liked sushi.

At best, Claire was attempting to make our lunch a "teachable moment" where I would learn how to be a big boy and do what real business-people did. At worst, and perhaps more likely, Claire was attempting to make our lunch a power-play, where I would recognize just how far beneath her I truly was, and that I would find this revelation permanently intimidating. And that would define our relationship from that point forward. This certainly was not the first time that a boss or co-worker tried to make me feel both subordinate and inferior. It probably would not be the last. These types of maneuvers were usually based on assumptions about Black people, and those assumptions were usually based on ignorance.

I had just completed three and a half years on the Carnation account. I practically lived in Los Angeles. And California is light years ahead of the east coast when it comes to embracing Japanese culture. Yamashiro, in the Hollywood Hills overlooking Los Angeles, was one of my all-time favorite restaurants. Hatsuhana, where we were eating that day, was also a place I had been many times before.

And by the way, the very first American pop star to record an album in a foreign language was Nat King Cole, who recorded in Japanese. When it came to cultural trends, Black people were almost always doing it first.

I ordered the sushi/sashimi combination, along with an order of Ikura, which was my favorite. Claire asked me questions about my background while we ate. I picked up a piece of sushi with my fingers (the proper way to eat sushi), and Claire paused mid-sentence to watch me. She shot a glance over at my chopsticks, which were beside my plate. Again, I saw that oddly curved smile. A few more minutes passed as we continued talking. I picked up my chopsticks to retrieve a piece of yellowfin tuna, waited a moment for another pause in our conversation before popping it into my mouth.

"You've used chopsticks before," Claire said the words as both a statement and a question.

I was not going to answer while still chewing my yellowfin, so I took my time to respond. And then, I looked at Claire and waited a few moments longer.

"Lots of Chinese take-out." I smiled.

And Claire made that oddly curved smile.

CHAPTER TEN

"And then I fired him"

In March of 1985, I was promoted to Vice President at SSC&B. It was often said around the office that people got promoted to Vice President as a way of pacifying them when they didn't get the raise they were asking for. There is some truth to that, however, I was 28 years old and had made VP before turning 30. I had gone from trainee to VP in less than seven years. To me at least, it felt like a big deal.

Unofficially, it was acknowledged that I was the agency's very first African American Vice President. Lots of handshakes and back-slaps, or hand-written notes scribbled on the announcement memo. So, I wasn't the only one who considered the promotion to be a very big deal. I was a first. A pioneer. Officially, however, the agency was loath to formally acknowledge such racial ground-breaking. They did not view this as a positive achievement, but rather as casting a harsh and embarrassing light on the fact that it had taken them this long to make this step forward.

There was also another implication of my promotion that SSC&B did not wish to have examined too closely. My Executive Vice President took me to lunch to congratulate me on my promotion and to explain to me in the most sympathetic way that it was a shame that someone as bright and talented as me had now risen as far I would ever go in the organization. Halfway through lunch, he was literally crying into his Manhattan highball glass because this was probably the last promotion

I would ever get. There was no room at the top for "people like me." He confessed it was "a crying shame."

Wait what?

Although I was very happy at SSC&B, and the agency had been extremely generous and supportive in my training, my assignments and responsibilities and my compensation, it was being made inescapably clear to me that any further advancement in my career would be frustrated, deferred or perhaps even thwarted. At age 28, I was being told to accept that I had gone as far as I could.

This was definitely not the career plan I had written for myself.

My circumstance was in many respects an analog for the situations of other Black professionals in advertising, or perhaps more broadly in corporate America. My company was glad to have me, and happy to show me off to the world when I celebrated some achievement, just as long as no one examined the context of that achievement too closely. Just as long as no one asked, "How come you have a 'first Black' anything in 1985?"

Lots of companies—lots of the agency's clients—already had Black VPs. Many of them were in departments like "Community Affairs" or "Urban Affairs", but at least they were there. Madison Avenue still had quite a long way to catch up.

I suspect that there were those in management at SSC&B who never thought that any Black person would make it that far or that I would ever make it that far. They never thought they would have to deal with the problem posed by the question, "What do we do with him now?"

I decided I should probably answer that question for myself. After seven years at SSC&B, I left in the summer of 1985 and went to Grey Advertising. Through an executive recruiter, Grey had been courting me for nearly 18 months when I finally accepted their offer. Grey was a much larger shop than SSC&B so I was hopeful that this would represent greater opportunities for advancement. I was also aware of Grey's history of being founded by Jewish advertising executives who had themselves experienced discrimination in the New York ad business. Instead of using the names of the agency principals, as was the tradition, they concealed their ethnic identities and chose the color of the walls as the agency's name. I was hopeful that this meant Grey had a more enlightened corporate culture with respect to racial discrimination.

Not long after joining the agency in 1985, I became Grey's first Black Vice President and Management Supervisor. The irony—or perhaps the pointlessness—of this accomplishment was abundantly clear to me. In addition to my account management responsibilities for clients such as Bristol Myers, SmithKline Beecham and Block Drug, I served as an adjunct to Grey's Market Horizons division, as researcher/investigator of acquisition candidates for Grey.

I remained at Grey for five years. And in those five years, I cannot think of a single event or experience that I feel compelled to write about here.

Well, alright, two very short stories.

I worked at Grey from 1985—1990, during some of the worst years of the AIDS epidemic. This was a disease that reached all corners of our country, but touched certain industries more than others. Madison Avenue had more than its share of AIDS tragedies.

One of the administrative assistants in my group was a tall, slender young man with shoulder-length blonde hair and an over-eager puppy-dog demeanor. When he became ill, he tried to keep his condition private, but eventually, someone outed him as HIV-positive. When my boss, an uptight, middle-aged Greenwich, Connecticut jackass named Ben, discovered this, he flew into an absolute panic. His first effort was an attempt to have the young man fired. When that failed, he sought to have him transferred to another group. That too, obviously failed. Finally, he demanded—and the agency agreed—to ban the young assistant from entering or using any of the men's room facilities in the agency.

To help him deal with what had become a pointlessly demeaning situation, several of the female administrative assistants discreetly arranged for the young man to use the ladies' room when he needed while they stood guard at the door. Sadly, however, before long, the young man went on disability, and we learned that he passed away at home.

PROTECTING MY OWN

On another occasion, one of the account supervisors in my team called me at the office from a print shoot that she was covering with the client. The young account supervisor was in tears on the telephone and asked me if she could leave the shoot and return to the office. I asked her to tell me what had happened to upset her, but could not get any meaningful details over the phone. She asked me to come down to the shoot and she would wait until I arrived before leaving.

When I arrived downtown at the shoot, the young woman was literally waiting at the door with her coat on. My efforts to ask questions were only moderately more successful in person. Apparently, the client, an officious, preening recent MBA who considered himself God's gift to brand management, was making endless "special requests" of the photographer during the shoot, while expressing his displeasure with how the day was progressing. My account supervisor attempted to be a mediating go-between so that the client did not harass the photographer directly. In response, the client brow-beat and bullied the account supervisor.

"Okay, I got it." I said to the young woman. "You go back to the office and write this up while it's fresh in your mind. I'll cover the rest of the shoot."

Once she had left, I checked in briefly with the photographer, then turned my attention to the client. I deliberately delayed my conversation with the client for those few moments, both so that I could collect my thoughts, and also to signal to the client that he was not my first priority.

I sat down in a chair next to him and leaned in close, so that our conversation would be private. "You know, she is a stellar account supervisor. She is super smart and totally committed to the success of your business. We all are."

I paused to allow those first few words to stand on their own. "But I want to be sure you understand something. Every one of us on my team, every one of us who is on *your* team, we're in the service business, not the servant business."

The client looked at me suddenly, his eyes opening wide.

"And if you ever treat one of my people unprofessionally again, you can expect me to respond in a manner that will be equally unprofessional."

The client lurched backward and was about to protest, when I cut him off.

"Why don't we both just cool down and make sure we have a great shoot today?"

And we did.

◆ ◆ ◆

Shortly after my two children were born, I interviewed for a job at The UniWorld Group, the largest Black-owned advertising agency in the country at that time. UniWorld had a reputation for truly breakthrough creative work. Byron Lewis, the founder/CEO, was an entrepreneur that I admired. He built UniWorld with his bare hands, his wits and his force of will, and been tremendously successful. Byron was a fascinating man and a colorful character; handsome, always dapper and elegantly dressed and effortlessly charming. I was definitely interested in coming to work for someone like him.

On numerous prior occasions, executive recruiters had asked me if I was interested in working for a minority-owned advertising agency. They pointed out that I had an excellent resume and would be highly sought after. Of course, I was also warned that the mainstream advertising industry did not have any love or respect for the minority agencies. They simply did not take them seriously. I was told, "Once you make the transition from mainstream agency to minority agency, you take the path of no return. It's a one-way choice." In essence, anyone who was lucky enough to have a good position at a mainstream agency would be giving it all away forever by going to work at a minority agency. Mainstream agencies would no longer respect my credentials (because they did not respect or value minority agencies or the work they did) and would never offer me a job again.

If I took a job at a place like UniWorld, I might never be able to come back to the mainstream side of the business. My career might be tainted forever by the "advertising ghetto."

Nevertheless, in 1989, I decided that my career needed some shaking up and some fresh energy. I had spent the previous 11 years working for two of the biggest and most respected ad agencies in New York; SSC&B and Grey, working on accounts like Johnson & Johnson, Carnation, Bristol Myers, and UniLever. I had learned the business and logged some noteworthy accomplishments. I had successfully launched five major national brands. But, I had also felt the cold, indifferent force of my face pressing up against advertising's glass ceiling.

And so, I arranged for an interview at UniWorld with the SVP, head of client services, the agency's second in command at the time. The interview seemed fairly positive for a while. It was mostly me talking about my background and the experience that I could bring to UniWorld. But about halfway through our discussion, things took a sudden turn. My interviewer thought I was very bright and had very strong credentials, but he said he needed to be honest with me.

I had heard that line in an interview before.

My mind began to race. He couldn't possibly be about to tell me that they don't hire Negroes. This was a Black agency. What the hell was he about to be so honest about?

"Frankly, I don't think you are Black enough to come to work for UniWorld. I think you're great, but I just don't think you'd fit in here. This is a special kind of place."

"Excuse me?" If I had been drinking, I would have done a spit take.

"You come from a mainstream agency background", He shrugged his shoulders. "You're accustomed to doing things the mainstream way. You would be constantly trying to get people to do things your way. That's not how we work."

I had never worked for a minority agency, so it was hard for me to rebut him, but the argument sounded pretty ridiculous to me. What kind of absurd ethnic stereotype was he suggesting was the everyday culture at UniWorld? I wanted to tell him he was crazy, but this was a job interview, and that wasn't the way this was supposed to go.

I didn't know what was worse; what he was suggesting about UniWorld, or what he was suggesting about me. Throughout my whole life, I had to deal with colorism from my own people, prejudice because of my light skin complexion. Throughout my life, there has always been someone who will look at my light skin and assume that I think of myself as superior to them because they are dark-skinned, who assume that I look down on them. As a result, I am treated with distrust and hostility by someone who ought to be a kindred soul. To be honest, this is not a common occurrence. Most Black people have too much empathy (and too much common sense) to be hung up on such petty prejudice. But there's always someone. And when it happens, it always stings.

I left the interview bewildered and disappointed. And dispirited. Shortly thereafter, I left the agency side of the business and went to work on the client side. I went to work for a company called The Danbury Mint. It turned out to be the worst professional experience of my career. I literally hated every single day that I worked there. I knew I had made a horrible mistake leaving the ad agency business, and in less than a year I was desperate to get back in.

Even though a year had passed, I was still bothered by the experience of my interview at UniWorld. I couldn't let it go. I decided to write a letter to that SVP. (This was 1990. People still wrote letters. I still write letters.) In my letter I told him that I would like to meet with him again. I told him that I felt he was wrong about me, and I told him why I would be an asset to UniWorld. I said if we were able to meet again that I would convince him of this.

I did not receive a response from the SVP. I did, however, receive a response from Byron Lewis, the founder/CEO, inviting me to come in for a talk. When I arrived at UniWorld's headquarters at the intersection of SoHo, Chinatown and TriBeCa, I was escorted into Byron's office, an ample L-shaped space tastefully decorated in African and contemporary art. Given Byron Lewis' colorful reputation, the office was surprisingly understated, suggesting a man who was very much in control of his own image and of the environment around him.

Byron greeted me as though I were a VIP guest. He got up from his desk and led me to a chrome and leather guest chair opposite a long sofa, where he sat down. On the glass coffee table between us was the letter I had written to the SVP.

"I read your letter," Byron began the conversation.

"He showed it to you?"

"He did," Byron said, looking down at the letter. "And then I fired him."

"You fired him?"

"I did," Byron nodded. "I don't know what is wrong with that child. (Byron often referred to the people who worked for him as "his children.") I can't have someone telling people that they aren't Black enough to work for me. I can't have people who think like that. As far as I'm concerned, if you're Black, you're Black. Period. What in the world is "Black enough"? For goodness' sake, we have a hard-enough time in this business without that kind of thinking. I need to have the best people working for me. I don't really care what they look like." And then he smiled. "And trust me, I have some funny looking people working here."

We talked for about three hours and the interaction never once felt like an interview. Occasionally the conversation was relaxed and meandering, frequently with Byron's reminiscences about the advertising business. But every now and then, we would hit a topic that excited him or me and the pace turned into a high-energy tennis match, with quick verbal volleying back and forth. He seemed especially to enjoy that. In the beginning, his assistant interrupted with a phone call or a question, but it soon became clear to her that he did not wish to be disturbed and the interruptions ceased.

About an hour into our time together, he paused as though something had just occurred to him. "In your letter, you wrote that you would really like to come work here. Is that true?"

"Yes sir. I want to learn from you."

"Good." He looked me in the eye. "Because you're hired. How soon can you start?" And then we went back to our informal conversation for another two hours.

I worked for Byron Lewis and UniWorld for six and a half years. Byron was the best mentor and teacher I have ever had in this business. And whenever anyone asks what was my favorite job or favorite place to work, without hesitation I tell them UniWorld. I loved going to work every single day. I learned multicultural marketing at UniWorld and took my own marketing skills to an entirely new level. Most importantly, for my own personal development, for my own "story", my UniWorld experience created for the very first time an intersection of who I am with what I do. My profession and my work were now a deeply personal extension of my sense of how I saw myself, how I defined and described myself. At UniWorld, we had a saying that we often told to clients and used in new business presentations; "Multicultural marketing is not just what we do. It is who we are."

This intersection of profession and personal identity had a significant yet unexpected benefit. My career as a multicultural marketer helped my two children, Sean and Lily, to create a picture and an understanding of who Daddy was. Kids in preschool and kindergarten have only the vaguest sense of what their parent does, or even what kind of person their parent is. And an understanding of ethnic or racial identity is still years away for most. But my job at UniWorld helped Sean and Lily see me more clearly and simply.

Dad was a Black man who helped companies sell their products to Black people.

It really wasn't any more complicated than that. Of course, as Sean and Lily got older, their understanding and perception grew more textured and nuanced. But it helped them tremendously to understand who they were by understanding who I was. I believe that it has helped them to develop a healthy and clear-eyed sense of the world in which they live and to be comfortable with their place in that world.

I spent six and a half very good years at UniWorld. Every day was exciting, challenging and rewarding. Although I am certain that most people at mainstream agencies looked down their noses in very condescending ways at the work done by minority agencies, the truth is that the advertising and marketing that is practiced at places like UniWorld is light years ahead of Madison Avenue. Integrated marketing was invented at minority agencies like UniWorld, and they were perfecting the art decades before Madison Avenue caught on. When we see mainstream agencies finally figuring out how to do experiential marketing, buzz marketing, and content development, we just smile and shake our heads.

And finally, after six and a half years at UniWorld, another opportunity came along—helping Spike Lee launch his own new ad agency—so eventually, it was time for me to move on. But I still look back nostalgically at my time at UniWorld. Byron eventually retired, and the place has not at all been the same since. It just isn't UniWorld without Byron. The agency's glory days are very much in the past, but that's okay. I am close to retirement myself, and I accept that all things have an expiration date. We were all "fresh" once.

CHAPTER ELEVEN

Working at home

I joined UniWorld at the beginning of September 1990. The agency was in its heyday and was the largest Black-owned advertising agency in the country. The agency had moved into its new offices in a SoHo high rise building at 100 Avenue of the Americas less than a year earlier. Everything was shiny and new and beautiful. It had an air of specialness. And it felt special to be there. But when a colleague asked me if I had a tuxedo during my first week there, I thought maybe things were going just a step too far.

But what my co-worker was asking was if I was ready for the upcoming CEBA Awards, which were just a couple of weeks away. I was embarrassed to admit that I had no idea what he was talking about. What were the CEBA Awards?

The CEBA Awards (Communications Excellence to Black Audiences) were the multicultural advertising industry's way of recognizing and honoring the great work of our peers. Minority agencies never won any of the mainstream advertising awards. The most polite thing that you could say was that the mainstream advertising award events did not even notice that we were there or the work we did. It was considered inconsequential and irrelevant. Nor was anyone from a multicultural agency ever a judge of a mainstream award. At least not back then. They knew we had our "colored" awards.

Jim Crow had drawn a big, bright line down Madison Avenue.

As it happens, I did not own a tuxedo. But I was a grown man and held a senior level position at the nation's largest Black-owned advertising agency. Renting formal wear was simply out of the question. It was definitely time for me to purchase my own tuxedo. I chose a very traditional, classic style from Brooks Brothers. (These days, I own three tuxedos.)

The awards that evening were held in the ballroom of the New York Hilton on 54th Street and Avenue of the Americas, an enormous and undeniably first-class venue. My colleagues and I were late to the event and missed almost all of the pre-event cocktail hour mingling. We had changed clothes at the office, something the women at UniWorld simply were not going to do. So that left a bunch of men fumbling with bow ties, cufflinks, and studs without any help. But the greatest challenge was trying to get a taxi to stop for a handful of Black men. Even in tuxedos, it was damn near impossible.

There were probably dozens of things that occurred during my first few weeks of working at UniWorld, new experiences, meeting my new co-workers, adapting to the new environment and new procedures. But most of those details fade from memory. What I remember, more than anything else, and what I associate most closely with beginning my work at UniWorld, was this night attending my first CEBA Awards.

I walked into the Hilton Ballroom, and it was like a scene from a Hollywood movie. The room felt magical, electric, as though everything had been sprinkled with a gentle touch of glitter. I saw hundreds of African American professionals in black tie and evening gowns, an image I had not seen since I was a small boy attending social cotillions at the Audubon Ballroom in Harlem more than twenty years before. I can honestly say that never in my adult life had I seen that many Black professionals looking their finest. This image was so powerful that I felt like the prodigal son finally returning home after a long, lonely absence. It was like the moment in the Wizard of Oz, when the images suddenly shift from black & white to vibrant Technicolor.

This was a through-the-looking-glass moment for me. And as I entered the ballroom that night, it almost seemed as though hundreds of people all turned in unison to acknowledge me and welcome me with an outstretched hand. I know that my recollection is blended with fantasy and imagination, but that is how I remember that night. I remember that I saw something that had been invisible to me before, but would never be invisible to me again.

I had no idea that so many smart, talented, creative people—Black people—were in the same business where I had just spent the past 12 years. I was so accustomed to working for advertising agencies where it was 'just me', or maybe 'just me and two others'. This was when I began to question the hiring practices of mainstream advertising agencies. This was when the problem first became real for me.

If you have ever been to a mainstream awards show, whether it was the Academy Awards, the Tonys, the Clios or simply some obscure industry event, there was always an element of ironic distance. There was always a hint of, "Yeah, we're all here, but we don't really take this thing seriously." It almost seemed like a repressed need to put down the thing they were celebrating.

That is not how Black people do award shows. There is none of that aloof air of above-it-all. When Black people do award shows, there is uninhibited joy and celebration. There is an explosion of individual and collective pride. There is kinetic energy. There can sometimes be—and often is—bad behavior at Black award show events, but that's because people become genuinely giddy about the experience. They lose themselves in the moment. For better or worse, it is to be expected.

Even so, at the CEBAs, there is no bad behavior.

From then on, working at UniWorld had established a new context, a new frame of reference for where I was working and who I was working with. In writing this chapter, I have struggled to find the right way to describe the changes that came with working at UniWorld; the shift in perceptions which in turn led to an adjustment in behavior, which led to a whole new set of emotions. It is very hard to explain to someone who has not had a comparable experience, but anyone who has come to work for a minority-owned company after working for a mainstream company knows exactly what I am talking about.

Most Black people in America live in two worlds; the mainstream majority world and the community of Blackness (not just Black people) that exists as a subset of the majority. W.E.B. DuBois wrote extensively and insightfully about co-existing in these two worlds. Language is one of the ways that Black people manage that dual existence. But there are also many, many aspects of dress and demeanor, both subtle and profound, that are signals and clues of that dual existence. Code-switching between two worlds is an essential skill set for Black professionals in most businesses, but it is absolutely critical on Madison Avenue, where the unfamiliar and uncomfortable can get you shunned, censored or fired.

When you come to work at a place like UniWorld, you leave all of that excess baggage at home. You save all of that stress-producing code-switching for client meetings. You don't have to be more than one person. You can just be you and perhaps discover that this person is worthy of dignity and respect without the performance element.

Because when you are working for a Black-owned firm, a place like UniWorld, you are working at home.

◆

Cash & Reputation

One of the unfortunate realities of most small businesses is that they frequently suffer from cash-flow problems. At the end of the quarter, money might balance out just fine, but on a week-to-week basis, money usually went out much faster than it came in. This is especially tough for advertising agencies. Profit margins are razor thin. Clients are notorious at seeing just how long they can stretch out a payment cycle. If you are a large agency, you find ways to move money around, and generally, you have enough of a cushion that cash flow is rarely a serious problem. If you are a small agency, managing your money is a preoccupation 365 days a year.

But even the largest of the large minority agencies, places like UniWorld and Burrell, are smaller than the typical small mainstream agency. The relative scale is completely different. At its peak, UniWorld had between 150—200 employees. A mainstream agency with 300 employees would be considered "quite small." There is nowhere on Madison Avenue where the pain of money management is more acute than at minority agencies. And because of this, two-thirds of minority agencies collapse financially sooner or later.

Minority-owned firms are much less likely to be approved for bank loans than white-owned firms, making it even harder to obtain the essential working capital to ensure that a business succeeds. According to a report issued by the U.S. Federal Reserve earlier this year, more than half of all loan applications from Black-owned companies are rejected. This is twice the rejection rate of white-owned companies. There is no mystery that Black-owned agencies struggle to survive.

There is no mystery that Black-owned agencies are nearly extinct.

UniWorld, however, has always had a secret weapon, something in its arsenal that none of its peers had. UniWorld had Josephine "Josie" Penzes and her team of Filipino female money mavens. Josie, UniWorld's Chief Financial Officer, and her team, including Stella Canlas and Cheri Baccani, ran all financial and accounting operations at the agency. CEO Byron Lewis never made a financial decision or spent a dime of agency money without their blessing. They were shrewd and gifted money managers with exactly the right instincts for the agency business. But most of all, they were incredibly disciplined. No one was permitted to break the rules. Ever.

So many minority agencies would find themselves financially squeezed, unsure how they would make next month's payroll. So they would move some money around—just this once. Borrow from Peter to pay Paul. Just this once. And as soon as they did, they tipped over the first domino. They were doomed. Sooner or later, their doors would close.

And once a minority agency closed its doors, there would be a fast-paced skirmish between the mainstream agencies and the remaining minority agencies. Minority agencies would pick up the suddenly unemployed workers while also reaching out to the former clients of the now-defunct agency, hoping to find opportunity in the other agency's misfortune. Mainstream agencies would talk to the defunct agency's former clients. They would tell those clients that they never should have trusted a minority agency in the first place. They (those minority people) are just not good business people, and they can't be trusted with a client's money. Mainstream agency folks would shake their heads and say it was such a shame, but after all, that's just how those people are.

But UniWorld had a reputation in the industry, and among all of the media companies where we placed advertising; our financial integrity was unimpeachable. And there were many times when all you had was your reputation to get you through a temporary crisis.

It also helped tremendously that in addition to being absolutely no-nonsense, Josie and her team were the sweetest, nicest people to work with. They were my friends.

CHAPTER TWELVE

Hair-brushing and Oprah's Favorite Things

Before joining UniWorld, I did some of my very first independent consulting for a place called Pleasant Company. They are the Wisconsin-based company that is the creator and maker of the American Girl Doll collection, some of the most expensive and most beloved dolls in America. Today they are an empire and a cultural phenomenon. In the early 1990s, they were just beginning to grow. The company was started by Pleasant Rowland, a former elementary school teacher who developed the idea of combining a series of semi-educational historical storybooks with a collection of beautiful dolls based on each storybook's respective little girl heroine. The books and their accompanying dolls inspire young readers, while teaching history in a fun new way. The company effectively created a new industry of ultra-premium priced dolls and accessories.

The American Girl Collection had four original highly successful dolls based on young girl characters living in different periods of American history: Felicity, an 'independent' girl living during the Revolutionary War era; Kirsten, who was part of a pioneer family in 1854 Minnesota; Samantha, who was an orphan in New York City in the early 1900s; and Molly, the daughter of a soldier in 1944. The dolls were sold in the company's mail-order catalog (pre-internet) for about

$99, with outfits and accessories that could cost $20 - $30 apiece. Despite the high prices, Pleasant Company had no trouble at all finding eager customers.

I met Pleasant Rowland, the founder and CEO, and an effortlessly warm and charming woman, when the company flew me out to Wisconsin for a job interview. Pleasant took me to lunch for our interview and we hit it off immediately. Instead of handing me off to the next interview after lunch, she decided to give me a personally guided tour of the company. Afterward, Pleasant tried to woo me to join the company, (and I was tempted) but I simply was not ready to relocate to Middleton, Wisconsin. I was, however, very happy to be invited to consult. Pleasant had a top secret, high priority project in mind. It was time to bring diversity to the American Girl Collection. Pleasant Company was going to introduce its first Black doll, Addy. Addy Walker was a proud, courageous girl who escaped from slavery with her mother and now lived in 1864 Philadelphia. The doll, about two feet in height, wore an authentic period dress in pink and white, with buttons down the front and a white lace petticoat.

Award-winning children's author Connie Porter wrote the Addy book series. And a panel of historians and academics (including Lonnie Bunch, who went on to become Director of the National Museum of African American History & Culture at the Smithsonian) served as an expert advisory board ensuring that all of Addy's details were historically accurate, including her doll outfits and the plots of her stories. Honestly, I could not even begin to describe the extraordinary lengths of meticulous care and research that went into the development of this doll. My job was to help ensure that whatever Pleasant Company created and introduced would be warmly received by African American moms and daughters. I felt incredibly privileged to be part of this project. I had none of the credentials of the other people involved, but Pleasant liked and trusted me, and that was sufficient for her. I took reassurance from the belief that, if Pleasant trusted me, she must know what she's doing.

In the beginning, I would ask, how did they expect their existing white customers to react to the introduction of Addy. Pleasant Rowland looked at me with the warm, maternal smile of a teacher in a one room schoolhouse and said, "If they're smart, they will love and welcome

Addy just as much as we will." And then she added, still smiling, "And if they don't, well that's not Addy's fault. That's their fault." These dolls, all of them, were Pleasant's children. She was not going to permit anyone to attack her children.

I actually played a role in the physical design of one key aspect of the Addy doll, her hair. Few things in America are more inextricably tied to Black culture and Black ethnic identity than Black hair. The way that our hair looks and feels, the many styles that our hair is worn, the connotations, perceptions and interpretations that our hair suggests, is a condensed encyclopedia of understanding and misunderstanding of Black people. Black hair is so central to Black history that it is even its own civil rights issue. And so, Addy's hair was the focus of considerable discussion and debate. Should it be short and natural? Should it be in cornrows or braids? What would be historically accurate, yet attractive to little girls? How difficult would the solution be to manufacture?

It might seem odd for a guy to be making recommendations about doll hair, but this is where my recommendation resulted in a team consensus. We had done quite a lot of consumer research and one of the key learnings from focus groups was that these little Black girls wanted to be able to have essentially the same "care experience" with their doll that little white girls had with theirs. And that "care experience" was to care for the doll the way that moms cared for their own little girls. And nothing signified this powerful and intimate care ritual more than hair brushing, having mom brush your hair lovingly. The bonding between mother and daughter that centered around hair rituals was such an important part of the lives of these little Black girls. That meant that Addy's hair had to be long and brushable. Of course, it also had to be authentically African American in look, feel, and texture, but it had to be very, very brushable. That was an emotional bonding experience that little Black girls never truly had before—brushing the hair of a little Black doll.

And so, Addy would have long, brushable hair, and would always be sold with a hair-brush.

In the fall of 1990, I joined UniWorld and concluded my consulting engagement for Pleasant Company as they continued to finalize the development of Addy. Two years later, in the final months of 1992, I received a call from Pleasant Rowland. It was time to introduce Addy to the world and she wondered if I (and UniWorld) would like to help. I was thrilled to be asked. Everyone loves new business that just knocks on your door, but this was going to be a special assignment, one that touched my heart. And my own daughter, Lily, would be turning five in just a few months, so I would be introducing Addy to her as well.

I knew that planning a successful launch for Addy would require an approach that would have far greater impact than simple advertising could ever accomplish. Black households had almost zero awareness of the American Girl dolls or any familiarity with their educational premise. We weren't just introducing Addy, we were introducing the entire company and the grand ideas and values that it stood for. Television, of course, was far beyond the limited reach of our marketing budget, but even if we could afford it, no TV commercial would ever suffice. We needed to be able to sit down and have a conversation with our prospective consumers. And our prospective consumers needed to be able to have an "experience" with Addy.

Our task was to build a marketing plan that could accomplish these objectives. We created three sets of live, interactive experiences with our target audience; two were intimate, one was grand. And—through good planning and good fortune—we rode the wings of a huge media event that worked out better than we ever could have imagined.

Looking back on the whole experience, I am pretty certain that the marketing plan we developed, the strategies and tactics we executed, could not have come from anyone but us, our team. No mainstream ad agency would have conceived such a non-traditional and bespoke path. And surely no mainstream agency would have the level of familiarity with the grassroots channels and contacts that we did. They simply could not have pulled it off.

Pleasant Rowland was right to place her trust in my colleagues and me.

For our first set of interactive experiences, we arranged for Addy author Connie Porter to conduct live readings from the first Addy book at community libraries in major cities across the country. Local librarians in African American communities loved the idea. Mothers brought their little girls to listen to the story, meet the author and buy the book. Mail-order catalogs were distributed (so that you could order your Addy doll), along with background literature on the American Girl Collection. We were able to deliver both the conversation and the experience. Local African American community newspapers provided generous coverage of the events.

Our second set of interactive experiences were a lot of fun and were helped along by some celebrity support. In middle class Black America, there are numerous organizations that combine positive social interaction with aspirational parent/child programs and events; organizations like Jack & Jill, Links, the Hord Foundation and others. The aspirational membership of these organizations was a perfect audience for an interactive Addy experience. At the same time, we reached out to actress (and the first Black Miss America) Vanessa Williams. (*Vanessa, by the way, was my dinner companion for the most extraordinary and most expensive dinner I have ever had in my life. But that is a story for a different chapter.*) She was a mother of two little girls and her daughter Jillian was the same age as my daughter Lily, the perfect age for Addy. We asked Vanessa if she would host a series of mother/daughter ice cream socials. She would read from the first Addy book and tell everyone about the doll and how it was such a great way for moms to promote reading and learning for their daughters. And of course, lots of mail-order catalogs were distributed.

Again, we were able to deliver both the conversation and the experience. And with Vanessa's participation we generated a ton of terrific publicity.

Our third set of interactive experiences was on a much larger scale. One of those organizations that I mentioned that combines positive social interaction with aspirational parent/child programs and events is the National Council of Negro Women (NCNW), a sixty-year old organization founded by Mary McLeod Bethune. Since 1985, the NCNW has hosted the annual Black Family Reunion Celebration, a three-day cultural event on the National Mall in Washington, DC celebrating the enduring strengths and traditional values of the African American family. Event attendance ranges between 10,000—15,000, and draws people from as far away as New York, Detroit, and Atlanta.

We set up a large tent on the National Mall and created an Addy exhibition with dolls, accessories, giant posters, books and catalogs.

Visitors could absorb all of the information and materials about Addy and the American Girl Collection. Most important; however, we set up roughly a dozen chairs with a dozen Addy dolls. And hair-brushes. Little girls could come into the tent, sit down and for ten minutes each, they could brush Addy's hair. At one point during the day there was a line of over 150 little girls outside the tent patiently waiting their turn to brush Addy's hair. By the end of the 3-day event, we had given out thousands of catalogs and created thousands of unforgettable bonding experiences.

One of the questions that we were repeatedly asked by the media (never by a consumer) was, "How can you justify asking Black mothers to spend $99 on a doll for their child?"

I think the media expected us to cower defensively from the question. But when you charge $99 for a doll, you know the question is coming. Our response was simple and honest. "Every day, parents must make careful choices how to make their family dollars stretch, how to make those expenditures matter. Sometimes those choices are about their children's happiness. Sometimes it is a desire to make an investment in their future. We believe that Addy and the American Girl Dolls are a unique way to combine reading and learning with simple childhood happiness. At the end of the day, that is a choice parents must make for themselves."

Parents were spending a lot more than $99 to buy their children Nikes and PlayStations. What we were offering was a lot more worthwhile.

The final leg of our launch marketing table was something of a gamble and a gambit. It was conceived and masterfully executed by UniWorld's PR Director, Lynne Scott. Every fan of Oprah Winfrey and her TV show knew that, every year in November, Oprah aired a special "Favorite Things" show where she showcased an array of items that she had personally fallen in love with and was sharing this information with her audience of millions of loyal viewers. Once the show aired, those "Favorite Things" would immediately become must-haves for millions of holiday shopping lists. The truth is, however, that many of those "Favorite Things" were products pitched to the show's producers by publicists and companies like ours in order to be included. Oprah might well be seeing the item for the very first time on air. That was how Lynne got Addy included among the "Favorite Things" that year.

If I remember correctly, Oprah had a woman who was a shopping expert of some sort on the show. This woman walked Oprah through the various items, telling Oprah a little something about each item. Oprah's responses would range from "That's very nice" to "I love that!" About two-thirds of the way through the show, the shopping expert finally got around to introducing Addy to Oprah. We were all on pins and needles, waiting to see Oprah's reaction. Was she going to complain about the doll's high price?

Oprah put her hand over her mouth. "Oh," she said. "I love this doll. I love this doll."

Oprah Winfrey proceeded to lose herself in the moment and bond with the doll as if she were an eight-year-old girl. The shopping expert had moved on to the next item, but Oprah clearly wasn't listening. Oprah walked away and sat down with the doll. She looked up at the camera and said, "We'll be right back after this commercial." When the show came back from commercial, Oprah announced, "THIS is my Favorite Thing and every single person on my Christmas list is getting Addy this year. That's all I'm buying." She and the shopping expert then returned to reviewing the other items while Oprah continued to hold Addy. But a TV show is timed right down to the second and they had lost time and weren't going to get to everything before the end of the show. One of the items that they did not get to was something new from Mattel's Barbie line, and the marketing executive from Mattel who was hovering on set nearby, had an absolute meltdown after the show. (Who knows, it might have contributed to Mattel's decision six years later to purchase Pleasant Company.)

The Pleasant Company order center phone lines were flooded after the show. People were going crazy to order this doll. And of course, Oprah now needed a few dozen. Placement of Addy on Oprah's show didn't just go better than expected, it went better than any of us could have imagined.

A full decade before "You get a car!" ever happened, there was Addy.

When we first developed the launch plans for Addy, the marketing budget was based on the company's projections for sales. African Americans represent roughly 12% of the population, and we were focused on a segment within that, the Black middle class. Consequently, it would be reasonable to project that sales for Addy would be 10% or less of the sales for Pleasant Company's other dolls. But Pleasant Rowland was gung-ho about Addy's prospects and believed that a chunk of their existing doll customers would want to own Addy as well. Pleasant believed that Addy sales might reach 30% of what the other dolls were doing.

All of Pleasant Company's sales came through either their 1-800 phone orders, or from orders that arrived in the mail. Consequently, the company was able to track sales on a daily basis, knowing exactly how every doll performed. We began our marketing activities in September, and the Oprah "Favorite Things" show aired in mid-November. By December 1, Pleasant Company was in an absolute panic. They had already sold out every single Addy doll produced and were now selling dolls that wouldn't be through the production process for a few more weeks. These were hand-crafted, high-end dolls. They couldn't simply crank out more. We were about to begin turning away and disappointing very emotional customers right before Christmas.

And we still had one more high-profile product placement that hadn't aired yet.

The TV sitcom, Hangin' with Mr. Cooper, starring Mark Curry and Holly Robinson, aired on ABC from 1992 to 1997. In season 2, the character played by 8-year-old Raven Symone wants—and receives—an Addy doll for Christmas. It is an adorable episode that aired on December 10, 1993, when ABC's TGIF line-up was at the height of its rating power. In the week leading up to that broadcast, sales of Addy were so strong that Pleasant Company actually asked the agency if we could persuade the network to air a different episode instead. (We could not.)

There were, unfortunately, a lot of moms and daughters who were unable to get their Addy dolls in time for Christmas morning, although the company did everything it could to satisfy every order. By the end of the year, in the final sales tally, Addy had out-sold Pleasant Company's #1 doll by 110%. Addy had out-performed its sales projection by a magnitude of almost 4x.

CHAPTER THIRTEEN

Black Coffee and Kool-Aid

One of the clients in my portfolio at UniWorld was General Foods. Technically, Kraft Foods had acquired the company, so they were now Kraft General Foods, but our relationship with the client pre-dated the acquisition, so we just kept calling them General Foods out of habit. When necessary, we called them "KGF." And KGF had given UniWorld an assignment that was truly rewarding, even though it involved almost no advertising at all.

Rather than spend their multicultural marketing budget on advertising, Maxwell House Coffee (a KGF brand) chose to target their funds to a major community relations goodwill initiative. They created and sponsored The Maxwell House Historically Black College Tour. And it fulfilled its objectives tenfold; tremendously impacting the communities it served and building strong, enduring brand loyalty among these consumers.

Historically Black Colleges and Universities (HBCUs) typically have extremely limited resources and finances. With the exception of two or three of the biggest names in Black colleges, none of the other schools have the money to conduct the kind of recruiting necessary to maintain healthy enrollment. And without healthy enrollment, they will never create the revenue they need. It's a catch-22. And most Black students at inner city high schools have never heard of these colleges, so they will never find them or consider applying without a helping hand.

That is where Maxwell House stepped in. They created—and funded—a tour so that two or three dozen admission officers from Black colleges could travel together to a half dozen cities in the northeast, mid-Atlantic and Midwest where they would rent a hotel ballroom or similar venue and conduct college fairs. This would be arranged in close coordination with the local school superintendent and high school principals, who would send busloads of bright young juniors and seniors eager to attend the college fairs. In each city, college admission officers would meet hundreds of curious and interested students.

It was quite something to be there when all of this was going on, to witness the excitement of the students, to hear the passion and the pride in the voices of the admission officers. It was a 'coming together' of the best kind.

None of this would have been possible without the generosity and commitment of Maxwell House Coffee. None of this would have been possible without the vision, imagination and marketing savvy of the agency team at UniWorld, a small but passionate team that worked tirelessly to sweat the details of all the logistics, all the local politics, and all the bureaucratic red tape.

I may have been the head of the account, but the person who did all of the work, the person who took all of the stress onto his own shoulders—and loved every minute of it—was Bernard Baskett. And although Bernard was the account supervisor who reported to me, he was ten years my senior. I was his boss, but he was quite often my mentor. He taught me a great deal about how to manage during a crisis and how to be a leader that others would follow. I am grateful for the privilege of our time working together.

The Maxwell House Coffee Historically Black College Tour is a perfect example of why multicultural marketing represents the most rewarding parts of my advertising career. It would be very easy to say that this program was nothing more than a feel-good community relations program, a nice philanthropic gesture, an attractive tax write-off. But that would fail to recognize the strategic planning that went into the concept and design of the program and would completely overlook the substantial positive impact on the Maxwell House bottom line. The reality is that the brand was building loyalty and market share among two high-volume coffee-drinking segments simultaneously; college-bound students and their parents. There was never a question in the minds of KGF executives. This program paid for itself several times over.

One of the principal architects of the program, and one of its strongest advocates, was Ann Fudge. Ann was a brilliant African American marketing executive (and Harvard MBA) who rose quickly through the ranks at General Foods and became president of the Maxwell House Coffee Division at General Foods. A few years later, she would advance again to become president of the beverages, desserts and Post divisions, a $5 billion unit of Kraft General Foods. She was a visible and revered face of the corporation. Under her leadership, Ann Fudge recruited, hired and mentored a coterie of young Black professional women who have each gone on to considerable success.

A few years after leaving Kraft, Ann Fudge made advertising industry history by being named Chairman & CEO of Y&R Brands, one of the biggest and most high-profile advertising agencies on Madison Avenue. This made her the first African American and the first African American woman to head a major ad agency. From the day she arrived at the bastion of old-school advertising, the senior executives at the agency did everything they could to undermine her presence and shorten her tenure, everything from daily passive-aggressive micro-aggressions to outright mutiny. By the second year of Ann's 3-year contract, she had effectively been pushed out of the agency, and control returned to the usual cast of white men.

One of the other brand assignments at KGF was Kool-Aid, which was fun and a bit crazy, but that is about what you would expect from Kool-Aid. For some reason, however, Kool-Aid always stubbornly resisted acknowledging the importance of African American consumers to the brand's success. No matter how much consumer research they saw, the brand manager and the category manager insisted that Kool-Aid was *"a **kid's** brand that happened to be popular among Black consumers too."* And when it came time to divide up the marketing budget, those Black consumers were a minor afterthought.

One day I finally had enough of their Saturday morning cartoon vision of the brand. I literally cut off the brand manager mid-sentence in a meeting and declared, "If Black people stopped buying Kool-Aid, this brand would be dead in a year."

"That is a totally ridiculous statement," the brand manager responded, angry that I had interrupted him. "You can't make any reasonable argument to support that."

I stood up from my chair, adjusted my jacket and said, "Watch me." Yes, I was being cocky, and this guy was my client, but he was a brand manager, and I was a senior vice president. Seniority had to stand for something.

Since the meeting we were in was a review of the latest consumer awareness and usage study, I literally had the data at my fingertips. "Among white households, almost 70% of annual consumption occurs in the three months from Memorial Day to Labor Day. For white consumers, Kool-Aid is a summer drink. Among Black households, however, there is only a minor bump in consumption during the summer months. It goes up in the summer but remains strong all 12 months of the year. For Black consumers, Kool-Aid is a year-round drink. We have a fundamentally different relationship with the product."

The brand manager sighed (and huffed a little). "We know that. But the summer months are still the most important months."

I shook my head. "Sure. The summer has your best volume, but you are overlooking the strategic importance of those other months. What would happen if Kool-Aid did not have steady sales in the non-summer months?"

He looked at me as though it were a trick question.

"If Kool-Aid did not have steady sales in the non-summer months, every major supermarket in America would remove the brand from the beverage aisle, where it has strong year-round presence and visibility, and it would be put in the 'seasonal' aisle and only be available for just three months a year, next to the charcoal briquettes. The rest of the year it would be gone from the shelves. You couldn't sell anything."

The brand manager looked at me as though I had smacked him in the face.

"And that's not the worst of it," I said, winding up for the final blow. "Once they take your SKUs off the shelf at the end of the season, you are going to have to pay millions every year in slotting fees just to get back on the shelf for the next summer season. With 20 different Kool-Aid SKUs, the brand would never be profitable again. It would die."

After a very long pause, where no one in the meeting spoke, the brand manager said, "I don't know if that would be true."

That was white brand manager-speak for "I have never thought about this before, and I don't have a response."

A few weeks later, the category manager sent the agency a memo advising us that the brand had decided to make a strategic reallocation of the marketing budget and would be increasing the agency's multicultural marketing budget "on a trial basis."

CHAPTER FOURTEEN

A Venezuelan Coup

One of the smaller accounts in my portfolio at UniWorld was Clairol hair products. Make no mistake, Clairol is actually a very big, glamorous, and prestigious client, but they gave UniWorld very little work to do, perhaps once every three or four years. The rest of the time they were dormant.

The Clairol assignment was a little bit different for me. It was targeting the U.S. Hispanic market, not African Americans, so it was a nice growth experience for me. (*It should be noted that I had not conducted a conversation in Spanish since high school. Even then, I impressed absolutely no one.*) UniWorld was the first African American agency to have a Hispanic division. We had several clients, like Lincoln-Mercury and AT&T, where we handled both consumer segments. For Clairol, we only handled their Hispanic marketing.

It would be at least another decade before Clairol or any other mainstream hair care brands did any advertising targeting African American women. You might see a Black model in a mainstream Clairol commercial, as long as she had long, straight hair. But none of these companies marketed specifically to Black women. The mainstream hair care companies left that turf exclusively to the ethnic hair care brands like Pro-Line and Soft Sheen and Johnson Products. They wanted nothing to do with that end of the market, no matter how lucrative it might be. (Remember that the next time a client tells you that the "only color they care about is green.") This marketing alienation actually went so far as to create a completely separate aisle in the drug store for "ethnic" hair care products. If you were looking to purchase a box of Dark and Lovely hair coloring, you would have to walk over to the 'colored' section of the drug store.

Toward the end of 1991, the Clairol client informed the agency that they would like to get back on the air (after a long absence) and needed us to develop and produce a new campaign. Cristian Dobles, the creative director for UniWorld Hispanic, developed a fabulous new campaign for the brand. Cristian and our TV producer, Darlene Samuels, proposed shooting the new commercials in Venezuela, which made good practical sense because it was January and we needed to shoot outdoors. February in Caracas would be summertime. (With Hispanic TV campaigns, shooting the commercials in Latin America was a popular way for agencies and their clients to circumvent the SAG and AFTRA requirements and avoid paying potentially costly talent residuals. This wasn't proper, but it was commonplace.) Latin American production companies also tended to be much less expensive than their American counterparts because of the comparatively low labor costs. Advertising agencies were constantly complaining to their clients that they were grossly underpaid, but these same agencies (ours included) were not above taking advantage of cheap labor when they could find it. Notwithstanding the financial advantages, the production company we chose was first-rate and was as professional and capable as any I have worked with.

Led by our producer Darlene, the agency team flew down to Caracas and were picked up at Simon Bolivar International Airport by the production company and escorted to our hotel downtown. The route from the airport to downtown took us past the almost endless vista of slums built one atop the other, covering and encrusting the mountainsides approaching the city. The expanse of poverty that went on mile after mile of dense barrio was something I had never witnessed before. I was no stranger to slums and ghettos, whether it was rural or urban. I knew many such places. Some I knew well. Just a few months later, I would be in Los Angeles only a few days after the LA riots, helping to open a new community literacy center in Crenshaw. But what I saw in and around Caracas was of an entirely different order of magnitude. This was a nation that had already begun to collapse in on itself. A few years after our time in Caracas, the city would become the site of El Torre de David, the Tower of David, a 45-story abandoned skyscraper that would become the world's tallest slum.

Meanwhile, we stayed at the Intercontinental Hotel, which was supposed to be one of the city's best hotels. It felt like it had not been updated since the 1950s, and that included the telephone and TV technology. Placing an international call often seemed more trouble than it was worth.

That evening, the director took all of us to dinner at his favorite steakhouse in Caracas. As we learned, the ranches in rural Venezuela are known for producing rich, flavorful beef. If you are a steak lover, as I am, authentic Venezuelan beef is a true bucket list experience. We dined on local wine, pabellón criollo, cachapas, and one of the finest steaks I have ever eaten. After dinner, we talked for hours about the country's problems and struggles while sharing Ron Pampero Anejo Aniversario, a Venezuelan rum.

The next day was our first full work-day in Caracas. We spent the morning scouting an exterior location that had been selected for the end scene in the commercial, where our very happy model's hair would look beautiful after using Clairol. The location we had chosen was the front of Palacio Miraflores, the Venezuelan presidential palace. The commercial would air on Hispanic TV networks in the U.S., such as Telemundo and Univision. It wasn't important that the setting be recognizable, but it was chosen for its beauty and its international atmosphere. We were planning to shoot early the next morning. There would be people on the street, but not too many and the indirect sunlight would be just right.

We returned to the production facility for lunch, and that is where I met our actress for the shoot. We had cast Carolina Izsak for the commercial. A few months earlier, Carolina had won the Miss Venezuela pageant, making her one of the most recognizable and admired women in the country. In the upcoming months she would go on to compete in the Miss Universe pageant (ultimately finishing in 4th place). More Miss Universe winners have come from Venezuela (7) than any other country except the United States. Miss Izsak was stop-traffic beautiful and a delight to work with. She was exactly the kind of gorgeous model you would expect to see in a Clairol commercial. We made some small-talk, but she mostly chatted with the director and Cristian about the afternoon shoot. After lunch we began prepping for the afternoon interior shoot.

The afternoon shoot was a shower scene, which is not that unusual for a hair care commercial. It was, however, my first shower scene, so I had a great deal of curiosity about how these things were done. It is perfectly natural to assume that shower scenes are shot in a bathroom somewhere. And sometimes that's true. Often, however, that is simply not practical. The way that most bathrooms and showers are constructed are extremely limiting for camera angles, especially given all of the big, bulky equipment necessary for a shoot. And low bathroom ceilings make it impossible to set up the lighting equipment necessary for quality filmmaking. Instead, for our commercial, the production company constructed a bath and shower in the center of a big empty studio room and surrounded it with lighting, camera and sound equipment. Water was pumped into the shower from a hose that snaked across the room and led off somewhere. It was quite an odd sight.

As I looked around the room, studying everything, our producer, Darlene Samuels caught my glance. "You noticed that there's no place for you to sit, didn't you?"

I made a point of looking around. "Uh, I guess."

She wagged her finger at me. "That's because you're not sitting in this room." She pointed off, over my shoulder. "You and the client are going to go and sit in that room over there where you can watch on the monitor." And then she let out a slight chuckle. "You little pervert."

Darlene was a petite, dark-skinned woman, five feet, two inches and maybe 100 pounds, dripping wet. But she had a wiry build that suggested that if she punched you, it would hurt. And she was practically a chain smoker, so whenever she laughed, which was quite often, smoke would come out. She also had a scowl that could make plants wither on the spot. She would use that scowl to great effect to create a sourpuss demeanor that actually concealed her tremendous affection and loyalty for her coworkers.

Advertising agency TV producers are the people who bring the copywriter and art director's creative vision to life. The production company directors get all the credit, but everything the director does, happened because of the producer. And Darlene Samuels was a producer who routinely made the impossible possible. I would rather work with Darlene than almost any other producer. I used to call Darlene "Miss Daisy", and she would look down her nose and say, "Oh, . . . it's you."

And when Darlene said "Oh" it had at least three syllables.

Carolina walked onto the set wearing a tiny bikini, ready for the shoot. Darlene watched me watching Carolina. "Now beat it. And take your damn client with you."

In the make-believe shower, the camera was framed from Carolina's shoulders up, so you never saw her bikini. After all, this was a hair commercial. Every time they did a take and the director called "Listo" (which means "ready"), right before calling "Acción", a crew member would turn on the water from the hose. Unfortunately, it was just a garden hose, and the water was not heated at all. And so, as the cold water hit her body, Carolina let out a high-pitched shriek that we could hear all the way in the other room. I was sitting in the other room (as instructed by Darlene) and chatting with the client when we both heard the shriek. Simultaneously, we both turned toward the TV monitor to see what had happened. For just a brief moment, an image flashed in my head of the shower scene from the movie "Psycho." Fortunately, what we saw on the screen was a shivering Carolina, clutching herself and laughing. For the next four or five takes, Carolina continued to let out that high-pitched shriek the moment the water hit her. After a while, however, she became accustomed to the water, and we were able to film what we needed. It was a lot of torture for poor Carolina for what would be just a few seconds in the commercial.

We were up early the following morning for our location shoot at the plaza in front of Palacio Miraflores. However, we were quite surprised to see that we were not the first to arrive at the presidential palace that morning. There appeared to be a full battery of tanks—military tanks— encircling the palace, along with dozens of other military vehicles. In fact, the closest we could get with our cars was several blocks away. As we all exited our cars, I looked at the director, as if to ask if he had arranged this.

"I don't know what this is." He looked baffled and a bit troubled.

Darlene looked around and shook her head. "No. This is not good. This is _not_ good."

Haltingly at first, and then in a determined march, we walked from our cars to the spot where we were supposed to be shooting. With Darlene hovering over him, the director was speaking frantically into a radio, attempting to get some answers.

I looked around in every direction, unsure what to do or what to say. As I turned around, a man in a uniform was standing a few feet away, speaking sternly in Spanish. Susan, the account supervisor from my team, translated for me, knowing my linguistic limitations. "He said we have to leave this area immediately."

I shook my head. "I'm not leaving. We have a permit. Tell him we have a permit from the government film office."

Susan started translating for the man, but he cut her off before she could finish a sentence. "No. No. No. Immediatamente."

I was convinced that our shoot was being ruined because someone in the government decided to conduct some random military exercise in front of the palace to impress the president.

There were several more moments of pointless three-way conversation before another man in uniform—this one older—approached us. The first man snapped to attention and referred to the newcomer as "Capitan." At first, the older officer ignored Susan and me and engaged in a rapid-fire Q&A with the other man in Spanish. When he was done, he turned to me and spoke in English. "I do not care about your permit. You need to leave this area immediately."

Showing my frustration, I snapped back at the officer. "So why did we bother to get a permit in the first place?"

After a few seconds of just staring at each other, the officer spoke. "There will be no more talking. If you do not leave this area, you will be taken into custody."

At that moment, from about 50 feet away, Darlene yelled my name and waved for me to come to her. I hesitated for a second or two, not because I wished to stand my ground, but because I was afraid that if I started walking, my knees were going to wobble. When the army guy said, "taken into custody," I knew it was time to retreat.

When I reached Darlene, she locked her arm around mine and began walking me away from the plaza. "We're pretty sure we have another location. Just give us a half hour and we'll be fine. Okay?"

Darlene, the director, and his crew found another location near the Plaza Venezuela, and we were able to begin filming after a short delay. Throughout the day, staff from the production company attempted to learn what was really going on at Palacio Miraflores, but it was not until that evening that we got the story.

That morning, we had walked right into the middle of an attempted military coup led by Hugo Chavez to overthrow the administration of President Carlos Andrés Pérez. Chavez had the backing of about 10% of the Venezuelan military and a sizable chunk of the civilian population, especially in the countryside. In Caracas, however, not so much. President Pérez was returning that morning from Davos, Switzerland, and the plan was to abduct him at the airport and assassinate him. The abduction failed and things went downhill from there. By the end of the day, Chavez had surrendered and was sent to jail, at least until his next coup attempt 10 months later.

We had gotten all of our work done that day and the commercial was almost finished, but when we discovered all that had transpired that day, we suddenly realized that we were "urgently needed back home" in New York. We told the director and the production company to finish the commercial without us and we booked flights home the next day.

The finished commercial, by the way, with a beautiful model and beautiful hair, all looked great.

CHAPTER FIFTEEN

"I don't like your clothes"

Beer companies make a lot of money. I mean, a whole lot of money. If you're in the beer business and you survive, you're going to be rich. But it is a tough business. The competition is ferocious. The profit margins are razor thin. The regulatory environment can be a bureaucratic nightmare. And the industry's growth rate has not exceeded +2% in decades. Growth is flatter than last night's beer. Beer companies are constantly trying product extensions and new product variations as a way to squeeze some fresh dollars from consumers. And they spend millions and millions of dollars on things like Super Bowl commercials just to maintain some brand excitement.

Although they don't spend nearly as much as they should, beer companies are reliable and enthusiastic marketers to multicultural consumers. In fact, across all the different product categories, beer brands are among the earliest consistent marketers to minority consumers. Back in 1956, when Nat King Cole had his TV show, Rheingold was one of his few regular sponsors. Unfortunately, like most beers in the 1950s, Rheingold was a regional brand, not national. The dominance of national beer brands came a decade or two later.

By the early 1990s, when I came to work at UniWorld, the American beer market was dominated by three mega-brewers; Anheuser-Busch, Miller Brewing and Coors Brewing Company. Coors was a client of UniWorld and one of the major brands in my portfolio. In the late

1980s, before I came to UniWorld, the agency had played a major role in launching Coors Light into the New York and Northeastern markets. This was not simply among minority consumers, but among all consumers. UniWorld put Coors Light on the map in the Northeast, and it was hugely successful for Coors.

But just a few years later, the brewery's mainstream agency had managed to claw back the general consumer assignments we'd been given previously and relegated UniWorld to strictly minority marketing that was mostly of a community relations focus.

We would need to find a way to "claw back" our status as an agency that was integral to the success of Coors. And we would use some pretty gutsy marketing magic, some celebrity star power and some sleight of hand to do it.

At the time, Coors did not have a multicultural marketing department or director. Instead, it had Community Relations. Its director was Ivan Burwell, a brilliant and savvy marketer who was probably the best client I ever had. I am tempted to say that Ivan's talents and abilities were wasted at Coors, but the truth is that under Ivan's direction, we did great things for Coors.

Coors Brewing Company is located in Golden, Colorado, possibly the heart of western redneck country (as opposed to southern redneck country). They celebrate the good old ways and the good old values, which are not necessarily bad things, but they do make people like me a bit nervous being around after sundown. In fairness to the people I knew at Coors, the vast majority of them were decent, friendly, good people to work with. The Coors family, however, had an entirely different—and well-earned—reputation.

Long before there were the Koch brothers, there were the Coors brothers, William and Joseph Coors. The two brothers were founders of the Heritage Foundation conservative think tank and were major donors and supporters of Barry Goldwater and Ronald Reagan, as well as various right-wing causes. They were acknowledged to be members of Reagan's "kitchen cabinet." Under their management, lie detector tests were given regularly to Coors workers to ferret out homosexuals, radicals, and union activists.

In 1984, Bill Coors attended a meeting of the Minority Business Development Center in nearby Denver. An African American business owner who was present at the meeting told Coors that "our ancestors were dragged here in chains against their will."

William Coors responded, "I would urge those of you who feel that way to go back to where your ancestors came from, and you will find out that probably the greatest favor that anybody ever did you was to drag your ancestors over here in chains, and I mean it." He went on to say that Africa's economic problems stemmed from "a lack of intellectual capacity."

In the ensuing uproar, the Los Angeles branch of the NAACP called for a boycott of Coors beer, and 500 liquor stores in Southern California joined in. Within weeks, the boycott had become a national movement. Months later, Coors surrendered to mounting pressure by signing agreements with Black and Hispanic groups to increase its minority hiring, to develop minority distributors, and to invest in banks, law firms, advertising agencies and other businesses in minority communities. Coors also committed to increasing sales in minority communities.

This led to the creation of the Community Relations department at Coors, run by the wise, occasionally wily, and tremendously capable John Meadows and his deputy, my client Ivan Burwell. Together, they built a national network of community relations managers dedicated to consistent, positive, effective outreach to minority communities and businesses, especially beer retailers. Person-by-person, market-by-market, and with the help and partnership of UniWorld, they rebuilt goodwill (or created it from nothing) for the Coors Brewing Company across the country.

Coors is perhaps a perfect example of why I love the work I do, why I love multicultural marketing. Coors used to be a company that was—in my opinion—an active and undesirable part of what is wrong in America. But circumstances brought the company to a point where it needed to change, it needed to clean up its act and do better. UniWorld, the minority agency where I worked, was able to step in and support the work of Coors Community Relations to make Coors a better company, bring meaningful programs to communities of color, and give minority businesses a hand up. We helped with the implementation of the Coors Literacy program and several other great programs and initiatives. We helped Coors become part of the solution instead of being part of the problem.

Yes, we helped Coors to sell a lot of beer. But we taught Coors how to do well by doing good. And if you ask anyone who works for a multicultural agency, they will tell you this is the biggest reward for us. It sure is for me.

As I said before, the vast majority of the people I knew at Coors were decent, friendly, good people to work with. The Vice President of Marketing, however, was a possible exception. He did not like the agency, did not like me, in fact probably did not like any of the people at UniWorld. We took it in stride. We're in the service business.

One day, after I had been on the account for three or four months and had been out to Coors a half dozen times, we had just wrapped up a meeting with the VP of Marketing at Coors when he said to me, "I don't like the way you dress."

"Excuse me?"

"I don't like the way any of you dress." He waved his hand as though painting a broad brush across the other agency team members in the conference room. "All of you New Yorkers, you come out here and you dress like New Yorkers. But, you're not in New York. You're in Golden."

We all looked at him and listened as though we were all receiving important information.

"You don't see any of us dressed like that. You look like you're putting on airs. You look like you think you're better than us." He pointed his finger. "Next time you come out here, dress like normal people."

Honestly, I don't think he really cared all that much about what we were wearing. That was just a convenient excuse. He simply did not like looking at us. He did not like seeing Black people walking around his company like we had a right to be there, like we were "equal" or something. The fact that we wore professional attire just made it worse. It made him feel uncomfortable. It made him feel insecure. And every single Black professional knows what it's like when you make a white colleague feel insecure.

We're in the service business. So, from then on, we dressed like normal people in Golden do. He still didn't like us.

THE BIRTH OF THE LIGHTSHOW

And then one day a new VP of Marketing was hired at Coors. He was a Chicago transplant. (Coors recruited a lot of talent from Chicago, but that was as far east as the company was willing to consider. Other than people from Chicago, they did not trust anyone east of the Mississippi.) And he was convinced that he was the smartest person in the room. Always. He was convinced that Coors was damned lucky to have him and convinced that all of the agency people were hustlers constantly trying to con their clients. Thank goodness he showed up.

In our first major meeting with the new VP, the agency had done weeks of preparation putting together a marketing review deck to show him all the work we had done and why we had done it; the research, the strategy, everything. Half a dozen of us had flown out to Coors to make the presentation in one of the company's big conference rooms. About five minutes into our presentation, the new VP announced that he was bored.

"Look, look… I'm sure all the work you guys did is very nice. But to be perfectly honest, I don't care about that stuff." He announced, calling a halt to the presentation. "Number one, that stuff is all in the past. I don't care about the past. I care about what are we going to do next. And number two," he gestured with his hand, "all that stuff is 'feel good' stuff. It doesn't move product off the shelves. This company needs to move product off the shelves. That's my job. If you want to be my friend, help me move product."

Actually, he was wrong on several counts. Most especially, the work we had been doing was moving product off the shelves. A lot of product. But we knew this only anecdotally, from retailers and even from distributors. No one from Coors was actually tracking sales by ethnic accounts. You see, that was (and is) the game in multicultural marketing that virtually every single client plays. They don't track ethnic sales of their brand or create the means to track it, so the multicultural marketing efforts never have objective value. It can never be proven that the work has value to the company, that it is growing their business. The result is that, whenever they need to, or whenever it is convenient, clients are able to cut the multicultural budget and argue that funds are needed for "core sales initiatives."

Everyone at UniWorld knew this. We had heard it a thousand times. It is how the playing field remains uneven.

"I know your agency wants a bigger budget. I know all you want is a chance to show what you can do. And I want to give you that chance." The Marketing VP wanted to show us that he was our friend, that he was our hero. "So, I am going to give you a challenge."

Then he paused and let the room fall quiet for dramatic effect. Everyone waited.

The Marketing VP spread his hands on the table. "The simple fact is that Anheuser-Busch has much more money and much bigger resources than we will ever have. We could come up with the best marketing idea and A-B would just outspend us 4-to-1 and it would be game over. That will always be true." He leaned across the conference table to look straight into my eyes. "So how do you beat that? How do you come up with a strategy and a game plan that can beat that?"

If I had to guess, I think this was probably a challenge that the president of Coors had given to his new Marketing VP, and it was a challenge that the new Coors Marketing VP had given to its mainstream agency. We were simply the last to be handed a lemon and told to make lemonade.

But if you know us, you know we make the best lemonade.

We told the client we would return in a month with a proposal. We explained that working with less money than everyone else was simply standard operating procedure for a multicultural agency. We know how to do more with less. That's our skill set. Of course, he didn't believe us. He assumed it was all talk.

He did not realize, however, that when you spend week after week, year after year, asking your clients to give you the chance to prove how really good you are and how really powerful the multicultural consumer really is, you also spend that time getting ready. If you are smart, and oh yes, we were, you don't risk not being ready when the client finally says yes and asks you what have you got. The stakes are just too high. Once lost, the opportunity is irretrievable. You smile and say, "Let me show you."

Our opportunity to "claw back" had come.

When we returned, we presented a plan that was based on insight, experience and a good deal of very smart research that we had already conducted. The plan was built upon two key concepts and a very unorthodox executional strategy. The first concept was that, for a young, extremely media-savvy ethnic consumer, messaging—no matter how good—would never be effective enough on its own.

"They say a picture is worth a thousand words, but the memory of a positive experience is worth a thousand pictures."

Our plan would need to be built upon delivering unforgettable positive experiences. And those experiences would have to be "ownable" by Coors.

The second concept was something we called "two kinds of real." To succeed with consumers, a brand must deliver on both:

- **"Personal Real"**—Friends and people that I know personally talk about it, (word-of-mouth, ethnic media, etc.) recommend it, use it.
- **"Big Real"**—It's important and high profile in the world beyond my own personal experience; on TV and visible in the media that I consume and the places I go.

"If 10 of my friends are down with something, then I see it on TV, then I really want it."

The final piece of the plan was our unorthodox executional strategy. "We are going to conduct asymmetrical warfare against our big competitors. They are the British Redcoats, a vastly bigger army, marching in formation. And we're going to be the scrappy American revolutionaries, shooting while moving. Always moving." I laid out our pitch.

"We're not going to have a test market that Anheuser-Busch can observe and study. We're going to have ten markets and we're going to do something different in each market. And as soon as we execute a program in one market, we pull up stakes and move to another. The competition will be spending all of their time trying to figure out what we're doing."

And then, just as the Marketing VP had done a month before, I leaned across the conference room table and looked directly into his eyes. "But they're going to be looking for the wrong thing. Because **what** we're doing doesn't matter half as much as **how** we're doing it. And Anheuser-Busch just isn't built for our kind of how."

The Marketing VP tried to conceal the fact that he was smiling. He probably thought we were crazy and full of crap, but there was something about the audacity of our approach that appealed to him. "And you actually think you can pull this off."

"I know we can," I said with typical account guy confidence.

"And what is this crazy plan going to cost me?" He folded his arms and leaned back in his seat, but I could tell that he was already beginning to think about how he would take credit for the idea if this "crazy plan" ever succeeded.

I put the budget up on the screen. The amount was more than we thought the client would approve and less than the client thought we would ask. The negotiation process was miraculously quick and painless. And just as the client was about to give us a final approval, I put up my hand.

"Before you say okay, there's one more thing we need to ask for, and it's kinda' big."

The Marketing VP withdrew into his chair and pulled back slightly from the table. He looked at me, both annoyed and suspicious.

"If you approve this, we will lay out as many plan details as possible upfront. But then we need to be able to run and just keep running. If we have to come back to Golden and schedule a meeting every time we need approval, this isn't going to work. We have to make it impossible for the competition to catch up."

The client shook his head. "There is no fucking way we are just going to hand you a check and send you on your way." He thought carefully about this. Clearly, he was unwilling to trust us that much, but he was also unwilling to let what might be a great opportunity just slip away. "I am going to assign someone from the Coors Light brand team to be your permanent watchdog. Wherever you go, he goes. If you need something approved, you talk to him. Either he approves it himself or he talks to someone who can. Those are my terms." He folded his arms. "And I want detailed quarterly reports from the field."

And that is how the "Coors Lightshow" was born.

CHAPTER SIXTEEN

A night at the Copa

The concept of the Lightshow was to share experiences with our target consumers the way friends share good times with each other. If we include these consumers in our good times, they will include Coors Light in their good times. A "Lightshow" became _any_ experience Coors Light creates to share with its friends; a party, a TV show, a basketball game, a comedy show, great music . . . As we said before, the **what** doesn't matter half as much as **how** we're doing it. So, we did crazy, different things all across the country.

We hired a guy, Marc S. Strachan, to be the producer of the Coors Lightshow tour. I had never met Marc before. He had his own consulting business and was recommended by a freelance copywriter who was working at UniWorld at the time. I didn't know the copywriter that well either, so I was especially nervous about accepting his recommendation. UniWorld was betting its credibility and relationship with Coors on the success of this program. If we succeeded, the rewards would be huge; but if we failed, we would almost certainly lose the business, one of our biggest clients. As much as I believed in our idea, the truth is that we had never done anything like it before. And now I'd have to put my trust in someone I'd never worked with before.

Marc turned out to be a consummate professional with the ideal skill set for managing what could be charitably described as a "moving circus." He kept things on track and within budget, and he became a trusted collaborator throughout. Since then, we've collaborated in a variety of capacities, including having him as my client (Diageo) and the two of us as business partners (The S/R Alliance).

Marc S. Strachan and I assembled a road crew of about a dozen people to cover all of the operational, logistical and creative needs of the tour. We created a schedule that put us on the road for 3-4 weeks at a time before returning home to rest, regroup, and plan the next burst. We did this for nearly two and a half years. In many respects, the traveling regimen was similar to my years shuttling back and forth to Los Angeles on the Carnation account. The big difference, however, was that I was single then. Now I was married with two children in elementary school. Now I was missing a lot of school concerts, parent-teacher conferences, and T-ball games. The absences were difficult on all of us. I was also ten years older, and all this travelling stuff wasn't fun anymore, especially since most workdays did not end until around 3AM. I spent a good deal of the time in a bad mood, which actually had the unexpected benefit of discouraging the crew from too much goofing off. Thanks to my bad mood and Marc Strachan's professionalism and skill, we were able to maintain a highly efficient and effective operation throughout.

One of the hallmarks of the tour was being able to feature one well-known music act and one up-and-coming act that was on the cusp of breaking out. This was strategically designed to give the audience the bragging rights to say they saw a particular star before he or she became famous. And this mattered a great deal to our audience. One of those "cusp" acts was a 16-year-old—and extremely well-mannered—Usher, who was thrilled to have the exposure. Another "cusp" act was the Goodie Mob.

The Lightshow tour treated all of our participants very well, especially the performing talent. Before going on stage, we gave the Goodie Mob Coors Lightshow satin jackets made just for them, hats, leather bags, all sorts of nice swag. We wanted them to wear our jackets on stage, which they did. During the performance, we had crew tossing Lightshow tee shirts into the audience. People loved getting stuff for free, no matter what it was. After the show, CeeLo came up to me and said he wanted one of the tee shirts like the ones thrown into the audience.

I explained to him that when there is a lively crowd (there always is) we can't hold back. We gave away every single shirt. There was simply nothing left. But he was insistent. We had to find him a shirt, even if it meant having a crew member take one back from someone in the audience. I told him that wasn't going to happen.

CeeLo became irate. I told him I would be happy to send him a whole bunch of shirts when I got back to New York.

He made several suggestions about sex acts I might perform. And he said he would be waiting for me in the parking lot.

Because I wasn't in the best of moods to begin with, I directed our security team to accompany Mr. Green to his limo (which we had paid for) and to make sure he doesn't come out until it was time for him to go. It was probably one of those talent-relations issues that I should have let Marc Strachan handle instead.

The Goodie Mob's debut single was released just a few months later and hit number 39 on the Billboard Hot 100.

◆ ◆ ◆

We brought the Lightshow to New York at least four times. New York was one of our most successful markets, but for a bunch of reasons they were also some of my least favorite shows. High on that list was a night at the Copa.

Most of the time, when we brought the Lightshow to a venue, it was a full turn-key operation. We brought in all of our own staff and resources. Most venues were happy to step back and let us do our thing. Some were not. The Copacabana in New York City was not. Management insisted that their in-house security team had full control over the event.

Right from the start, we knew we were going to have problems. Rather than direct attendees to form a single line outside the club, Copa security set up a semi-circular barricade in front of the entrance. When the size of your crowd is modest, this helps create the illusion of a big crowd that can't wait to get in. When the size of your crowd is large, however, this creates complete chaos. And that is precisely what happened. There was no orderly way to admit people into the club. This slowed the admission process to a crawl, which dialed up the chaos and the crowd's frustration, which dialed up the anxiety of their security team.

In the midst of all of this, a caravan of eleven SUVs began to arrive on the street and pull up in front of the club. It was Sean Combs (Diddy), bringing Biggie Smalls (Notorious B.I.G.), Total, the Lost Boyz and a small army of "friends" from Bad Boy Records. They were late and needed to get inside the club and get backstage to get ready to perform. Unfortunately, the entrance set-up—and the chaos—created by the Copa's security team was going to make it impossible for anyone to get inside. Diddy expected the crowd to part like the Red Sea and allow his entourage to enter. That wasn't happening.

He seemed to feel that yelling at me would somehow solve this problem. "Do you know who I am?"

The noise from the crowd had grown quite loud, forcing the two of us to stand inches apart in order to be heard. I put my hand on his shoulder in the friendliest way that I could and with a half smile, I said, "Son," (Yes, I really said "Son.") "If you have to ask people if they know who you are, then you really aren't all that. So, let's work this out."

"If my people can't get in there, then there ain't no show."

"We'll figure this out," I said. "I promise." That's about when I heard a voice in my headphones. It was Greg Freelon, our stage manager. He informed me that the Copa had a rear entrance around the block, where the street was deserted. We then arranged for the caravan of cars to go around the block to the rear entrance. The plan might have gone smoothly (well, maybe) if they had just walked over to the driver of each SUV and discreetly explained the plan. But instead, one of Diddy's guys yelled out to all of the SUVs at once, "We're going around the block to the rear entrance!"

So that is what the caravan did, followed closely behind by nearly 200 members of the crowd that had been trying to get in the club. What remained at the front entrance was now a large but manageable crowd that was making its way inside in an orderly fashion. The Copa's security team thought the problem was solved. I thought the problem was solved.

I was a complete fool.

A few minutes passed and then suddenly, there was pounding on the back door to the nightclub. Inside the back door was one security guard standing in the backstage area. He went to the door and asked who was there. He heard voices from the other side, but couldn't quite make out the response. So, the guard unlocked the door and opened it just a few inches to speak to whoever was on the other side.

What happened next could easily have been an animated Looney Toons cartoon. The door opened with such force that it completely came off its hinges in one quick motion and landed flat on the floor. That might have been comical, except that the security guard was behind the door and was now flat on his back underneath the door. Then came a tidal wave of humanity rushing through the open doorway. The first few stepped right across the door with the man underneath. Biggie Smalls, who was one of the first to come in, saw what had occurred and directed those behind him to step around the door and not on it. Amazingly, just about everyone obeyed.

No, actually, that was not the amazing part. Here is the amazing part. As soon as Biggie and Total and the Lost Boyz had all gotten inside the club and brushed themselves off, Biggie yelled, "Let's go!" and they all formed a conga line behind him and danced out onto the stage and started their performance as though everything had been carefully choreographed. The show itself was a huge success. No one in the audience had any idea what had happened. A couple of the guys from our crew accompanied the security guard to the hospital. Miraculously, he suffered just two broken wrists.

Before we launched the Coors Lightshow program, we made sure that a sales tracking mechanism was in place. We reminded the Marketing VP of his own words to us, "If you want to be my friend, help me move product." We said the program wouldn't be worth doing if we couldn't prove success.

We took nothing for granted. We met with local retailers in every market we toured. It would have been standard procedure to do a whole sales presentation to the retail accounts, explain the whole program, even give them sell sheets with bullet points. That would have been the standard way to go. We didn't do that. We were the #3 beer company. We knew that any sales materials we gave to these guys would end up in the hands of Anheuser-Busch or Miller by the end of the week.

Instead, we just told them about the event that was happening in their market right now. We invited them to come to the lightshow and experience it for themselves, to see their own customers enjoying Coors Light. We invited them to just hang out with their own customers and talk to them. They did. And the result was an immediate bump in product orders from the retailers to the distributor.

At the end of the first quarter that the program was in place, we were able to track an increase in Coors Light sales. In a product category that had not seen an increase in sales of more than +2% in over a decade, we grew Coors Light sales by +7%. By the end of the second quarter of the program, sales in the Lightshow tour markets had increased +11% versus the prior year. In the two and a half years of the program, we kept this pace going.

A few years later, Miller Beer decided to poach several Coors marketing, sales and brand personnel in an effort to recreate their own version of the Lightshow. Of course, none of the people that Miller poached had actually worked on the program, but that may not have been what the executives said in their interviews. Around the turn of the millennium, Miller launched their own program, claiming to have invented the idea. I'm told it did reasonably well.

UniWorld had succeeded in "clawing back" its status as a vital player in Coors marketing and advertising success. After the Lightshow, the Marketing VP came to us and said that Coors was planning to launch a major out-of-home advertising campaign on billboards all across the country. Ordinarily, this would be an automatic assignment for their mainstream agency in Chicago.

"I'm going to make this a creative shoot-out," the Marketing VP announced. "Whichever agency shows me the best work wins."

We won.

Not only did we get the assignment, and the nice money that came with it, but we got something else that meant almost as much to all of us at UniWorld. Maybe more. Coors presented our agency with a set of custom-made hunting jackets (someone even found out our correct sizes). Over the left breast was the Coors Light logo. And embroidered over the left front pocket, it read:

Golden Colorado
1997 Creative Shoot-Out Winner

Twenty-five years later, I still wear my jacket.

CHAPTER SEVENTEEN

My dinner with Vanessa

I mentioned previously that Vanessa Williams was my dinner companion for the most extraordinary and most expensive dinner I have ever had in my life. Well, this is the story of that evening.

My Coors client, Ivan Burwell, was an astute marketer with an empathic sense of how to communicate with the African American community in ways that relate and resonate. But Ivan was also a bit of a bon vivant. When you were in Ivan's company, you did everything first class. You traveled first class. You stayed in four-star or five-star hotels and you dined in the very best restaurants. Ivan believed that we were all doing very difficult, very important jobs for a very big company, and we should all be treated accordingly. Everyone's conduct on the job was totally professional and responsible. No one ever abused the privilege. And Coors never challenged an expense.

Ivan also had a seemingly endless list of contacts and friendships in the African American entertainment world. Ivan had no problem helping Coors connect with a celebrity or artist to become involved with the company's community initiatives. These Black artists did not have any loyalty or affection for Coors, especially given its reputation for being 'unfriendly' to minorities, but they rarely ever turned down a heartfelt pitch from Ivan. Adult literacy was a very important community initiative for Coors, and Ivan had secured Danny Glover and Vanessa Williams as spokespeople for the program. Both Vanessa and Danny recorded radio commercials for the Coors Literacy program and were featured in print ads and collateral materials. Danny was particularly active in doing personal appearances at local community events for Coors. In her radio spots, Vanessa used the soundtrack from her Top 10 pop single "Dreamin" as background.

I'm not sure how literacy was chosen as the major community initiative for Coors, but it is an issue and a problem that is far greater than one might imagine. Less than half (48%) of all Americans of any race can read and write at an 8th grade level or above. 14% of Americans have "below basic" literacy skills (4th grade level or below), and 4% are entirely non-literate. There are many causes of illiteracy, including lack of educational access, physical and cognitive impairment and learning challenges. Danny Glover was drawn to the Coors Literacy program because he is dyslexic and struggled with reading well into his adulthood.

I don't recall if this was the agency's idea or Ivan's, but together we decided to reach out to the national leadership of the Delta Sigma Theta Sorority as a potential partner for the Coors Literacy program. Delta Sigma Theta is a historically African American sorority, founded a century ago at Howard University (a historically Black college). Since its founding, Delta Sigma Theta has created programming to improve political, educational, and social and economic conditions within the Black community. The sorority consistently collaborates with community organizations and corporations to further its programming goals. With a membership in excess of 300,000 nationwide, DST is one of the largest sororities in the country and wields tremendous influence throughout Black America.

We arranged a meeting at UniWorld's New York office. The Delta representatives came in from Washington, DC and Ivan flew in from Colorado. Together we made a presentation to the Deltas about the Coors Literacy program, including the new advertising campaign. The three Delta women talked among themselves in hushed tones and knowing glances. If I were to guess, I would say that these women were probably a few years older than the rest of us, perhaps in their early fifties. But it wasn't so much an age difference that I observed. It seemed more as though they were living in an older time, perhaps the 1950s or 60s. They were very proper, very formal.

"Mr. Burwell," one of the women addressed Ivan. "Coors Literacy certainly seems like a wonderful program. We fully support its goals and objectives."

"Yes . . ." Ivan leaned in, sensing there was a 'but' coming.

"We see that the advertising campaign that UniWorld has created for you features Vanessa Williams as a spokesperson." She spoke with her hands folded on the conference room table. "That is a concern for us."

In September 1983, Vanessa Williams became the first Black woman to be crowned Miss America. But just weeks before the end of her reign in 1984, Penthouse magazine published unauthorized nude photos of Vanessa that had been taken years before. Vanessa was forced to relinquish her crown and the first runner-up assumed the title. Four years later in 1988, Vanessa released her debut album, which went platinum and included four Billboard Top 100 singles. At the time of the meeting between Ivan and the ladies from Delta Sigma Theta, Vanessa Williams was about to release her second album, which included the chart-topping single, "Save the Best for Last."

"We believe that Miss Williams is a lovely young woman, but her career is marred by scandal of a terrible sort." If the three women had been wearing pearls, I think they would have been clutching them. "It would be irresponsible of us to agree to associate Delta Sigma Theta Sorority and the work that it does with someone who could cast the organization in a negative light."

> *(It is not my purpose or intention to portray Delta Sigma Theta Sorority in any disparaging way. The organization has an outstanding record of accomplishment and a legacy of tremendously worthy and worthwhile good works. But this is the conversation I witnessed on this particular day.)*

Ivan and the agency tried to reassure the representatives that the 1984 scandal was ancient history. Vanessa had successfully put this behind her and the country had moved on. She had received a 1988 NAACP Image Award. Her career was continuing to rise. But the ladies weren't having it.

With his usual diplomatic charm, Ivan said, "Ladies, I was really hoping that we could be partners." He extended his hand. "But we're sticking by Vanessa, so I guess we're not going to be partners."

I'm not sure this was the response the ladies were expecting from Ivan. I can't imagine they thought he might agree to change the campaign, but who knows. They seemed surprised that our meeting was ending so abruptly.

◆

Months later, Ivan was back in New York and at UniWorld's office. At the end of our meetings, Ivan said, "Hey guys, Vanessa is going to join us for dinner, okay?" As if he needed our consent. "We'll swing by her hotel and pick her up."

And so the four of us left the office and waited for Vanessa in the lobby of her hotel. This is how we began; Ivan Burwell, Moses Brewer, Bernard Baskett and myself. Moses was Ivan's associate at Coors Community Relations. Moses was about six foot, four inches; all height and no width. Moses, who was from rural Alabama (and never lost his accent), received a basketball scholarship from the University of Denver, and later became a Dean of Students and basketball coach. In 1982, he joined Coors and had been working with Ivan ever since. Bernard was the account supervisor at UniWorld who worked for me on both the Coors and Kraft General Foods accounts. Bernard was the old hand on the Coors account. I was the relative newcomer, being there roughly a year.

While waiting for Vanessa, Danny Glover's attorney and his wife appeared in the hotel lobby. The attorney asked us what we were doing, and Ivan explained that we were waiting for Vanessa to come down to join us for dinner. And that's when the attorney said, "Well, Danny will be down in a little bit, so I guess we're all going to have dinner together."

Danny Glover was also a spokesperson for the Coors Literacy program, but I'm not sure that we knew that Danny was also in the hotel. In fact, I'm not entirely sure that he was. We had not discussed or mentioned Danny being part of dinner, but now Danny was coming and so was his attorney and the attorney's wife.

Vanessa arrived in the lobby accompanied by her hair-dresser. She apologized for making us wait and asked Ivan if it would be alright if the hair-dresser came with us to dinner. Not a problem. One more in the group. What started as a party of five, was now a party of nine.

We asked the attorney if Danny would be coming down soon. He walked off to a phone and placed a call. "Danny says he'll meet us at the restaurant."

As we headed to the doors to leave the hotel, two women entered the lobby from the sidewalk outside. They were Vanessa's cousins. "Where are you going, girl? We're supposed to have dinner."

Along with hugs and kisses, Vanessa said, "I'm so sorry, but I have a business dinner tonight." Vanessa stepped over and whispered to Ivan, "I didn't make any plans with them. I just told them I would be in town. It's okay."

That's when I heard Danny Glover's attorney say, "It's not a business dinner. It's just dinner! Come on girls, join us."

The cousins looked at Vanessa and said, "Is that okay?"

Vanessa turned to Ivan, communicating the same question with a glance.

And Ivan turned to me and said, "It's up to you, because you're going to be picking up the check."

I said, "Let's go before we pick up anybody else."

Bernard and Moses were both trying very hard not to show any expression on their faces.

It took a caravan of taxicabs to shuttle all of us from the hotel to Jezebel, the soul food restaurant at the edge of the theater district on 45th Street and 9th Avenue, with the best Charleston She-Crab soup in the city. One of Jezebel's memorable features was its décor. Inside, the restaurant resembled an elegant parlor that might be found in a Charleston, South Carolina, mansion. Dozens of evocative paintings covered the red-painted walls and eccentric antique lamps sat on the tables. There was even a table where diners ate their meal sitting in a white wicker porch swing that hung from the ceiling.

Unfortunately, the restaurant was not very happy to see us. Jezebel can be damned near impossible to get in under the best of circumstances. We were more than a half hour late for our reservation and our party of five was now a party of eleven. Yes, we had Vanessa Williams with us, but the answer was still no. No.

Quick strategic huddle.

"Let's go to the Shark Bar."

I knew immediately that this was probably a bad idea. The Shark Bar was another extremely popular New York soul food restaurant, but we had no reservation, it was 30 blocks uptown, on 75th and Amsterdam Avenue, and it was a much smaller restaurant. There was no way this was going to work, yet somehow with almost no further discussion, we were all packed into another caravan of taxicabs, headed for the upper west side.

We got to the Shark Bar and half of us didn't even make it inside the building. It was that crowded. We had entered that time of the evening when the dinner scene begins to overlap with the bar scene. And Shark Bar was packing both in.

Ivan looked at me plaintively. "What do you want to do?"

"My choice?" I quickly asked Ivan. "Let's go to China Grill."

China Grill was an ultra-upscale Asian restaurant in the lobby of the CBS Black Rock Tower at 53rd Street and Avenue of the Americas. Back in the 1990s, before the wave of young, renegade chefs from Hong Kong and Shanghai began coming to New York and opening their own avant-garde restaurants, China Grill was the most radically creative Asian cuisine in New York. The food was write-in-your-diary good. People would take photos of their food. And this was before the invention of camera-phones or the existence of Instagram. Just as important, China Grill was quite accustomed to people arriving for dinner at 10pm.

China Grill was extremely expensive. After all, the location was some of the most expensive real estate in New York. The rent must have been astronomical. The dinner bill was going to be steep. If this had been dinner for five, which was the original plan, dinner would have been expensive, but it would not have caused alarm. It was just how we rolled. But dinner for eleven would undoubtedly get flagged. It was the very definition of an abusive expense. But the time for back-pedaling had long-since passed. We were taking this journey all the way.

When our band of merry travelers arrived at what was now restaurant #3, I asked the maître d' if he could accommodate a group of eleven.

(It is entirely possible that we were twelve now. We may have picked up someone somewhere. I can't swear to it.) He smiled and said, "Of course. If you just give me a moment." After conferring with his staff, he turned back to me and said, "Would you mind terribly if we gave you two tables next to each other?"

"Not at all. That would be wonderful." I said. And asked him to lead the way.

We had two large round tables of six (which is why I think there were twelve of us now) right next to each other in an excellent location to see and be seen. And even though typically jaded New Yorkers do not make a fuss over celebrities, Vanessa was radiantly beautiful that evening (as always) and she drew the attention of everyone around us. By now, of course, everyone of us was famished. There was much conversation during the menu review process as everyone decided what to order. But as soon as the food arrived, silence enveloped the group, and the business of eating took precedence. By the time we got to the second course, conversation resumed, and everyone made jokes about our misadventures earlier in the evening.

At one point, I happened to look over at the other table and noticed the attorney reviewing the wine menu with the waiter, and I heard him say, "Let's get a couple of bottles of champagne for the table."

As discreetly as I could, I reached over and literally tugged at the hem of the waiter's coat. The waiter turned sharply and looked at me. "Yes sir, can I help you?"

I gestured for the waiter to lean in for a whispered communication. "Excuse me," I said. "I don't wish to be rude."

The waiter nodded his head.

I reached into my jacket, removed the American Express card from my wallet, and showed it to the waiter. "This is the card that will be paying for tonight's dinner. I don't wish to embarrass the gentleman at the other table, but if I didn't order the wine, it isn't going on this card."

The waiter nodded again. "I understand completely sir." The waiter excused himself and returned to his other duties. He did not say anything to the attorney, but the champagne never arrived.

Speaking of "never arrived", Danny Glover never arrived to join us at dinner. That is actually pretty understandable, since he would have no idea which restaurant was our final destination. He might have gone to Jezebel and never found us. That's a shame, because I met and spent time with Danny on other occasions and found him to be warm, friendly, very down to earth and quite passionate about the Coors Literacy program. Years later, after I had launched Heritage Apparel, Danny and I reconnected regarding my company's Buffalo Soldier Cavalry Jacket. Danny starred in and executive-produced the movie "Buffalo Soldiers" and gave me his thoughts and feedback to our design.

At the end of the evening, which was well past midnight, the check arrived, and I saw just how much our evening had cost. Bernard, who was dying of curiosity, leaned over my shoulder to look at the check. He started to chuckle. "You're in trouble now, my friend."

"Don't say that."

Bernard suggested that we split the check so that it didn't all fall on one card. That probably wasn't necessary, but we did it anyway. Bernard put $1,500 on his card, and I put $2,500 on mine. That covered everything, including tax and tip, which was generous and well-earned.

Ivan put his hand on my shoulder. "Mark, no matter how much that is, I promise you Coors will approve it."

"Thanks," I said. "Come to the office tomorrow. I'm going to give this to Josie in the morning. I won't be able to sleep until I turn in these expenses."

Moses looked at us both and shook his head. "Oh man, I'm just glad I'm not either one of you."

As we said our goodbyes for the night, Vanessa gave me a big hug and said, "Thank you for turning an insane evening into a wonderful evening. . . . And thank you for introducing me to my new favorite restaurant." She smiled.

The next morning, the first thing I did in the office was complete my expense report and turned it in to Stella, who immediately took it to Josie, UniWorld's CFO. Josie called me into her office, which was right next door to mine.

"Mark," Josie put her hand to her forehead. "What did you do last night?"

"There's more," I said as I sat down in one of the chairs. "Bernard has more."

"Is the client going to approve this?"

"Yes." I nodded my head. "Ivan's coming in this morning. He'll come see you. But he personally guarantees he'll get it approved."

Ivan came by a short while later and spoke to Josie. He reassured her that the dinner was entirely "client-directed" and UniWorld would not get stuck with the bill.

Also that morning, Byron Lewis came by and poked his head into my office. Before he said a word, I said, "You heard about the dinner."

He smiled, which let me know he knew that everything was okay. He said, "With a dinner bill like that, there should have been doggy bags."

CHAPTER EIGHTEEN

Calendars, Posters and the Pinewood Derby

One of the staples of multicultural marketing—perhaps a very tired and overused staple—is the annual Black History Month ad. Companies and brands that never bothered to spend a nickel the rest of the year, and never gave the African American consumer a second thought, would nevertheless trudge out an ad for the month of February and run it in Ebony and Essence Magazines, giving a "big salute to Black achievement" so they could check-the-box of the company's "long-standing commitment to diversity." These ads rarely demonstrated any creativity or originality, and made no effort to connect the audience to the brand's values or positioning. The tagline for these ads might as well have been, "See you next year."

On the other hand, there were several companies and brands that had a substantial ongoing commitment to minority consumers. These brands were present in the multicultural marketplace all year-round. And, in February, you could expect something extra, something a little bit special from these brands. In some cases, a brand might offer a special consumer promotion or consumer premiums. Coors, for example, each year published their Black Heritage Calendar in February. These calendars featured a series of original illustrations and stories of Black history, all centered on a Western theme befitting the Coors

Rocky Mountain heritage. Each year, these calendars were a highly sought-after item by both consumers and retailers. Anheuser-Busch had their own Black History Calendar featuring the kings and queens of Africa (befitting the "King of Beers" legacy of Budweiser). These promotional giveaways were a guaranteed home run with consumers.

One year, however, in spite of the calendar's immense popularity, our Coors client, Ivan, decided it was time to change things up a bit. Time for something fresh. Of course, a factor in Ivan's decision might also have been the practical consideration that printing and distributing a calendar is both expensive and quite labor-intensive. The challenge he put to the agency was to come up with an alternative promotion that would be equally popular, yet easier and cheaper to produce.

After going back to the drawing board to brainstorm ideas, the agency's recommendation was to create a 20" x 30" poster featuring a dramatic illustration of the Tuskegee Airmen of WWII. The posters would be produced on large tear-pads of 20 posters each. The tear-pads would be given to retailers based on how much Coors Light product they purchased to sell. The retailer would display the tear-pad of the poster in-store to highlight the promotion. Consumers could obtain a free poster (while supplies last!) with the purchase of two six-packs of Coors Light. Ads on local radio stations would announce the promotion and direct consumers to get the poster where they buy Coors Light.

The UniWorld creative team that developed the concept and the poster layout featured two of the most talented art directors/designers I have ever worked with, Aaron Bell and Ben Marshall. And the team was led by Valerie Graves, a brilliant creative leader and mentor. In developing the concept, the creative team studied the archives of photos of the Tuskegee Airmen, in training and in action. They reviewed Negro magazines from the WWII period, as well as a very limited number of books that wrote about these Black aviators. The posters featured six Tuskegee Airmen standing proud and tall in flight coveralls and looking skyward. In the background were two P-51 Mustang fighter planes emblazoned with the red tails that were the trademark of the 332nd Fighter Group. The poster included the squadron insignia of the 332nd Fighter Group (the 99th, the 100th, and the 301st Fighter Squadrons), the Tuskegee Airmen. The image was bold, dramatic and heroic.

The Tuskegee Airmen story began as an experiment in 1941. *Were colored soldiers really smart enough and brave enough to fly modern aircraft into combat?* But by the time WWII had ended, the Black pilots who trained at Tuskegee Airfield in Alabama had become more than heroes.

They were legends of the skies.

The soldiers who trained at Tuskegee Airfield became the elite corps of all-Black fighter pilots of the 332nd Fighter Group in World War II. "The Tuskegee Airmen" flew over 15,000 combat sorties escorting and protecting Allied bombers over Germany, shot down 409 enemy aircraft and never lost a single bomber to enemy fighters. Known also as the "Red Tail Angels" for the distinctive markings of their P-51 Mustangs, the men of the 332nd were a soaring example of bravery and determination.

In 1995, most Black Americans were not familiar with the story and heroic exploits of the Tuskegee Airmen. Unless you were alive during World War II, you had very little exposure or opportunity to learn about the critical role that these aviators played in defeating fascism and Nazi Germany. Schools weren't teaching any of this. The media didn't know any of this. Hollywood didn't know any of this. But at UniWorld, it was our job to know these stories. It was our job to be fully immersed in African American history and culture. It was our job to be the "subject matter experts." As one of my mentors used to say, "This ain't my hobby. This is my profession."

Ivan loved the idea. Everyone did. But still, the calendars were proven winners. This was something new. How many posters should we print? Just how popular would it be? No one could be sure, so the consensus was to err on the side of caution. We would print 75,000 posters. If we could sell enough Coors Light to give away that many posters, it was a winner.

Consumer promotions can be a tricky business. There are lots of details and lots of moving parts, and everything has to be in the right place at just the right time or things fall apart. So, naturally, that's precisely what happened. The posters, which looked gorgeous, were being shipped from the printer to the various distributors across the country, but there was a slight delay, a few days or so. That delay was further compounded by the fact that the distributors don't make calls on every retailer every day, especially not the smaller ethnic retailers. The visits and the deliveries are part of a routine schedule that cannot be disrupted.

So, at the beginning of February, the radio ads began airing, announcing the promotion and urging consumers to get to the stores to get their posters "while supplies last." The stores, however, did not have their posters yet. All across the country, African American consumers were rushing to the store, buying their Coors Light, asking for their poster, and leaving the store empty-handed. All across the country, retailers were harassing their distributors to deliver the posters. And all across the country, consumers were overwhelming the phone lines at Coors, demanding their Tuskegee Airmen posters. If Coors wasn't in such a remote location in Colorado, I'm sure that mobs of angry consumers would have been standing outside the brewery gates with torches and pitchforks.

The delay was only one week, but it seemed like it lasted forever. Finally, the posters were in the stores. Consumers were probably visiting the stores every day, either as part of their regular routine, or simply to check back for the posters. By the end of the next ten days, in African American neighborhoods in key cities across the country, there was no Coors Light left on the shelf and there were no more Tuskegee Airmen posters anywhere. Gone. 75,000 completely sold out. Thank goodness the radio commercials had stopped airing. And there were still almost two weeks left to the month.

For about a minute, everyone contemplated the idea of trying to rush-print more posters and get them into the markets. But it was simply impossible to get them done and distributed fast enough. It was better to have a promotion that was so hot it became a rare collectible.

The enormous popularity of the Tuskegee Airmen poster made an indelible impression on me. The Black consumer appetite for images and stories of African American history and heroes was virtually insatiable. It represented an unmet need that was bigger than anyone imagined. There was so much undiscovered history of African American achievement, so many stories of the essential and pivotal part that people of color have played in America's journey. No one—neither white nor Black—learned these stories in school. And so, when images and messages like the Tuskegee Airmen poster were presented to an audience starved for inspiration, starved for aspiration, they were more than an attractive novelty. They were a tonic for the ailment you didn't realize you had.

In the months that followed the Tuskegee Airmen poster promotion, I began brainstorming plans for a business idea, a company of my own. I had always hoped—or perhaps expected—that I would start my own company someday. Since I was 10 years old, and had the largest lawn mowing service in the neighborhood, I have been a lifelong entrepreneur. I love starting things and building things. I started a successful business in college and employed 20 other students. (People absolutely crack up when I tell them that I owned a highly successful discotheque in college. Hey, it was the 70s.) Once I began working in advertising, I assumed that I would someday open my own ad agency. But I was falling in love with this new idea of launching a company that marketed products that celebrated African American history and heroes. I gave every free moment I had toward planning to bring this idea to life.

My embryonic idea would be called "Heritage Apparel." The name was meant as an explicit acknowledgment that the product that I would be selling was pride; pride in one's self, pride in one's history. It would be a company that manufactured and marketed apparel and collectibles. And it would be a company that would take the multicultural marketing skills that I had learned and put them to work for me. I was also fascinated by the idea that the internet was maturing as a commercial marketplace. Businesses were able to reach vast potential audiences of customers that they could not have reached except at great expense. This created an asymmetrical opportunity for small and start-up businesses. The moment seemed ripe for an entrepreneur to go seek his fortune.

I had been at UniWorld for roughly six years. The only opportunity for my advancement would be to inherit Byron's job as CEO, and that was highly unlikely. I loved UniWorld, but Byron loved it ten times more than I did. It was commonly understood around the office that the only way that Byron would leave UniWorld was on a gurney. I certainly wasn't wishing for that or waiting for it. But I had not yet reached my 40th birthday and forward career momentum was still very important to me. I spent more and more time thinking about launching my own company.

And then, unexpectedly, a phone call came along and put my plans on hold, at least for a while.

◆ ◆ ◆

"OBVIOUSLY, I CAN'T RESPOND
TO THAT IN ANY WAY."

Sometime in September of 1996, I got a call from an executive recruiter, a headhunter who had tried to lure me away from UniWorld on a few prior occasions.

"I have an opportunity I'd like to talk to you about," he began. "I'm afraid a lot of the details are highly confidential, so I can't tell you very much."

I listened. "Highly confidential" could be either very good or very bad. I was curious.

"A creative celebrity is going to open his own advertising agency." The recruiter led with his headline. "He's going to run the creative side of things, obviously. But he needs someone who can run pretty much everything else. He needs an account guy who's more than an account guy. He needs an entrepreneur with a solid head on his shoulders. Somebody who's ready to run their own agency." He paused for a beat. "And . . . it needs to be somebody he feels he can work with."

So far, things sounded pretty cool. "Uh huh."

"So, if you think you would be interested, I need you to send me the latest copy of your resume." There wasn't going to be a lot of Q&A in this conversation. "Obviously, I can't tell you who the creative celebrity is unless he decides that he would like to speak with you."

And then, without hesitating or even thinking about it, the words spilled out of my mouth. "So, Spike is finally going to start his agency."

Filmmaker Spike Lee had, on several occasions, expressed a desire to start his own agency. He had said so both publicly and privately. I knew this because my work on the Coors account had brought me together with Spike for a joint project. Spike is an alum of Morehouse College in Atlanta. Spike was helping Morehouse to promote their minority business development efforts in a section of Atlanta called Atlanta University Center. My client, Ivan Burwell, brought Coors Community Relations aboard to help support the program. We produced some advertising together. The collaboration was a success and Spike was grateful for our participation.

There was a very long silence at the other end of the phone. "Obviously, I can't respond to that in any way."

Now it was my turn for a very long silence at my end of the phone. "Okay," I said finally. "I'll fax you a copy of my resume by tomorrow."

A week or two later, the executive recruiter met with Spike and presented him with ten resumes of African American advertising professionals that the recruiter felt were his best candidates. My resume was among the ten.

Spike looked at each resume one at a time. He read them. Then he spread them out on the table in front of him, examining them as a group. Spike picked up one resume from the group and handed it to the recruiter. "I know this guy. Have him come in. Give him a call and set it up."

It was my resume.

"What about the others?" The recruiter asked.

Spike shook his head. "Just this one." Apparently, Spike remembered me from the Morehouse project. He liked my resume, and he knew we worked well together. I think that as the process unfolded, he did end up interviewing a few other candidates. But for all intents and purposes, I was the only finalist on his list.

Damn. I wish I had known that at the time. I surely would have negotiated a much better deal for myself. But this key detail was not shared with me until many months after the fact.

Well, since I had now made the "short list", the recruiter briefed me on a handful of previously "confidential" details. The new agency was a partnership between Spike Lee and the mega-agency DDB (once known as Doyle Dane Bernbach, the creative powerhouse of the 1960s). Specifically, the partnership was with the Chicago office of DDB, with the involvement of a handful of the Chicago office executives. Spike had recently directed a handful of commercials for the Chicago agency, and that is where "exploratory conversations" began. The new agency would be called Spike/DDB and despite the Chicago connection, the offices would be in New York.

It was easy to understand why Spike wanted so badly to have his own agency. As a cinematic director, Spike approached his films as an auteur. He developed the story idea for the films and often wrote the screenplays himself. And when filming was done, he was intimately involved in the editing and post-production details. Spike touched everything from beginning to end. But with TV commercials, Spike's role was much more boxed in. He did not participate in the concept development or script, and once the shoot day was over, he had no involvement in editing or post-production. All of that was handled by the agency creative team and it drove Spike crazy. He did not like being just one of the steps in the commercial-creation assembly line. If he had his own agency, he could bring his creative vision to every step in the advertising process. That is exactly what he wanted.

Before interviewing with Spike, I was scheduled to meet with George Lewis, Spike's father-in-law. Spike placed a great deal of trust and faith in the judgment of his father-in-law, and for good reason. George Lewis began his career in the mid-1960s as a financial analyst for General Foods, working on Kool-Aid. In 1967, he was hired by Philip Morris as a corporate analyst. By the time I met him in 1996, he was Vice President and Treasurer of Philip Morris Worldwide, one of the highest-ranking and most powerful African Americans in corporate finance. The following year he would become President and CEO of Philip Morris Capital Company. When it came to making financial decisions, George Lewis was in a league all his own.

George Lewis called me directly to schedule our interview. I wasn't expecting that. He lived in Stamford, Connecticut and I live in Ridgefield. He proposed getting together in Connecticut that Saturday afternoon so we could have a relaxed conversation. That would have been great, except for one thing. Saturday was my son Sean's Pinewood Derby race for the Cub Scouts. We had built the racecar together. My nine-year-old son was extremely excited about the race and what we had built together. This was an important father-son event. Missing it was simply not an option.

I explained this to George and apologized. I told him to pick any other date and time I would move everything to be there. He didn't seem to mind at all, and we ended up meeting at his very elegant Manhattan office at Philip Morris the following Tuesday.

Sean came in second place among the Wolf-level scouts in the Pinewood Derby.

Again, I did not learn of this until many months later, but apparently, George Lewis made up his mind that he liked me even before he met me. George told Spike (who had a two year-old daughter and a son on the way), "This young man puts his family first. That's the kind of father I expect you to be."

Over the next several weeks, I interviewed with Spike, with DDB's HR Director and with an executive from DDB Chicago who was designated as the "Godfather" or chaperone of the partnership between the two agencies. Ultimately, this led to a job offer to become Managing Director and co-founder of Spike/DDB.

You might be surprised to know that I did not say yes immediately. In fact, I was not entirely sure that I was going to say yes. I had spent nearly a year investing all my emotional energy in planning the creation and launch of my own company, something that was mine, something that was a completely different direction from another job at another agency. It wasn't simply an entrepreneurial impulse, although that was a very big part of it. I have had that entrepreneurial impulse and desire since I was ten years old. It was always going to be part of what drove me. But I was also driven by the extraordinary inspirational heroism of the Tuskegee Airmen, by the spirit of dramatic adventure. It was like reliving the excitement of the comic book heroes of my childhood. Only this time the heroes were very real.

Even a glamorous, important job working alongside a celebrity at an ad agency was going to have a very hard time competing with that.

It was time to seek advice from someone much wiser and more level-headed than myself, so I went to my wife, Laura. She knew that I was restless at UniWorld and ready for a change. She knew about the months of planning and my excitement about the idea of starting my own company. And she knew about the interviews and the job offer from Spike/DDB. She was—and is—my life partner, and no important decision could ever be made without her.

"What will you have to do if you take this job?" She asked.

"I'll be managing all of the business and operational aspects of the agency, while reporting to Spike", I said.

"So," she tilted her head slightly. "You will be launching a new company and running it, but using other people's money." It was both a question and a statement.

"Basically."

"Is there any reason you couldn't put the Tuskegee Airman plans on the shelf for a year or two and come back to them?" She probed.

"Just that I want to do it."

"But you could still do it two years from now." Again, it was both a question and a statement.

"So, you think that's what I should do?" I pressed for a definitive point of view.

"Do whatever feels right to you." And then, after just half a beat, she added, "but I know what I would do."

And so, in mid-November of 1996, I accepted the offer to become Managing Director and co-founder of Spike/DDB.

CHAPTER NINETEEN

Community Service

I accepted the Spike/DDB offer in mid-November, however, I explained to Spike and the others that I couldn't fully start until January. I was in the middle of wrapping up a big project for Coors that included a handful of travel. In good conscience, I could not walk out in the middle of that. It would have been unprofessional and terribly unfair to my colleagues at UniWorld and to my Coors clients. They had all treated me well. I had to give them the same respect.

Spike was very understanding, but the delay drove the DDB folks crazy. They had planned a big publicity wave for the agency launch announcement, and I was upsetting their timetable. I hadn't even started and already I was their "problem child."

Even though I hadn't officially started, I was able to attend a number of pre-launch meetings and actually spent a good deal of time helping to make needed adjustments and revisions to the agency's business plan, which—in my opinion—included quite a few pie-in-the-sky assumptions and forecasts for revenue. I told the Chicago executives that parts of the business plan included more wishful thinking than a ten year-old boy on Christmas Eve. They told me that the plan had been vetted by far more experienced hands than me and that I was attempting to set the bar too low.

One of the plan points that made me particularly skeptical was the assertion that $2 million in revenue in the agency's first year would come from business obtained from DDB's existing clients. These existing clients would feed incremental business into the new agency. Since that was going to be a sizable chunk of our revenue forecast, I pressed for more specifics.

"Which clients? Have they already committed to do this? How certain are we?"

In response, I was told that this had been in the works for months and it was not necessary for me to come in at the last minute and ask 20 questions. In hindsight, this was a moment that did not pass the smell test. This was a moment that felt like somebody was papering over bullshit, and perhaps I should have put more trust in my own instincts. But I was the new guy on the team. I did not create the business plan. And I was eager to fit in, eager to make a good impression, even though it was also being made clear to me that I would be held responsible for delivering those financial projections.

Right after the New Year of 1997, I was fully on board at Spike/DDB and ready to tackle all of the new challenges, which were many. We had no staff. We had no clients, and we had no offices. On January 6, 1997, I showed up at the cafeteria (my temporary office) at DDB New York with my laptop and my cellphone and immediately began trying to do something about each of those things. Actually, we did have one staff member, an executive assistant who greeted me when I arrived at the cafeteria. She had just arrived from Chicago over the weekend and apparently knew more about her new assignment than I did.

I told the folks at DDB Chicago that Spike and I would need an executive assistant right away, since we had so many things to do, but I intended that to mean that Spike and I would choose and hire someone right away. I wasn't expecting to have someone sent to us from Chicago, especially not someone neither of us had ever met. And given the fact that we were a minority agency with a multicultural marketing focus, I suppose that I also expected that our executive assistant would be a person of color. That wasn't who our Chicago-transplanted assistant turned out to be. Apparently, the executives at DDB Chicago never considered that, or simply didn't care. She was a self-proclaimed Midwest country girl who hated New York, was not especially familiar with Spike Lee's work and had never worked in a multicultural environment before. Clearly, these were not relevant considerations.

My new assistant's previous boss in Chicago had left the agency suddenly, perhaps not of his own choosing, and she had no boss and no assignment. Senior management in Chicago decided to offer her this opportunity and she accepted, literally sight unseen. To be fair, she was definitely smart, quite professional and hard-working. But she was accustomed to functioning within the infrastructure of a large, corporate agency with hundreds of employees, and where virtually every task was delegated to someone else. She had never worked for a small, start-up company, where you not only changed the printer's toner cartridge yourself, you also went to the store and bought it yourself. The very idea seemed incomprehensible to her.

When I called Chicago, which I did every single day to cover a myriad of tasks and inquiries, I was told, "I hope you don't mind that we took care of this for you."

Which roughly translates to, "We really don't care if you mind, but we wanted to be polite about it."

My new assistant also spent a great deal of time on the phone to the Chicago office, often just to stay connected to the Chicago gossip, or for her friends to ask her what Spike was like. Before too long, however, I began to sense a different tone and purpose to her calls.

The senior executives at DDB Chicago who helped engineer this new agency partnership were constantly in a state of anxiety and worry about two things; 1) that they had entered into a partnership with a highly unpredictable and independent-minded creative celebrity, 2) that we were operating nearly 800 miles away and not under their roof. As any psychologist will tell you, there is no fear quite like the fear of the unknown. So, it was not a surprise to me or to Spike that a high priority for the Chicago executives was the installation of "an observer" that could keep an eye on the Black folks in New York. We both agreed, however, that there was no point in taking offense or creating a confrontation. Spike's attitude was, "Let's just be great. She can report that."

I had gotten to know Spike a little bit during our prior interaction a few years earlier, but now I was spending a tremendous amount of time with him and getting to know him quite well. People who know only Spike's public persona would be very surprised to learn that Spike is actually quite introspective and introverted. Spike is always observing, always listening and always processing what he sees. But rarely speaking. Although very different in personal style and demeanor, Spike is like Barack Obama in how carefully he chooses his words. In fact, Spike is so economical in his speaking that most people in the office assumed that he did not like them or did not wish to speak with them.

As our office eventually staffed up, that was a common refrain. People would come into my office, close the door, and confide to me that Spike does not like them. I would ask why, and they would say because he never speaks to them. I would then explain that if Spike did not actually like them, they would not still be working here. Most left my office feeling less than fully satisfied by the reassurance.

Truthfully, Spike did not wish to chit-chat and did not wish to have agency staff casually walking into his office to chat. Frankly, that's true of almost every CEO or senior executive I have ever worked with. People simply don't realize how terribly unproductive it is. Spike expected me to deal with all of that and relied upon me to be the gatekeeper at the office. This was a role that led to an endless amount of stress for me, as well as a ton of needless office drama. Almost everyone at the agency believed that I was embracing the gatekeeper role purely for my own benefit and ambition and to prevent anyone else from enjoying proximity to Spike. Countless hours were spent with agency staff trying to figure out ways to get around me or get me out of the picture entirely. It became mentally and emotionally exhausting, and made it almost impossible for me to have the relationships with my staff that I wanted. It also made it very hard for the agency to cohere as a team.

Spike's detachment from everyday office affairs was further exacerbated by the fact that he was right in the middle of production of his next film, "He Got Game." It was common for Spike to be gone from the office for a week or more at a time. And when he was there, he would have a dozen things on his mind other than the agency. Spike was a chronic multi-tasker, always doing six things at once, which usually made him extremely dependent upon the people close to him to help juggle all of the balls that were constantly in the air. All of this contributed to creating an office atmosphere that often felt like a combat MASH unit where each of us clung to whatever survival mechanism kept us from having a complete nervous breakdown.

It was completely inexplicable to me how the folks at DDB never discussed or anticipated Spike's film production schedule before locking in the agency's launch timeline. When asked (after the fact) about the obvious conflict of commitment, they would brush it off by saying they always knew that this would occur, but that Spike was capable of doing many things well. In private, however, the issue had caught them unprepared and ultimately unable to offer constructive solutions.

One of the many things that Spike did exceptionally well was publicity. The agency's launch publicity was extremely effective and made a big splash in the industry and throughout the media. In fact, it got to the point where we had to establish a cut-off date for cooperating with the publicity machine so that we could get on with the agency's actual work. A by-product of all that great publicity was that the agency was flooded with calls and inquiries from prospective clients wanting to talk to us about their business. At first, we thought this was great. We were going to be fending off new business overtures with a stick. We were going to exceed our revenue forecasts by a wide margin.

Well, not exactly.

What we had were dozens—literally dozens—of clients that wanted to arrange a meeting with Spike. Sure, they held out the carrot of prospective business, but all it took was a few well-chosen follow-up questions and it immediately became clear that all they really wanted was an opportunity to meet a celebrity, to meet Spike. They had no intention, and in many cases no authority, to award us any new business. This became a problem we needed to solve very quickly. I developed an "Agency Inquiry Questionnaire" for prospective clients, designed to gauge how sincere and concrete the inquiry was. This narrowed the list down considerably.

One of the earliest clients that we pitched was Finish Line, the national athletic shoe retailer. The client's corporate headquarters was in Indianapolis, so Spike and I grabbed an early morning flight from LaGuardia Airport. Whenever we were out in public, and especially when we walked through airports, people would stop and point at Spike and say, "You're Spike Lee." Spike would smile and say, "A lot of people say I look just like him." After several moments of hesitation and careful examination, the person would nod their head and say, "You do, man. You do." On this morning, it was the dead of winter, so when I met Spike at the airport gate, he was wearing a big puffer jacket as protection from the cold weather. Once we boarded the plane, however, Spike removed his jacket, and I could see a golden-brown stain roughly the size of a silver dollar on the left shoulder of Spike's suit jacket. I almost did a double-take staring at it.

"What?" Spike caught my look.

Upon closer examination, it appeared that Spike's newborn son, Jackson, had spit-up on his shoulder, probably while Spike was holding him. I summoned the flight attendant, who immediately knew what to do. She was happy to offer special attention for Spike and "flew" into rescue mode. A little club soda and a clean white cloth napkin and Spike was as good as new. We went on to the pitch meeting with the Finish Line client and won the business. Finish Line went on to become one of the agency's very first clients, and we were not just their multicultural agency, but we were their "agency of record", handling *all* of their advertising. They were a fun client, and we did terrific work for them. Those early commercials were written and directed by Spike and shot on the streets of Brooklyn.

You People

By the end of the first quarter, we were fully operational with offices on Fifth Avenue, just off Union Square, four solid clients and a preliminary staff of about a dozen good people. It was time for a financial recap with the executives in Chicago. Unfortunately, the "recap" felt more like a reckoning and a dressing down by Lionel Barrymore at the bank.

Start-up agencies spend a lot of money up-front in order to establish themselves and create the necessary infrastructure and operational momentum, like trying to get a freight train moving from a dead stop. It takes a tremendous amount of energy and fuel. But revenue from new clients is the opposite. The money generated by client media expenditures does not come until after all the agency's other work is done, at the end of the process. This never looks good on an agency balance sheet and is one of the key reasons that so many agencies suffer from cash-flow problems. In our case, it did not help that Spike/DDB spent a sizable chunk of its first few weeks conducting press interviews, posing for photos and attending dead-end new business meetings instead of doing work that generated revenue. From an accountant's point of view, we looked like an enormous waste of money, a bad business decision.

And so, when I walked into that first quarterly board meeting in Chicago, I thought I was going to share how proud I was of all the things our agency had accomplished in just three short months. Instead, I was asked to rationalize every dollar our agency had spent in just three short months. I could have had all of the appropriate good reasons in the world. It didn't matter.

"Where's our money?"

I could have said that I knew all along that this was what the quarter was going to look like. It didn't matter.

"Where's our money?"

The finance people stay completely disconnected from the daily operation of the business for a reason. They don't want to know. They don't care.

"Where's our money?"

I have dealt with finance people throughout my career. They are usually tough because they take their job and their fiduciary responsibilities very seriously. It's not personal. They don't dislike you. In fact, it's great to have a tough finance director by your shoulder when you are negotiating fee contracts with the client. They are great negotiators.

But in the wake of that difficult first quarter board meeting, I began receiving memos from the DDB Chicago CFO that went noticeably beyond "tough but fair." Contrary to what I just said about finance guys not getting personal, these memos were definitely personal, and they had a strong whiff of condescension. By the time I got my second memo, I was seeing language like "you people" and "learning to be responsible." We were admonished that running our business "like other minority agencies" would not be tolerated.

This was not going to be okay with me. I sent the memos to the EVP at DDB Chicago who was designated as our agency's godfather. I told him the CFO's next memo had better include an apology or I was going to take this to HR. He told me that I was over-reacting. He told me the CFO "didn't have a racist bone in his body." (God, how I hate that expression.) I never received the apology, but the memos stopped. This only made the next board meeting twice as awkward and uncomfortable.

By the end of the second quarter, we were in the black. Thank goodness the agency was making more money than it was spending, but we were still below our forecasted revenue target. That's when I began asking, whatever happened to that $2 million in guaranteed revenue from existing DDB Chicago clients? Our doors had been open for six months and we had not heard a single word about any business referrals from DDB. And I reminded the board that they had written that into the business plan, they had made the promise, even though six months earlier I had loudly voiced my skepticism.

Yes, awkward and uncomfortable.

I think the Chicago executives were expecting me to be easier for them to manage. I think they were expecting me to be someone much more eager to please my corporate masters. Perhaps if I had come to Spike/DDB directly from a big, mainstream agency (like my first two agencies, SSC&B or Grey), my orientation and inclination would be to think and act just like them. But I had spent six and a half years at UniWorld, which turned my head in a different direction and afforded me plenty of opportunities to bump heads with mainstream agency types. When it suited their needs, they would not hesitate to run over me like the cross-town bus.

Perhaps most important, Spike had entrusted me to manage his agency, to handle the business side of things and to represent his wishes and his voice in the way that I did my job. Spike would not want me to be a passive or submissive empty suit in dealing with our corporate partners in Chicago. That would be letting him down.

So, I pressed and pushed and kept pushing until we finally got invited to a meeting with one of DDB Chicago's biggest clients, Anheuser-Busch. The St. Louis mega-brewery was known for big, bold-statement, terrific advertising (of a certain very all-American style) and for showcasing their best advertising in hugely expensive Super Bowl commercials each year. To their credit, as soon as Anheuser-Busch saw that they had the opportunity to 'tap' the creative firepower of Spike Lee's new agency, they asked to meet with us as soon as possible.

Anheuser-Busch was not going to take any business away from DDB Chicago and give it to us. That would have been terrific, but definitely expecting too much. They did, however, give us a chance to snatch away an attractive piece. They asked us to develop a Bud Light commercial for the Super Bowl. If they liked our work best, our ad would run.

We flew home from St. Louis amped up about the assignment and confident that we could kill this. Spike wasted no time calling together the creative team and brainstorming. Spike knew that we could not simply give the client a good idea, or even a few good ideas. DDB Chicago was going to give them a dozen good ideas. We had to give Anheuser-Busch something that could only come from Spike/DDB. No idea was considered too far outside the box. In fact, the more outrageous, the better.

As the team pitched ideas to Spike, you were very lucky if you actually got to read the whole commercial script before Spike yelled, "Next!" Occasionally, he would say, "I'm sure DDB would love that idea. Next!"

After much work and trial and error, we had a handful of ideas that really broke through and would be polished up for presentation to the client. But we had one idea that rose above the rest. When Spike saw the idea, the side of his mouth curled up into the beginning of a mischievous grin and his eye began to twinkle, Spike announced, "Now *that's* a commercial you can't get anyplace else but here."

James Brown, (the R&B legend, not the sportscaster).

Throughout his adult life and professional career, wherever James Brown was, mayhem and brushes with the law were not far behind. Sometimes he just seemed to be a magnet for trouble. Between 1987 and 1996, he was arrested four times on domestic assault charges. But despite all his troubles and scandals, James Brown was beloved by his fans and there was an element of his popular appeal that crossed over to the mainstream.

When we were brainstorming ideas for a Bud Light Super Bowl commercial, James Brown was being sentenced to 200 hours of community service.

Our commercial opens on a crane shot down the center of a typical all-American suburban street, the kind of street you might expect to find Beaver Cleaver playing catch with his dad and brother. You see handsome homes with well-maintained lawns and white picket fences. And you see—somewhat off in the distance—a silhouette of a man riding a bicycle down the street. It's not some fancy racing bike or dirt bike. It's an old-fashioned bicycle with a basket on the front and a little squeeze horn next to the basket.

The camera cuts to show a suburban dad mowing his lawn happily, with just the first few beads of perspiration on his brow. He hears the squeeze horn from the bicycle and looks up to see that the rider is James Brown.

"Community service. Bud Light for my friend!" As James hands the man a cold, refreshing Bud Light from his basket. James smiles and keeps riding down the street.

At his next stop, James meets a man who is washing his car in his driveway, and the scene is repeated. "Community service. Bud Light for my friend!"

There's some announcer copy in the middle, and the spot closes with a long shot of the silhouette of James Brown riding down the street, and you hear, "Bud Light for my friend!"

The advertising managed to take one of the Blackest entertainers in show business (the singer of "Say it loud, I'm Black and I'm proud!") and placed him—successfully—in one of the most traditionally ultra-white American settings, while simultaneously giving a knowing wink to his run-in with the law in a way the audience found perfectly okay. And all of this was wrapped around cold, refreshing Bud Light as the hero of the story. In the competition for most talked-about commercial at the water-cooler the day after the Super Bowl, this was guaranteed a seat in the top five.

The client loved it. This was the commercial for the Super Bowl. The client had only one question; could we get James Brown to do it?

Spike nodded his head. "I think I can get him."

And Spike was right. He got James to say yes. And for 24 hours, we were elated. Everyone was happy. We had won a high-stakes creative shoot-out against some of the best advertising professionals in the business and we were going to put an outrageously good commercial on the Super Bowl. But the next day, Spike got a phone call. James Brown had placed a condition on his willingness to do the ad.

"What?" I said, as Spike was breaking the news to me in painfully slow pieces.

"You know that Reverend Al Sharpton is James Brown's godson."

I said nothing. Frozen.

"James wants Sharpton to be in the commercial with him. They're both riding the bikes," Spike said in a flat monotone.

I said nothing. Still frozen.

"That's the only way James will do the spot. Him and Reverend Al or nothing." Spike looked at me with a rueful smile. Then he pantomimed taking a shotgun and shooting a clay pigeon out of the sky.

Before the day was over, the Anheuser-Busch client would confirm what we already knew. The spot was dead. They would go with one of the DDB Chicago ads.

CHAPTER TWENTY

Red Carpets and Travel Irons

For the average person living in New York or Los Angeles, a close encounter with a celebrity is really no big deal, and most New Yorkers and Angelinos are pretty good at being nonchalant about celebrity encounters. They might be impressed. They might be a fan. But they work hard not to show it.

A simple, "Hey, how you doing?" And they go about their business.

In my work in advertising, however, I have met and worked with dozens of celebrities; from A-list to stars before-they-were-stars. The practical reality of the job, my job, was to treat each one with professional respect, but not much more than that. Fawning really gets in the way of doing your job, and it gets annoying pretty fast. Most of the celebrities that I have worked with are simply decent, good people, professional and easy to work with. Some celebrities expect more—both in the way they are treated, and in the demands listed in their contracts—and, within reasonable limits, they usually get it. My colleague, Marc S. Strachan once sent a white stretch limo to the airport to pick up a certain R&B singer. She took one look at the white limo waiting at the curb and turned around and boarded the next flight home. She informed Marc that "White limos are for prom dates and drunken bachelor parties. They are undignified." She would return only when he provided a black limousine.

I shot a series of Jell-O ads for Kraft General Foods with Bill Cosby. I had heard countless stories from colleagues about his kindness and generosity, and they are probably all true. But that was not the man I worked with. The man I worked with was an impatient and, at times, irascible Hollywood veteran who commanded the set and made people jump at the sound of his voice. This man was 100% in control of his brand, and when the camera was on, he turned on the charm that lit the room by itself. He could perform magic. He knew how to be "Bill Cosby." Of course, that was back in the days when the Bill Cosby brand was still quite popular, wholesome and appealing.

This was in stark contrast to people like Vanessa Williams, who was simply the sweetest, warmest and most down-to-earth woman you are ever likely to meet. A pleasure to be with. Giancarlo Esposito might be TV's most evil villain, but he is a charming, regular, good-hearted guy to be around. I am privileged—and grateful—to have had the opportunity to get to know quite a few celebrities just as the lovely people that they are.

As a consequence of my work, it is very difficult—and very rare—for me to become star-struck. Even meeting a hero like Gregory Peck back in my college days did not rattle me (although it came close). But in all my years in this business, it did happen twice. And both occasions occurred during the year that I worked for Spike.

The first occasion came early in the year. DDB New York was the agency handling the promotion of the 39th Annual Grammy Awards, which would be held at Madison Square Garden on February 26, 1997. Keith Reinhard, chairman of DDB Worldwide, and the architect of the Spike/DDB partnership, was fond of Spike, both personally and professionally. He took it upon himself to make sure that both Spike and I had tickets to the Grammys. And these were not just tickets, they were VIP tickets. My guess is that this was not Spike's first time attending the Grammys, although I never asked him, but it was definitely my first time.

Yes, yes. I am going to tell you all about just how incredible it was to attend the Grammy Awards. Because, well, it was. But first, I have to tell you that the coolest feeling I have ever had in my life was going home and telling my wife that we had tickets to attend the Grammys. That feeling just cannot be beaten. Our kids were still in elementary school, so I am not sure that the news had much of an impact on them, though they sensed it was some kind of a big deal.

My wife went into an immediate panic. She had roughly one month to shop for a dress and whatever else she needed. She wasn't sure it was enough time. I was confident that she would look amazing. After all, she was—and is—the most beautiful woman I have ever met. No celebrity could ever hold a candle to her.

Ten years earlier, we were on vacation in Deauville, France, right in the middle of the Deauville Film Festival. The little French village and every hotel in it was packed with hundreds of celebrities. The Normandy Hotel, where we stayed, was the festival headquarters. The only way to enter or leave the hotel was by way of an official red carpet that was lined with paparazzi. Laura was photographed hundreds of times by photographers who were convinced that she was Veronica Hamel. I told my wife that Veronica Hamel wished that she looked as good as she.

The afternoon of the Grammy Awards, I was still at work. I had brought my change of clothes to the office with me that morning. After all, for guys, you put on the tux and there isn't that much else to do. You get someone to help you with the bowtie and the cufflinks and you're all set. Our limousine picked up Laura (who was stunning in a floor-length slinky Black dress) at home in Connecticut and drove her to the office to scoop me up as well. Together, we headed uptown from Union Square to Madison Square Garden. The tickets came with detailed instructions for our driver; where to go and how to get there. Everything around the Garden had been blocked off to normal traffic. Only cars with a special sign inside the windshield would be permitted through. The procession of cars moved slowly along 34th Street, then right on Seventh Avenue, pulling up to the front of Madison Square Garden.

When we arrived, the limo door was opened for us by someone waiting at the curb, and we stepped directly onto the red carpet. Although there was an unmistakable sense of grandness and pageantry to the moment, almost as though the whole world was standing there, waiting to see us arrive, there was also an ultra-efficient assembly-line dynamic at work. The photographers were given a certain number of seconds to take our picture before we were politely but firmly ushered forward on the carpet so that we could keep things moving and make room for the next arrival.

And just like our red-carpet experience in Deauville ten years before, there is a moment of stillness when you step onto the red carpet. The paparazzi, and everyone else who has come to see celebrities, stop what they are doing and take you in with a long, frozen, deep stare. Time stops for just a second. An algorithm conducts complex data processing inside their brains and determines whether or not you are "Somebody."

Although a few seemed unsure, most quickly decided that we were not.

We kept moving forward, but as we were walking, our heads were on a 360-degree swivel as we tried to see everything and take it all in. Everywhere we looked, there were celebrities, in front and behind us. Off to the sides were celebrities being interviewed by E! and MTV reporters. All the while, you can hear the polite voice of one of the attendants saying, "Please keep moving forward," as they gently touch their hand to your shoulder. The whole experience caused sensory overload, and if the attendants hadn't kept urging us forward, we might have just stood there all night.

Once inside the Garden's main lobby, forward progress was now divided into several divergent paths leading to different seat sections. Off to the far right was a path with the shortest line. This was the path for admission to the executive suites, the luxury skyboxes. The tickets we had been given were for the "official Grammy suite", where the president of the Academy was to sit, along with his family and a handful of luminaries. As Garden security was checking our credentials, two men in tuxedos brushed past us and stepped onto the escalator.

Laura squeezed my arm. "Those two guys that went past. Did you see them?"

I shook my head. "No. Why?"

"Those were the 'Crashers,'" she pointed discreetly. "They're famous for crashing big events and award shows. They went by without showing any tickets." These two men, in their mid-thirties, fully understood that if you are a well-dressed white male, and you walk and move with a certain confidence, no one questions you. No one challenges you.

"Well, they're in now." I smiled. "Let's hope they're not sitting with us."

We heard later that security eventually caught up with them, probably at another check-point, and they were summarily tossed from the Garden.

Once we arrived at the skybox suite level, there weren't any more celebrity sightings. All of the celebrities were seated down in front, where the TV cameras would be, and where, if necessary, they could walk onstage to receive their awards. The executive suites were for a different kind of VIP, those not seen in front of the camera. And tonight, apparently, Laura and I fit that description.

The suite was actually bigger than the apartment that Laura and I used to have when we lived on 44th Street and Second Avenue, just starting out. You entered a very roomy lounge area with couches, leather chairs and low marble coffee tables. Along the wall was an extravagant hot and cold buffet, with both a full gourmet dinner and endless snack foods. I am certain we sampled almost everything. I know that I did. There was a fully stocked bar with a bartender, as well as a hostess, in case you preferred to have your drink brought to your seat for you. Facing into the arena were two rows of comfortable leather seats with a marble counter for your food and drink.

When we walked in we were warmly greeted by DDB Chairman Keith Reinhard, who was the only person I recognized. I am always a bit uncomfortable when attending social functions where I don't know anyone. Part of that uncomfortable feeling, I suppose, is the very self-conscious awareness that I am often the only Black person in the room. That awkward reality happens far more often than you would guess. It happens to me and to every other Black professional in advertising that I have ever known. I always feel as though everyone knows each other except me. Everyone was very friendly and there was no legitimate basis for my anxiety, but it didn't help when I looked around and saw that Spike was not there, especially when several people asked me where he was.

"I haven't spoken to him all day. I assumed he would be here."

Apparently, the person from the Grammys who was responsible for sending us tickets, intuitively decided that Spike would prefer to sit down in front, where all the other celebrities and the TV cameras were, while I sat in the skybox. They were probably right, but no one had told me. So, I naturally worried that sooner or later someone was going to come up to me and say that if, Spike wasn't there, we should probably go. Fortunately, no one did.

That year, the Grammys were hosted by Ellen DeGeneres, which seemed like an odd choice to me. She never quite matched the rhythm of the evening or the mood of the audience, and seemed to be trying a little too hard to prove her bona fides in a music context. It could have been worse. The following year the Academy chose Kelsey Grammar to host the award show.

About halfway through the evening, Spike showed up at the suite. He spent about five or ten minutes saying hello to everyone before finally coming over to me with a plateful of food in his hand.

"Damn, Mark. Why didn't you tell me y'all had food up here? We've been starving down there."

I looked over and saw Spike's wife, Tonya, preparing a plate for herself at the buffet.

I invited Spike to sit with Laura and me.

"From now on," Spike said, "I'll just assume you got the hook-up. I'll go where you go."

CHANCES ARE

The second occasion of 'celebrity overload' came four months later, at the end of June. Another one of our earliest clients was Showtime Pay-Per-View. They hired our agency to promote the rematch fight between former heavyweight champion Mike Tyson and current champion Evander Holyfield. Both fighters were previous champions. Both fighters were engaged in "career comebacks."

In 1992, Tyson was convicted of the rape of Miss Black Rhode Island in a hotel room while attending the Indiana Black Expo (an event I attended numerous times) and was sentenced to six years in prison. He was paroled after serving three years and began his comeback in 1995. Tyson regained his WBC championship title in a fight against

Frank Bruno. Next he regained the WBA championship in a bout with Bruce Seldon.

Evander Holyfield retired in 1994 after losing the WBO championship bout to Michael Moorer and subsequently being diagnosed with a heart condition. After a year of retirement, however, in which Holyfield went on a religious crusade, he claimed that his heart was healed, and he was returning to the ring. Holyfield's comeback record was somewhat uneven, defeating Olympic gold medalist Ray Mercer, but losing a third fight to Riddick Bowe. Most sports writers and commentators considered Holyfield to be a "washed up" fighter.

In November of 1996, Mike Tyson gave his first "renewed" heavyweight title defense fight against Holyfield at the MGM in Las Vegas. Tyson lost in the 11th round by a TKO. The referee stopped the fight as Holyfield pounded him defenseless, taking his championship title. It was the biggest, most successful pay-per-view event in Showtime history.

As soon as our agency publicly announced our launch, we received a call from Showtime. They wanted to retain our agency to market Showtime's pay-per-view of the rematch, which would occur in June. They wanted—if possible—to beat the pay-per-view sales record set by the first fight. They wanted the biggest boxing box office of all time.

I am a huge boxing fan and have been one for a long time, so this assignment was a great big gift for me. As crazy and as challenging as this project often was, I had fun for every minute of it. This was not a project that I was going to delegate to anyone else.

Showtime knew who their core audience was. They knew who would most likely shell out $100 for a pay-per-view sporting event. They had been "working" that base for years. But their core base was only going to get them so far, and it wasn't going to break any box office records. They would need to attract a large swath of fans who had never purchased pay-per-view before, people who had considered it, but never pulled the trigger. Our job was to figure out who those people were and figure out how to push them across the finish line.

We conducted research among boxing fans, among fans of other sports and among people who did not consider themselves avid sports fans. We wanted to know what kinds of events got them excited, what kinds of events would they go out of their way to watch or be part of. All of the learning and all of the focus groups led us to develop a strategy that elevated the event above and beyond sports, a strategy that positioned the rematch as an important cultural and collective social event. Like Woodstock. A lot of people went to Woodstock to hear their favorite bands play. But what made Woodstock a phenomenal, record-breaking cultural and social event was all of the people who went simply because they didn't want to miss being part of it. Our goal was to present the fight as something "other" than a sporting event, to present it as "an event" where perhaps anything could happen.

Our principal client at Showtime was a senior marketing vice president named Sheila. If you looked up "cougar" in the dictionary, Sheila's picture would be there; slim, tanned, blonde, botoxed and ultra-white teeth. Always dressed to the nines. A fresh glass of white wine was never entirely out of reach. Despite her appearance—or perhaps because of it—she was a consummate professional. She knew her business better than anyone and was usually the smartest person in the room. And most important of all, she trusted Spike and me.

As we began the creative development process, Sheila asked, "Is there any way that we can do this using existing footage of Mike and Evander? Without having to bring them back to shoot? We can give you tons of footage to use."

Naturally, we figured we probably were going to use and need footage from the first fight. That was to be expected. But we also figured that we were going to have to bring them in to shoot whatever new idea we developed.

"Is there a problem?"

"Trust me," Sheila said, "it would really make everyone's life a lot simpler if we didn't have to do that."

Sheila had already shown us a great deal of trust and given us free rein to explore unorthodox ideas, so we felt obligated to reciprocate. "Sure," we said, but there was hesitation in our voices.

"Okay," Sheila said, taking a long drag on a cigarette. "I'm going to tell you a story."

And here is the story that Sheila told us.

Back when we were making the ads for the first fight, we had a shoot scheduled with Mike and Evander. We would only get one shot at interrupting their training for the fight, so everything was packed into this one big shoot.

It's the day of the shoot and we're at the production studio setting up. A lot of big-shots from the network are there. Everybody is running around getting ready and Evander walks in. Early. He's just walking in by himself and he's carrying a gym bag. He's looking around at everything and doesn't seem to know what to do with himself. So, I said, "Evander, what's in the gym bag?"

Evander rests the gym bag down on the table and unzips it. He reaches in and pulls out his boxing trunks and smiles at me. "I brought my trunks" he says. "But they're all wrinkled, so I brought my travel iron. Is there someplace I can plug this in?"

I practically fell off my chair. "Evander, you brought an iron? What are you going to do with your iron? I'm sorry. Stupid question. My fault. Evander, you don't have to do that. We'll take care of that. You should just relax till we're ready.

So, we get Evander all settled in with the make-up people and we finished setting up for the shoot and we're waiting for Mike to arrive. And we're waiting.

Mike finally shows up. Three days later. Three fucking days later. Do you know what it costs to hold up a shoot for one day? (Sheila glances at Spike.) Sorry, of course you do. Who am I talking to?

Mike shows up and he's got ten people with him. And he announces that they're all hungry and need to eat first.

"And so," Sheila smiled wryly, "It would be really good if we didn't have to go through that all over again."

Spike and I kept giggling over that story for a solid half hour afterward, but we agreed to find a way to work with whatever footage already existed.

The direction that Spike gave the creative team was to "think beyond sports" and the team definitely delivered against that objective. When we presented our work and our creative recommendation to Sheila and her colleagues, I did the set-up. I reminded the client of the approved creative strategy and I summed up the promise. "Our goal is to make the viewer believe that absolutely ANYTHING could happen in that telecast. And whatever happened, everyone would be talking about it afterward, because they saw it live." I paused for dramatic effect. "So, we have to present an image and an idea to the viewer that is not at all what they were expecting to see."

Then we showed the client a 15-second montage of footage from the first fight. "Everyone knows what to expect. So, we can't do that." I said. "We need to show them something they won't expect."

I turned and looked at Spike.

"Johnny Mathis." Spike grinned. "We're gonna have Johnny Mathis."

Spike then took out the storyboards and presented the commercial idea to Sheila. We would film Johnny Mathis singing "Chances Are" (one of his biggest hits) and use CGI to place him in the ring with Holyfield and Tyson (using footage from the first fight) beating each other's brains in. Johnny's movements would acknowledge his presence in the ring and occasionally he would just barely avoid getting clobbered by a punch. We hired the technical geniuses at Industrial Light and Magic (the people who created all of the Star Wars CGI) to create all of the special effects. The lyrics to "Chances Are" carry the implied message that just about _anything_ could happen. And the juxtaposition of the song and the mayhem in the ring was just absurd enough to underscore that very real possibility.

This was not going to be a sports event. It was going to be an *event*.

We didn't have to bring in Mike or Evander. We brought in Johnny. Most people today are probably not that familiar with Johnny Mathis. He hasn't performed in over a generation; his heyday was in the 1960s.

But when I met him on the commercial soundstage on the day of the shoot, he was still—unmistakably—the smoothest man in show business. He was dressed impeccably in a bespoke Italian suit and looked as though he had already spent the morning with the hair, make-up and wardrobe people. Mathis is African American and Native American, with a coffee-brown complexion. But his face had the extra glow of a man who spends his time in sunshine and leisure. In fact, as we chatted, he boasted that he only accepted work engagements in places where he could squeeze in a round of golf. For the entire day of the shoot, a smile never left his face. This was a man who had discovered the secret of life.

In the 1950s and 1960s, it was quite common for African American recording artists to be exploited, cheated and financially screwed by the big record companies. After all, where were they going to go? What were they going to do? Johnny Mathis wasn't having any of that. In the early and mid-1960s, Mathis launched his own record label, his own music publishing company and his own live concert promotion company. As Billie Holiday would say, God bless the child that's got his own. And, boy oh boy, Johnny had amassed lots of his own.

Although his image was as a singer of smooth, romantic ballads, Mathis was actually a star athlete in high school and college as a high-jumper, hurdler and basketball star. In fact, in 1954, Johnny Mathis beat future NBA legend Bill Russell in a high-jump competition.

Because of licensing and publishing rights that would have taken months to unravel, we were unable to use the original recording of "Chances Are" in the commercial. No matter. Johnny laid down a fresh track for us and it was pitch perfect. When the long day of singing and filming and lining up shots was all done, Johnny Mathis looked as fresh and relaxed as he did when he walked in that morning. He shook hands, signed a few autographs (including an album cover for my aunt), and was on his way.

While we were in post-production, we were contacted by people from each of the two fighters. They heard that Spike shot a commercial to promote the fight, but that their fighter was never asked to come in for a shoot. What was going on? We explained that we "worked with footage from the first fight" but did not provide any additional details.

When the commercial went on air, all of the sports reporters thought we were crazy. They thought the commercial was mocking their beloved sport and that we had made a huge mistake. They thought that Showtime had made a huge mistake by hiring non-sports veterans.

I remember having a very brief conversation with legendary boxing writer Bert Sugar at the fight weigh-in. Bert was never without his trademark fedora or his unlit cigar. He looked at me and said, "You work for Spike Lee?"

I said, "Yes."

"I think your commercials are stupid." And he turned on his heels and walked away.

To her credit, Sheila recognized that the strategy was working. "Not only is everybody talking about the fight, they're talking about our ad. We're getting twice the exposure." She took a long drag on a cigarette and then put it out. "Either we're all a bunch of fucking geniuses, or I'm going to be out of a job."

Spike and I were invited to Las Vegas to watch the fight as guests of Showtime. On fight-night, Showtime hosted a pre-fight party at the MGM for all of the celebrities who had come to town to witness the rematch. The party was held in one of the MGM ballrooms because anything smaller would not have accommodated the huge crowd. When I arrived, the room was already packed, and a steady stream of people were continuing to pour in.

I had barely stepped into the room when a hostess carrying a tray of champagne flutes handed me a glass. A few seconds passed and another hostess was upon me with crabmeat-stuffed mushrooms and salmon and caviar on melba toast. In the span of those few seconds, I had begun to glance around the room and my brain had already recognized about a dozen fairly major celebrities. I was thinking to myself, "Wow, there's a lot of A-list people here", when I realized that my glance had barely covered 20% of the room. So, I began to move about the room and "mingle" with the crowd. There were probably 200 people there, and easily 80% of them were famous or ultra-famous. I started to do a little exercise in my head; how many famous faces have I seen tonight? How many famous names can I remember when I retell the story of this evening? Almost certainly, I had a goofy, inner-focused look on my face when Laurence Fishburne stepped alongside me.

"So, how do you like working with Coach?" Fishburne looked at me and probably wondered if I was having a stroke.

"Excuse me?" Not only did I look stupid, but now I sounded stupid too.

Fishburne gently tapped the lanyard around my neck, the one that granted me admission to the party and to the fight afterward. It had my name and "Spike/DDB" underneath. "You work for Spike, right?"

"Oh… Yeah. Sorry. I was thinking about something else." I tried discreetly to shake off the fog. "I work with Spike. We did the ad campaign for the fight."

"Yeah, I know." Fishburne laughed. "Coach here tonight?"

"He should be. Haven't seen him so far."

"Well, if you see him, tell him I said: 'Hey'." Laurence Fishburne nodded at me and walked away, obviously not expecting our conversation to get any better.

I know I spoke with four or five other people in the ballroom that night, but I don't think I could tell you who. Some were from the Showtime marketing team working for Sheila, some were just random people. But the entire time I was preoccupied with mentally cataloging each celebrity I saw.

And then, all on its own, my brain said "Stop." It was like a computer warning me that if I don't take a moment to click "save" I might lose my data. I put down my champagne glass, said "no thank you" to the chicken skewers, and turned and left the ballroom. I went straight back to my hotel room and grabbed a yellow legal pad from my suitcase. I sat down at my hotel room desk and wrote down the names of every celebrity I had seen at the party. When I was done, I had filled every line on two pages. Somewhere in my files, I still have those two pages of yellow legal pad paper.

When I went back down, I went straight to the MGM Grand Garden Arena and found my seat six rows back, ringside. I was close enough to get spattered, if blood or sweat went flying, which it usually did. I still had not caught up with Spike, who was somewhere in the arena, but I was sure he was fine. I got to my seat in time to watch the undercard fight and see Christy Martin win a TKO victory over Andrea DeShong in the 7th round. Christy was an impressive athlete and fighter who gave credibility and respectability to women's boxing.

As soon as the bell rang to begin the first round of the night's main event, Evander Holyfield came out swinging, eager to assert his dominance in the fight and to put Tyson on the defensive. Tyson countered Holyfield's aggression with strong punches of his own, but he was clearly uncomfortable fighting from a defensive posture. The second round dialed up the action even further, as the two fighters spent most of the round trading blows while standing less than two feet from each other. The close contact reached an inevitable climax when Holyfield head-butted Tyson, tearing open a cut over Mike's right eye. Whether the head-butt was accidental or intentional depends on who you ask. The referee ruled it accidental. Mike protested loudly.

Watching a fight on TV is great. The multiple cameras ensure that you get all the angles, and you never miss a detail. But it is no substitute for the adrenaline rush of being there and watching the fight from ringside. Everyone is shouting. You are shouting. Emotions are communal. You can hear leather make contact with flesh.

At the start of round three, Tyson came out of his corner not wearing his mouth guard. His cornerman shouted to the ref and called Mike back to put in his mouthpiece. The fight resumed. About halfway through the round, something happened. Everyone sitting at ringside reacted the same way. What just happened?

Evander Holyfield violently thrust himself away from Tyson and began jumping up and down in the ring. It didn't make sense. The only time that you ever see a fighter jump up and down in the ring is after the fight is over and he is declared the winner. But the fight wasn't over.

After another second or two, you could see blood streaming down from Evander's right ear. It was a lot of blood.

And then another strange thing happened. The people in the front row were close enough to see exactly what had happened in the ring. And now they were all talking over their shoulders to the people in the second and third rows, explaining it to them. And a few seconds later, the people in the third row were turning around and explaining it to the people in the fourth and fifth rows. And a few seconds later, someone was telling me, "In the clinch, Tyson bit Holyfield's ear. He bit off a fucking chunk of Holyfield's ear."

Referee Mills Lane was explaining the situation to the boxing commissioner while a doctor was examining Holyfield's ear. By now, microphones were picking up the conversation and putting it on the arena PA system. From his corner, Tyson insisted that the injury to Holyfield's ear was the result of a punch. Mills Lane looked at Tyson and yelled "Bullshit!" The referee was ready to disqualify Tyson, but Holyfield swore he was ready to continue the fight.

The two fighters resumed the remainder of round three, which had only thirty seconds left, and then proceeded to round four. It did not take very long into round four before the two fighters were in a clinch. And then it happened again. This time Mike Tyson bit into Holyfield's left ear and provoked the same response from Evander.

The referee reacted immediately. "That's it. This fight is over." Bedlam erupted in the ring as dozens of people stormed through the ropes. Holyfield's wound was being tended to by his cornermen, but Tyson was charging across the ring, arms swinging. MGM security formed a protective barrier around Holyfield, while Las Vegas Police attempted to restrain Tyson and his entourage.

Nothing more could possibly happen. Until it did. There was a sudden loud pop from somewhere in the audience. The sound triggered complete chaos in the packed arena, as people began to flee what might have been a gunshot from somewhere in the crowd. The Vegas PD moved in.

I moved out.

About a half hour later, from the safety of my hotel room, I learned from the TV news that the "pop!" that everyone heard was the opening of a champagne bottle by someone celebrating the bet they had just won with Holyfield's victory. The mayhem resulted in two or three people being taken to the hospital.

It was an insane night. And as our advertising had promised, absolutely anything could happen. And it did. Even though the fight lasted less than four full rounds, everyone left feeling they got their money's worth.

A few days passed, and everyone was back at the office by the time we heard from Sheila. The fight had generated a total of $180 million in revenue, eclipsing the draw of the first fight. It was the biggest pay-per-view event in history. Another decade would pass before the match between Oscar de la Hoya and Floyd Mayweather in 2007 would break our record.

CHAPTER TWENTY-ONE

A Favor for a Friend

After a year at Spike/DDB, I was restless to move on. The most important part of the experience, the most rewarding for me, was the launch. I was a key part of the collaboration that created something from nothing, that took an idea and transformed it into a real thing, a successful, money-making enterprise. In one year, we had grown to a $35 million agency with a solid roster of enviable national clients. And we had a team of professionals who were doing outstanding work.

But I felt like the archetypal western hero (if I may be allowed to call myself that) who knows when it is his time to get back on his horse and move on. I had other business elsewhere that was calling me. It was time to attempt to fulfill my dream of launching my own company.

I left Spike/DDB with little or no fanfare. I went into Spike's office at the end of the day and handed him my letter of resignation. He read it and looked at me somewhat forlornly. He knew the letter was coming.

"Mark, I can't think about this right now. I have to get to the Garden." And that was the last we ever spoke of it.

Because I had spent so much time planning and preparing, it did not take long to get my new company up and running. I had vendors and contractors already lined up. The designs for the apparel line were completed and already broken down into production patterns by the factory that would produce the clothing, all made in the U.S.A. Logos were developed and trademarks were pending. We were as ready as we could be. By mid-spring 1998, Heritage Apparel was operational and beginning to manufacture our Tuskegee Airmen leather aviator jackets and other clothing that celebrated African American history and heroes. By the fall, our first products were ready, and our ads were out in the market.

But that is a story for another day. Sorry, but this book is about my life on Madison Avenue. Heritage Apparel is a story, perhaps, for another book. For now, I'd like to explain what pulled me back into the advertising agency business right when I thought I had left for good.

In late January of 1999, I received a phone call from Jeff Burns, the Vice President of Advertising for Johnson Publications and Ebony Magazine. Jeff and I had gotten to know each other well professionally during my time at both UniWorld and Spike/DDB. Jeff met with my team and me frequently to present special advertising packages being offered by Ebony and we would put together deals on behalf of one of my clients. Jeff managed to track me down at home by reaching out to my mother. Both Jeff and my mother, Rita Robinson, served on the board of directors of the New York Urban League. So, Jeff asked Mom for my home number.

Jeff began the conversation with an obvious attempt to butter me up by heaping conspicuous praise about my success launching and managing Spike/DDB. "…And now I hear that you started your own company! I shouldn't be surprised by anything you do."

"Jeff, stop, please." I interrupted. "All this butter is not good for my heart. You're calling because you want something. Tell me what's up."

"I want to ask you a favor." He said, his tone becoming serious.

"I figured that's where we were headed."

"Do you know Caroline Jones?" He asked.

"Well, I know of her, of course. But we've never met." I paused to anticipate his next words. "But I'm not looking for a job, Jeff. I'm doing something else."

"I know. I know." He said. "But Caroline needs your help. She has cancer. It came back. Four years ago, she went through chemo treatments and the agency almost completely fell apart in her absence. She has to do treatments again and she needs you to come in and hold everything together."

I was silent for several moments. "That's really awful, Jeff. I'm sorry to hear that, but I already have a company to run. Even if I wanted to help, I can't walk away from Heritage Apparel."

"Mark, listen to me." There was a firmness in Jeff's voice. "How many Black folks are out there who can run an ad agency? Run it and not screw it up." He paused. "Come on, we both know the answer to that question. This lady is a legend. We can't let her agency come apart because she's sick. She deserves better than that."

"Jeff, I can't do two totally all-consuming things at the same time. I would just do both things badly."

Jeff Burns was right about at least one thing. Caroline Jones was indeed a legend, and she was someone I admired and always wanted to meet. I had worked with Byron Lewis. I had worked with Spike Lee. Working with Caroline would have been a great experience.

Ironically, the circumstances that drew Caroline Jones to a career in advertising were somewhat similar to my own. During her senior year at the University of Michigan, Caroline attended a campus recruiting seminar hosted by a woman executive from J. Walter Thompson, who encouraged her to apply. J. Walter Thompson was—and is—one of the landmark agencies of advertising. It has been an industry leader since its founding around the turn of the century. JWT is also known as the agency that hired advertising's first female copywriter, Helen Lansdowne Resor, in 1908. It was a fitting place for Caroline Jones to begin her career.

Caroline came to New York in the summer of 1963 and was offered a secretarial position just two days later. The turn-over rate among secretaries at Thompson was so high that the personnel director assured her that "on any given Monday" there would always be positions available.

At J. Walter Thompson, all women, regardless of age, education or experience, started as secretaries. Men, on the other hand, were hired directly into junior art director or copywriter positions in the creative department. Within weeks of being hired, Caroline applied to Thompson's Copywriter's Workshop, a training program offered annually to selected female employees. Ultimately, she was one of 18 secretaries, from an applicant pool of 200, that were admitted to the training program. And she was the only Black woman. She became the very first Black person—man or woman—to be trained as a copywriter at Thompson.

Despite her successful completion of the Copywriter's Workshop, Thompson assigned Caroline to the agency's Research Department, where she developed and refined the analytical and strategic skills that would later make her copywriting so exceptional. After a year in the Research Department, however, Jones saw several other secretaries promoted directly into copywriting and she threatened to quit. This finally got her the junior copywriter position she desired, which led to assignments on the Prince Matchabelli fragrance account and the Breck Shampoo account. Later, Caroline would ask her management why they never cast Black women in any of the Breck ads. She was told, "Because Black women don't have blonde hair."

Although her career advanced and she became a Creative Director, Caroline eventually became frustrated by the regressive and restrictive culture at Thompson and left in 1968 to become one of the founding members of Zebra Associates, a Black-owned multicultural agency. This was the beginning of Caroline's industry activism. She became a member of the National Association of Market Developers (NAMD), a networking and support group of Black advertising and marketing professionals, and one of the founding members of GAP, the Group for Advertising Progress. Caroline became a sought-after speaker at advertising industry conferences, often as the only female event speaker.

In 1975, Caroline was hired by BBDO, another of the mega agencies of Madison Avenue. She was recruited by BBDO president Jim Jordan, the same Jim Jordan who would return to his alma mater, Amherst College, just two years later, to seduce an impressionable college junior (me) to the advertising profession. Jordan offered Caroline a vice presidency, making her the first Black woman to become an executive officer of a major advertising agency. It was an historic moment, and the appointment generated a ton of media publicity, both for Caroline and for BBDO.

Unfortunately, good publicity was probably BBDO's principal motive for the hiring. BBDO got lots of kudos for their bold hire, but Caroline was responsible strictly for marketing work targeted to Black consumers. What's worse, many of her white co-workers did little to conceal their feeling that she was not entitled to be a Vice President. She felt unsupported, exploited and isolated.

Two years later, in 1977, she left BBDO to join Frank Mingo, a Senior Vice President and account management supervisor at McCann Erickson, to form the new Black-owned agency, Mingo-Jones-Guilemenot (later, just Mingo-Jones). The new agency had a unique and noteworthy "godfather" as it debuted on Madison Avenue. The Interpublic Group, the giant holding company that owned McCann, SSC&B and a portfolio of other major agencies, was providing seed money, credit support and multiple back-office resources to the minority start-up. This was an historic first in the advertising business and gave Mingo-Jones a better chance for success than any of its peers.

The new Black-owned agency announced its intention to take on mainstream clients and create advertising for the total market, but the opportunity—and the clients—never quite materialized. No client stepped forward to give them that chance. Instead, Mingo-Jones was yet another (quite successful) multicultural agency developing ads for minority consumers. Ironically, one of the ad campaigns that Caroline created while at Mingo-Jones was "We do chicken right" for Kentucky Fried Chicken. The campaign was so successful and resonant that the client forced their main agency, Young & Rubicam, to adopt the campaign for all of their advertising. The thought of shifting their main advertising business from Young & Rubicam to Mingo-Jones, however, never occurred to KFC.

Pretty much everyone assumed that with her name on the door, Caroline was a full equity partner in the hot new agency. The reality was that she was merely a salaried employee (and not an especially well-paid one, either), as Frank kept all of the profits for himself. After numerous prior clashes, in 1986, Caroline gave Frank Mingo an ultimatum, make her a "real partner" or she would leave. He refused and she left and launched Caroline Jones Advertising.

Within a year or two, Caroline's new agency was billing (the metric commonly used to measure agency size) roughly $12 million, which placed her in the middle of the pack for minority agencies at the time. Her clients included blue-chips like American Express, Prudential and Anheuser-Busch, as well as the Partnership for a Drug-Free America. Caroline Jones Advertising racked up more advertising and creative awards than Caroline had shelves to display them. The work was reliably top notch.

Unfortunately, when a company is built around the brilliance of a single leader, the company's destiny is inescapably tied to that leader's destiny. And in 1993, Caroline's destiny was a diagnosis of breast cancer. In 1993 and 1994, Caroline withdrew from the daily operations and affairs of the agency to undergo chemotherapy and do everything to battle her illness. In just a matter of months, the agency lost half of its clients. The clients that remained cut back their budgets. By the end of 1994, Caroline Jones Advertising filed for bankruptcy and was no more.

By the middle of 1995, Caroline was well enough to return to work and announced the launch of the new agency, Caroline Jones Inc. With new clients such as the U.S. Postal Service and McDonald's Tri-State Coop, the new agency was on its way to a successful rebirth. By 1998, the agency already had plans for bigger, nicer office space. Unfortunately, by 1998, Caroline's cancer had also returned. She realized that she needed to do everything she could to fight this illness, and she needed someone she could trust to look after her agency.

"Caroline asked me to call you." Jeff Burns pressed forward. "She wants to meet you and talk to you. You gotta at least do that."

"Jeff…"

"Mark, if you're going to turn her down, you're going to have to do it to her face."

I closed my eyes and braced myself for my own response. "Okay."

A week later, I was in Caroline's office sitting with the advertising legend. She wore a well-tailored pantsuit in the way that a very attractive woman seeks to emphasize her business side when making a first impression. Although Caroline welcomed me warmly, her demeanor was quite serious, businesslike. Rather than a casual, getting-to-know-you conversation, our talk quickly took on the air of a negotiation.

"I understand your reluctance to get involved with my agency at this time," she said, almost in a monotone. "You have started a new business of your own." She nodded her head and then did a bit of a mental gear-shift. "And by the way, congratulations. You must be very proud." She smiled, and a little bit of sunshine broke through. She made a subtle choice to let down her guard, to let me "see" her.

"Thank you."

"I'm sure you think I'm horribly selfish," she apologized. "All I care about is my business."

"I understand that completely," I interjected. "I think we are probably the same."

"I need you, Mark." Her voice softened measurably. "My agency died because I was sick. But I got it back. I fought. I fought, like I have my whole life. And I got it back." She started to choke up, just slightly. "I can't let that happen again."

"I understand, but I don't know if I can help you." I wasn't entirely prepared for just how difficult this conversation was going to be.

"If you agree to do this for me," she leaned forward. "I will come into the office every day. Every day." She shook her head. "No matter what." She took a deep breath. "I won't leave this all on you. I just know that sometimes I won't be able to focus. I won't be able to come to meetings. And our clients need to know that there is a leader in charge."

We talked for a while longer. We negotiated. I said I couldn't come into the office every day. And when I was there, I might have to work on Heritage Apparel. She accepted. I accepted. It wasn't what I intended to do when I entered her office, but it was what I had accepted when I left.

◆ ◆ ◆

For about a year and a half, I helped Caroline run the agency. More than any of the other aspects of the experience, I truly valued the time we spent getting to know each other. It was, however, a stressful time. I would come into the office probably three days a week. I would work a full day at the office, come home to have dinner with my wife, and then go to my home office to do Heritage Apparel business until 1:00 or 2:00 in the morning. Heritage Apparel's first year Christmas rush was an absolute nightmare. Every day there were hundreds of angry customers wanting to know when their order would arrive. I almost had a complete breakdown that year. The two jobs were ridiculously more than I could handle. I don't know what my family thought of me that year. I'm not sure what I thought of myself. Thank God I got through that somehow.

Over the course of my career, I have had the pleasure to work with a few wonderful clients; smart, sophisticated and good-hearted. And I have worked with a few truly awful clients; pig-headed, mean-spirited and thick as a brick. But none of my old clients were ever as bad as some of the clients at Caroline Jones Inc. They were beyond bad.

In the case of one client, the U.S. Postal Service, their awfulness was pretty comical. At least I can laugh about them now. When I first met the client in a highly formal orientation session, they had prepared a 150 slide presentation on the elaborate and arcane process for authorization and approval of all work projects and budget expenditures. At one point, the presenter paused and set aside her prepared remarks to be sure that I understood something very clearly. I doubt that I remember her words exactly as she delivered them, but this paraphrasing is nevertheless pretty accurate.

> *"The Postal Service process for project authorization requires multiple approval steps by each member of our marketing team. This process may take as little as ten days or as much as three weeks. It is important that you budget planning time accordingly, so that the approval process does not jeopardize the implementation and completion of a project by the appropriate deadline. You must build that into every timeline for your work.*
>
> *Furthermore, you must never initiate work on a project before you have received authorization to do so. The government will not pay for any work that you do that has not been authorized in advance. I'm sorry, let me say that*

again. The government will not pay for any work that you do that has not been authorized in advance.

There is a reason why it is so important that you understand this. From time to time you will receive a phone call from one of the members of the team. You might get that phone call directly from me. And we will tell you that we need something done. We will tell you to get started right away. We will tell you NOT to wait for authorization. That we need it now. We will probably yell at you to get it done. But if you do the work without waiting for proper authorization, the government will not pay you for it.

Do you understand me?"

And she was right. That's exactly what happened. Several times.

Whenever I am asked—which client was my absolute worst—my immediate answer is always the same. McDonald's. I won't even put them on my resume, that's how awful they were. While I was still at UniWorld, McDonald's tried recruiting me to work for them. They even flew me out to their corporate headquarters in Oakbrook for a day of interviews and classes at Hamburger University. (Yes, there really is a Hamburger University.)

Tucked away in a pleasant Chicago suburb that could have been the setting for "Father Knows Best", the McDonald's corporate campus could be mistaken for the campus of a small, midwestern college. On the inside, however, the environment more closely resembled the 1999 dark comedy "Office Space", with endless rows of identical anonymous cubicles. At a company with the brand identity of McDonald's, one would expect to find a high energy, even fun-filled workplace. It was the most mirthless office I had ever seen. And that's compared to the Postal Service!

The two clients who took me to lunch that day were like transplants from the 1960s Mad Men era. They both wore sharkskin suits (not kidding!), chain-smoked, and had steaks and scotch for lunch. By the end of the day, I was so creeped out by the experience that on the plane-ride home, I was already composing in my head the note I would send declining any offer I might receive.

And so, I was not the least bit happy to learn that the McDonald's Tri-State Coop was a major client of Caroline Jones Inc. I would be spending a lot of time with people who made my skin crawl. Burrell Advertising in Chicago had the McDonald's national account for African American advertising, but Caroline had the Tri-State (NY-NJ-CT) Coop, the local "owner-operators", as they were called. The Coop actually spent quite a bit of money on local advertising, mostly to feature their own specials and promotions. There was a marketing team from McDonald's Corporate that worked with the leadership from the Coop organization. Together, they interfaced with the agency.

Sound efficient? It wasn't. "Organization" was a word that could be applied to the Coop only if you closed both eyes and whistled loudly. The Coop was a collection of people who owned local McDonald's restaurants, each person a millionaire, each person the king of their own hill. You could tell them nothing. Each one knew better than you. After all, each one was a millionaire. You weren't.

Never was this chaos and lunacy more on display than at the quarterly Coop meetings at the Meadowlands Sheraton in New Jersey. One hundred or more owner-operators packed into the hotel ballroom while their advertising and PR agencies (including the Hispanic and mainstream agencies) attempted to present plans, programs and new advertising. Owners would yell at you from the audience while you were presenting. They would pepper you with questions, or simply heckle their disapproval. On more than one occasion, I have seen junior level agency presenters, men and women, flee the stage in tears.

But what bothered me most about this client was their attitude that they were God's gift to agencies. They would tell agencies—without the slightest bit of shame—"We will pay you next to nothing. And you will take it gladly. Because we're McDonald's and you're goddamn lucky to have us on your client roster. Our logo on your roster brings you business." And when they said they would pay "next to nothing", they meant it.

The Black owner-operators in the Coop, however, had demanded a codified fee formula for paying their Black ad agency, Caroline Jones

Inc. It wasn't a lot of money, but it was a fair formula. Unfortunately, no one was tracking enforcement, at least no one with a head for numbers. And McDonald's had almost never lived up to the terms. I did not uncover this until a year had passed and it was time to determine the fee for the coming year. When I met with the client and laid out all of the information, they responded matter-of-factly. "That's not what we have in the budget for next year. That's not what we're going to pay you."

I was taken aback. That certainly wasn't the response I was expecting. I couldn't think of anything more substantive to say, so I just said, "We have an agreement. We expect you to live up to the terms of the agreement."

The client pushed back quickly and firmly. "Well, we hired Caroline Jones Inc., and you're not Caroline Jones. So, we're not exactly getting what we paid for."

I stood up from the table. "I'm going to have to discuss this with Caroline. But I would hate to see this bring an end to our relationship."

They did not flinch. "You don't want to burn that bridge. You won't be able to cross it again."

The next day I sat with Caroline and told her about meeting with the client. I explained that we weren't making any profit on the account. We were just treading water. The account was monopolizing agency staff that could be better utilized on more lucrative assignments. I recommended that we resign the account.

"I need to know how you feel about burning that bridge."

Caroline took her time answering. "I don't believe in burning bridges", she said thoughtfully. She was quiet for nearly half a minute before completing her thought. "That's why I always carry dynamite." She smiled at me the same way that she smiled the first day I met her.

"Are you sure?"

"Fuck them", she said. "You can't move forward if you're looking over your shoulder."

So, we told McDonald's we could no longer be their agency.

A few months after that, I left Caroline to return to running Heritage Apparel, which needed my attention. I was also planning the next thing, a new company in partnership with my friend Marc Strachan.

Caroline's health improved. Until it didn't. I visited her several times at Memorial Sloan Kettering over the span of several weeks. She received daily deliveries of the New York Times, which she read and offered her opinion on this or that news story. But she asked me to bring her copies of Advertising Age, the industry's weekly trade publication, and we would sit and discuss the latest things happening on Madison Avenue. In early 2001, Caroline transferred to a hospice facility, and on June 28, 2001, cancer took Caroline home.

CHAPTER TWENTY-TWO

Forging an Alliance

It was now 2000. The new millennium. I had spent the past decade as a practitioner of multicultural marketing, at UniWorld, at Spike/DDB, at Caroline Jones Inc and at my own company, Heritage Apparel. I was, and I am, an adman. A Mad Man, through and through. But with each year and with each experience, I grew to love the multicultural side of the business more and more. And I grew to embrace the mainstream side of the business less and less.

By the year 2000, I had been working in advertising for 22 years. In many professions that is a full and complete career. In all that time, the advertising business had changed and transformed in dramatic and radical ways. The industry was no longer shaped by the individual styles and colorful personalities of iconic advertising agencies. Agencies that were once thought of as giants were now simply "operating units" within gargantuan holding companies whose "Holy Grail" was shareholder value. Interpublic, Omnicom, WPP, Publicis; these were the names that mattered now.

And by the year 2000, the advertising industry was climbing to what seemed to be an infinite crest of digital possibility with the birth and booming rise of the internet in the late 1990s. Everyone was predicting that advertising budgets would be 100% digital in just a few more years. Advertising agencies were in a panicked rush to hire young, tech-savvy recruits who inhabited and understood the digital new world, even if they had no aptitude for marketing or advertising. Even if they didn't have a creative bone in their bodies.

In the year 2000, there was one extremely important change to the advertising agency business that the new millennium did not bring, one aspect of ad agency life that seemed destined never to change. Madison Avenue was no more diverse then than it was when I began 22 years earlier. There were, in fact, more Black professionals in advertising. This much was true. In 2000, there were many more minority agencies than 22 years before. And that is where most of the Black people worked, not at the big, booming, mainstream agencies. The 1990 Census brought about a dramatic expansion in Hispanic marketing in the U.S. and a steady increase in hiring at advertising agencies. African Americans, however, were not benefitting from this trend.

And so, in 2000, I was quite content not to be working for a large, mainstream advertising agency. Of course, if I had felt differently, I probably would have had a pretty hard time finding a job.

For the time being, my job was running Heritage Apparel. The company had exceeded my wildest expectations. We had a product line of over a dozen different apparel items celebrating African American history and heroes. And every one of these items was made in the USA. We had resisted the temptation to save a few dollars by manufacturing overseas. We wanted our customers to see that "Made in the USA" label on our clothes. Our Tuskegee Airmen leather aviator jacket was a big hit, worn by two US presidents, the Chairman of the Joint Chiefs, and hanging in the Smithsonian. Our jacket. My jacket. And the Heritage Apparel website was selling our merchandise online at a time when Fortune 500 companies were just dipping their toes online. Black Enterprise magazine listed Heritage Apparel as one of the "Top 10 minority-owned companies doing e-commerce" in 1999.

Of course, nothing was ever that simple or that easy. The company had two problems, and each one was a pretty big problem. I had tried for two years to enlist investors to be part of the company. I faced the same challenges and the same closed doors as countless other Black entrepreneurs. Of all the start-up funds invested by venture capitalists (and the 90s were a time when everyone was investing in something), only slightly more than 1% was invested with Black entrepreneurs. I went to incredible lengths to solicit start-up capital. In the end, however, I was pretty much on my own, launching with just my own money, a fatal error that was both naïve and arrogant. That was problem number one. The second problem was that sales were good whenever we advertised, but when the advertising stopped, so did the sales. And the advertising was very expensive, even more, expensive when it's all your own money. It's pretty easy—and a bit glib—when you are just the account guy at the ad agency telling your client to increase the budget and do more advertising. It's another thing entirely when that "budget increase" is taken from your family's savings, from your children's college fund.

Sadly, I knew enough about new product launches to know that I was going to run out of money before Heritage Apparel was mature enough to survive on its own. The company was doing well, but not well enough. The company that I built, the company of which I was so proud, was going to die. The only question was whether it was going to wipe out all of my savings with it. This was a hard reality to face, but I knew that I wouldn't be much of a businessman if I couldn't shoulder that responsibility.

Back in 1997, shortly after the splashy and celebrated launch of Spike/DDB, another giant Chicago ad agency took note of that sudden success and decided to launch its own urban marketing agency spin-off. This time the Chicago agency was Leo Burnett, and the new spin-off was called Vigilante. The man chosen to take the reins of the new spin-off as its inaugural CEO was my good friend, Marc Stephenson Strachan. Vigilante was one of the first advertising agencies to position itself as "urban" marketing, an intersection of youth, multicultural and something edgier. Leo Burnett was the classic midwestern, white-bread, middle-American advertising oracle, creating messages of wholesome, happy American consumer life. Vigilante was everything that Leo Burnett was not. Vigilante was their way of saying, "We can do everything Spike/DDB does, but bolder, fresher and more daring."

Having two agencies both claiming this particular piece of real estate on Madison Avenue, was very healthy for the industry overall. It meant that this particular "brand" of marketing was not merely some eccentric one-off, but was an emerging trend, an undiscovered country that needed surveying. And I enjoyed knowing that my friend and colleague was right across town doing his best to deliver spirited professional competition. There was something very invigorating about it. It was, however, a shame, and a missed opportunity, that as the advertising industry aggressively recruited young people to help agencies tackle the digital and techno-logical transformation of marketing on the eve of the new millennium, they overlooked and neglected to leverage the insights and perspective of diverse young staffers to address marketing's cultural transformation.

For an industry that proudly boasts that it is the vanguard of popu-lar culture, that considers itself on the "cutting edge", Madison Avenue often seemed to be a day late and a dollar short. Madison Avenue never understood Black culture and did not believe that it ever had to. Black culture has always had a pervasive and intrusive influence on popular culture in America. But by the 1990s, Black culture—Black and Brown culture—was not simply influencing popular culture, it was supplant-ing it. And without a diverse workforce, advertising agencies lacked the tools and the perspective to represent this culture.

When I finally decided to leave Spike/DDB in early 1998, I was fed up with the paternalistic manipulations and constant micro-aggressions of DDB Chicago, the snarky emails, the commands to attend meetings in Chicago, the questions about what were we doing in New York. The "every day" of it got to be enough. I knew eventually that day would come when Marc would feel the same way about his Chicago overlords at Leo Burnett. Marc and I went to lunch at the outdoor café alongside St. Bartholomew's Church on Park Avenue shortly after I left Spike/DDB. He knew how I felt and why I left. He felt things would be different for him at Vigilante. Vigilante was still new and the relationship with Burnett was still new for him, although he already had war stories to share. Even so, he was optimistic.

"If you ever decide to leave Vigilante," I said to him, "the next thing should be something we do together. Create something together."

"That's a promise," he said as he extended his hand, and we shook on it.

Now it was 2000, and Marc Strachan and I were spending the day playing golf. Yes, golf. At the time, I was serving on the local board of directors of A Better Chance, a national non-profit organization that takes academically gifted minority high school students and provides them with the opportunity to transfer and attend some of the finest high schools in the country. This particular day was the annual fundraising golf tournament for A Better Chance, and I invited Marc to join me. I played golf once a year for our fundraiser. Marc was a serious player who never missed a chance to be on the links. In a scramble tournament, we were a perfect match.

As we played, Marc let me know that he was leaving Vigilante. Twice in the past year, he had won a piece of new business and he was ordered by Leo Burnett to resign the business because it conflicted with one of their accounts. At the same time, Chicago was hammering him for revenue growth.

I shared with Marc the grim outlook for Heritage Apparel and the emotional toll it was taking on me.

"It's time for us to do something together," he said. "The two of us together would kick some serious ass."

That day on the Ridgefield golf course, we did not discuss or develop any detailed plans. We did not attempt to nail down any specifics. But we came to a mutual decision, and we made a deal that was as firm as any legal contract. For the two of us, the next move would be a business together.

Both Marc and I started our careers in advertising courtesy of the 4A's MAIP Program. I had a four-year head start on Marc. That program made it possible for us to be in this business. The value and importance of that program cannot be overstated. And now we were two entrepreneurs who had accumulated our fair share of successes over the years.

It did not occur to either of us at the time, but looking back on it now, I am struck by the irony of two Black men closing a major business deal on the golf course. The golf course. I don't know if that meant we had "arrived", or if it meant we had been completely assimilated. Frankly, I hope it meant neither.

Marc and I spent the next four or five months meeting two or three times a week, each session lasting several hours, brainstorming and researching ideas for what our new business might be. Much of that time we spent at the giant study tables in the New York Public Library on Fifth Avenue and 42nd Street, except when we were tossed out for talking too much, which was often. We spent time at the research library of the 4A's, enlisting their help with our investigations. And we spent time meeting with and talking to people, all kinds of people, but most especially to prospective clients. If we were going to build a business, we needed solid reassurance that clients would be interested and would want to work with us.

The first decision we made was that we were going to continue to work in multicultural marketing. That was where our hearts were, and where we felt we could make a strong offering. I had worked with Byron Lewis, Spike Lee and Caroline Jones. Marc worked with Frank Mingo. We learned from the best.

We thought about whether we should open our own multicultural agency. We thought about it long and hard. It was the obvious next step. The fact that it was obvious felt wrong. What's more, we did not feel as though we were bringing anything new to the game. Even if we thought that we were smarter, better, it would still be just another ethnic agency. So what.

We kept talking, for hours and days and weeks. We talked about the history of multicultural advertising agencies. We talked about how the big mainstream agencies ignored the minority agencies for the longest time, as if they weren't even there. And then, when data from the 1990 Census revealed the size and potency of the ethnic consumer market, a flood of brands began recognizing the need to speak to this audience. More and more clients began allocating budgets for multicultural marketing. Mainstream agencies immediately saw this as a zero-sum game and stepped in to claw back their money. They told their clients they could do multicultural marketing just as well as the minority agencies.

It did not take very long, however, for most clients to see that they could not. Mainstream agencies never considered the possibility that there is actually a skill set and a science (as well as an art) to good, effective multicultural marketing. The thought simply never occurred to them.

Mainstream agencies shifted to "Plan B." If you can't beat the minority agencies, just acquire them. After all, buying Black people has always been an American tradition. All of the giant agency holding companies began buying up the important players in multicultural marketing. Whatever money clients chose to spend chasing ethnic consumers would find its way into the big agency pockets at the end of the day.

And then the magic lightbulb appeared over our two little heads. We figured it out. We knew what we were going to do. We were not going to open another multicultural agency. We were going to launch the industry's first multicultural marketing holding company.

Go big or go home.

We would create the world's first ethnic version of Omnicom, Interpublic or WPP. We did not yet know how. That was going to take more brainstorming. But now we knew the target we were aiming for. And as we brainstormed, we recognized three important truths that guided us in creating our business model.

1. We absolutely did not have the capital necessary to begin buying companies. Furthermore, it was likely to take months, if not years, of courtship before we could successfully conclude those kinds of acquisition deals. So, we weren't going to "buy" anybody. We would find another way. The way that we devised was to form a chain of interlocking covenants, contracts between all of the agencies in our network, that would bind them to each other and to us, more like a giant, multi-company merger. Believe it or not, the concept worked extremely well.

2. Minority agencies were typically launched by entrepreneurs with either a client-service or creative background. The back-office operations (finance, traffic, legal) were almost always thin, an Achilles heel vulnerability. We would provide a strong, centralized back-office operation that all of the agencies in our network could rely upon.

3. Minority agencies have two ways of chasing new clients and new business; either completely on their own (with very limited business development resources), or as a "tag-along" junior partner with a large mainstream agency. This latter approach was fairly commonplace, because mainstream agencies often needed to demonstrate to the prospective client that they had multicultural capabilities, or a minority-owned set-aside partner. Of course, when the business was won, the minority agency often got stiffed. We would provide a new business development "gang approach", where we were constantly mining and cross-leveraging client relationships within the network, while also pitching business as a team.

Of course, we had pages and pages of notes, strategies, diagrams and supporting data that were the building blocks of our concept, but these three points were the foundation. We knew how we were going to build our network.

Coming up with a name for our new company took us all of about ten minutes; the S/R Alliance. There was no argument over which initial should go first. We simply said them out loud and S/R Alliance sounded better than R/S Alliance. The "S" slipped onto "Alliance" and sounded funny. That's all it took.

Although it was our least favorite element of our business model, we knew that we needed to establish a strategic partnership with a large, mainstream agency. They would provide the critical back-office resources that our network would rely upon, as well as start-up capital, momentum and legitimacy. In return, we would provide comprehensive multicultural marketing resources, capabilities and credentials that would otherwise have cost them many millions of dollars. It would be a relationship where all sides could benefit. It would also be a relationship where each side would selfishly seek to exploit the other. It would be a law-of-the-jungle relationship, so we knew we had better walk into it with our eyes wide open.

Marc and I both had contacts at several major agencies, and we began meeting with them to explore the idea of a strategic partnership. In most cases, there was a lack of interest or a failure to understand our business concept. We would hear, "It's great to see you. Sounds like you are doing something really interesting." But it was clear to us they did not find it interesting at all. Multicultural was another world to them, and they had gotten by just fine so far without ever bothering to explore that world.

But then, one of our contacts at Omnicom referred us to this guy at BBDO New York. "This guy" was John Osborn, an EVP at BBDO and the Director of Integrated Marketing for the agency. Exploring new worlds was actually part of his official mission. Even so, we probably would not have gotten our first meeting with John if not for the referral from our Omnicom contact. It always pays to build and nurture your relationships in the business. If your network is anemic, so is your career.

When we met with John in his office, he was genuinely curious what we were all about. He had done his homework beforehand and knew something about our backgrounds, but he had been told we would be bringing a proposal for his consideration, and he seemed eager, like a little boy on Christmas morning, excited to unwrap his present. I have known John Osborn now for 20 years and he has never lost that boyish enthusiasm. It is central to what makes him a great adman. As Marc and I began laying out the elements of our business concept, John was running two steps ahead of us. We had not yet gotten to the part about a big agency strategic partner, but John was already interrupting us.

"Guys, guys. We should partner with you. You should let BBDO be your partner." John leaned across his desk with his arms extended. "I can think of a hundred ways this would be great."

That's how quick John was (and is). He sees possibilities and uses sheer force of will and a shot of adrenaline to make things happen. And that was probably the last time we called him "John."

"Call me Ozzy," he insisted. "My friends call me Ozzy."

By the time we had our second meeting with Ozzy, he had already lined up an official approval from Bill Katz, president of BBDO NY, and had probably also begun a half dozen other steps to advance the partnership deal. And within just a few short months, our partnership was being announced to the world in a full-scale PR blitz.

FOR IMMEDIATE RELEASE

BBDO NEW YORK AND THE S/R COMMUNICATIONS ALLIANCE FORGE STRATEGIC PARTNERSHIP

Urban/multicultural holding company gives BBDO instant access to burgeoning communications area and enhances BBDO's strategic communications offerings

BBDO New York announced today that is has formed a strategic partnership with The S/R Communications Alliance, a unique holding company focused on the establishment and/or acquisition of urban/multicultural communications companies. Through its companies, The S/R Communications Alliance provides a full-range of urban and multicultural marketing services including: strategic planning, advertising and creative development, consumer insights and market research, promotional services, media buying and planning, and more.

Under terms of the agreement, BBDO New York will gain instant access to the resources available through The S/R Communications Alliance.

There were six companies in the Alliance network when we launched in the first quarter of 2001, and by the middle of that first year, there were ten companies. Ten companies. The Alliance had agencies covering the African American, Hispanic, Asian and LGBT consumer markets. We had a media buying agency, operating units in both quantitative and qualitative research, a field marketing unit and a guerilla marketing street team. We covered every aspect of multicultural and urban marketing. Within our first 16 months, we had grown to be a $250 million network.

Nothing like the Alliance had ever existed before, nor has ever existed since. Over the course of my career, there are many things for which I am very proud, but in 2001, I wrote my own chapter in the history of Madison Avenue. And that will always be true.

At the end of the year, Marc Strachan and I were recognized by New Ventures Magazine with the Entrepreneur of the Year Award. I have been an entrepreneur since I launched my lawnmowing service when I was ten years old. This award meant everything to me.

2001 also brought September 11, and the tragic and calamitous events now known simply as "9/11." I was walking across the Today Show plaza in Rockefeller Center that morning, on my way to the office, when news of the first plane-strike was announced and most of the media still thought it was an accident caused by a small private plane. Looking back, my memories of that morning, of that day, are like my memories of the day that President Kennedy was shot. Those memories will never fade. The terror attacks were a blow to our country in many different ways, including to the American economy. 2001 was also the year that the dotcom bubble burst. Within weeks or months, thousands of internet-based companies were out of business and hundreds of thousands of investors lost fortunes. The "irrational exuberance" of the new millennium came to a sudden screeching halt, as though someone dragged the needle straight across the turntable.

The Alliance survived, but this took the wind completely out of our forward momentum. Multicultural marketing budgets—as always— were the first to be cut. Belt tightening hit our part of the business first and longest.

CHAPTER TWENTY-THREE

We told you so

In a previous chapter, I mentioned that McDonald's was my least favorite client of all time. Now I can mention which client was my most favorite. My best client ever was HBO.

HBO was a BBDO client. Marc and I leaned on BBDO, asking when they were going to introduce us to one of their big clients. As it turned out, the lead account person on HBO had been quite friendly and welcoming to us during the first days of the BBDO/Alliance partnership. She now offered to make introductions to her clients. Our first meeting at HBO was with the BBDO account team, our chaperones. When we met the HBO clients, they already had an assignment in mind and were eager to see what the Alliance could do for them. HBO was planning to debut a major new series. It would air on Sunday nights after The Sopranos, the most valuable piece of real estate on the network. The storyline and characters of the show would have particular appeal to a young, urban audience. The expert resources of the Alliance could not have come along at a better time for HBO.

Although we would have been very happy to take on the entire assignment, it was too big and too "plum" to give all of it to us. That would have caused serious tension with the BBDO account team. And after all, they brought us to their client. Keeping the peace was just smart business. So, the client split the project in half; all of the above-the-line paid advertising work would be handled by BBDO. All of the below-the-line non-traditional marketing work would be handled by the Alliance. And that was going to be quite a lot.

We were about to launch "The Wire."

In the briefing meeting, the client gave us the first two episodes of the show, along with some behind-the-scenes materials. They told us the airdate and how they wanted the audience excitement to build toward that airdate. They did not waste time with a lot of details. Their direction was simple and clear.

"You have two objectives," the client explained. "Number one; draw as many eyeballs to the show as possible. Number two; we want you to make our competitors look at what we did and say, 'How the fuck did they do that?' We want you to do all the crazy shit they would never think of doing."

Marc and I shot each other a quick glance. This is why people say they love working for HBO.

It would be impossible to list or describe all of the things we did to create attention and interest for the new show, unless I devoted an entire chapter to it. But we did do some 'crazy shit.' We were the first to use a special spray paint made from chalk, so we could spray paint stenciled logo images onto sidewalks everywhere without getting into trouble with the police for vandalism. We let loose giant inflatable balls with The Wire logo into the stands (and onto the field) at televised baseball games. We got hip hop artists to wear Wire apparel in performances. My favorite, however, was our army of "Pixmen", guys with portable video monitors strapped to them, who would show up outside of nightclubs, where people were waiting in line to get in. The Pixmen would screen trailers of The Wire for people to watch.

We developed a campaign to promote Sex and the City to the LGTBQ market and a campaign for The Rolling Stones' first-ever concert at Madison Square Garden, which aired live on HBO.

The Wire was never the general audience ratings smash that The Sopranos was, for obvious reasons. The setting, subject matter, and cast—by design—all appealed to a very specific segment of the TV audience. Within that audience, the show was a ratings blockbuster, which drew a substantial number of new viewers, and new subscribers, to the network. HBO knew exactly what it was doing with this bold new program.

Critical reception for The Wire was over the moon. More than a handful of the medium's most respected critics have named The Wire as the single best show in the history of television. We were just lucky enough to play a small part in the show's introductory fanfare.

In 2002, a new competitor to the Alliance emerged. Don Coleman Advertising was a Detroit-based minority agency owned and led by former pro football player, Don Coleman. The agency, which had been around since 1988, managed to be fairly successful financially without ever really distinguishing itself in terms of the quality of its creative work.

In 1999, Don Coleman Advertising was acquired by True North Communications, one of the 2nd tier mainstream holding companies. All of the holding companies were buying up minority agencies. True North purchased 49% of the minority agency. This was a familiar transaction. DDB owned 49% of Spike/DDB. Y&R owned 49% of UniWorld. Publicis owned 49% of Burrell. And so on, and so on. Whenever a mainstream agency or holding company purchased a minority agency, they always took 49%. That way, on paper at least, everyone could claim the agency was still "minority-owned" and keep a straight face. The reality, however, was that the percentage was irrelevant. The mainstream company held a vice-like grip over the finances and operations of the minority agency. The mainstream company had the final say on every important agency decision.

As I said, however, True North was just a 2nd tier holding company, and in 2001, True North was acquired by Interpublic. Everything that once belonged to True North was now assimilated into Interpublic, including Don Coleman. In 2002, with capital funds probably supported by Interpublic, Don Coleman acquired Montemayor y Asociados and Asian-American agency Innovasia Communications, to become GlobalHue. Don Coleman and Interpublic announced GlobalHue's 3-piece network to the world as the advertising industry's first multicultural marketing holding company.

This pissed us off tremendously, but pissed off BBDO even more. Of course, the media came straight to us for comment, and we did our best to set the record straight, as did BBDO. But in our business, the one who lies loudest and most shamelessly usually wins. Today, most people couldn't tell you who was first. Most people don't care. I care.

◆ ◆ ◆

Later that year, Daimler Chrysler issued an RFP for its multicultural advertising account. Chrysler was determined to make an aggressive attempt to capture as much of the minority car-buyer market as it could. The advertising budget for the account was going to be huge. The Alliance intended to make a play for the account. We were exactly the kind of minority-owned marketing organization that Chrysler was looking for. We were tremendously excited about the potential opportunity and went to our BBDO partners to seek some operational support for the pitch effort.

Instead, we were invited to a big meeting convened by Andrew Robertson, the new President/CEO of BBDO North America. In the large, formal conference room were Andrew, Ozzy, Doug Alligood (BBDO's SVP of Horizontal Markets), and two others, Peter Arnell and Steve Stoute. The gist of the meeting was that BBDO was asking the Alliance to "stand down" and not pitch the Chrysler account. They acknowledged that they could not "order" us to do so, but they made it clear that they would be backing another team on the pitch.

The "other team" was Peter Arnell and Steve Stoute. Peter (who is white) was a graphic designer and self-proclaimed world-class brand and marketing guru. Steve (who is Black) was a music executive that had been with various labels over the prior decade, and was probably best known for being assaulted with a champagne bottle by P. Diddy. Together, the two men were forming a new agency for the sole purpose of pitching Chrysler's multicultural account. If the prospective account was big enough, creating a new agency just to serve that account was often a slick strategic move. Omnicom (BBDO's parent company) was going to back the enterprise. Peter Arnell asserted that he had a close personal relationship with Chrysler's Senior Vice President of

Marketing, and on the basis of that relationship, Peter guaranteed they would win the business. For any white, male advertising agency executive, this proposition seemed perfectly normal and reasonable. Just a bunch of white guys giving business to their friends. Just another day on Madison Avenue.

Steve said nothing, spending most of the meeting texting on his Blackberry and hardly ever looking up.

"Uh, . . . hang on a second." After a very long silence, it seemed like the right moment for me to say something. "Chrysler has engaged Reverend Al Sharpton to be part of their agency review process. There is absolutely no way that he is going to allow Chrysler to hire an agency that isn't minority-owned."

"He will get overruled," Peter rebutted.

"This won't be some closed boardroom where they can shout down the reverend." Marc Strachan shook his head. "He'll make this a very public thing. And it will get ugly fast."

"Our agency will be minority-owned." Peter asserted.

"How, exactly?" Both Marc and I asked.

"The RFP submission will show that we are a minority agency."

"Yes, but how, exactly?" We insisted.

"We have that covered." Peter Arnell waved his hand, not interested in arguing any further.

Andrew Robertson placed both hands on the conference table and smiled at us. "Are we clear?"

Marc and I looked at Ozzy and at Doug Alligood. We said nothing.

Ozzy came by our office afterward. "Guys, this is how Andrew wants to play it." Ozzy knew we were unhappy, but there wasn't a damn thing that he—or we—could do about it.

"Oz," I said. "Let's put aside for a second the fact that you are totally screwing us. Totally fucking screwing us. But forget that. The Arnell-Stoute thing is never going to work. It's not minority-owned. I don't care what kind of accounting BS they pull. It's not going to fool anybody."

"Do you really think that this is the first time anybody has tried to run that game?" Marc asked. "Sharpton has seen that okie-doke a hundred times before."

"This is going to blow up and turn into a major embarrassment for you guys."

Ozzy was a bit shaken by the certainty of our gloom and doom. "Well, maybe it's a good thing that you guys aren't involved."

As the RFP and pitch process moved forward, the Arnell-Stoute team made it through the first round and was advancing to the next round. The next time we saw Ozzy, he was upbeat. "I don't know, guys. It looks like Arnell and Stoute are going to make it happen."

I gave Ozzy a quick dirty glance. "Please resist the urge to provide us with progress reports."

A few more months passed. The Arnell-Stoute team were now in the finals. But we were hearing back-channel rumors that the client had repeatedly asked for documentation that verified minority ownership, and each time they were given an excuse and a promise that the documents were forthcoming. With increasing pressure from Sharpton, the client finally told the Arnell-Stoute team that they would not be permitted to continue in the pitch unless they could present the documentation.

Amid a flurry of emotional protests that this was unfair, unreasonable and unprofessional, the entire enterprise finally collapsed in on itself. The Arnell-Stoute team was not only out, but it almost seemed as though they were never there in the first place. Poof! They were out, gone.

Ozzy came by to tell us what had happened, but we already knew. "Do me one favor, guys." Ozzy asked. "Just please don't say 'we told you so' to Andrew. Okay?"

The Chrysler account was awarded to GlobalHue. That outcome was preordained from the beginning. It was obvious to Marc and me that no one had made the slightest effort to check out their competition. If they had, they would have seen immediately that Don Coleman was a major financial supporter and an officer of the National Action Network, which was the Reverend Al Sharpton's organization. For this pitch, that was the only relationship that mattered.

And speaking of relationships, the Alliance relationship with BBDO did survive the Chrysler pitch debacle, but just barely. Things were never the same afterward. Omnicom was embarrassed. Andrew Robertson had backed the losing team and was pissed about it. But he wasn't pissed at Peter Arnell. That would be too logical. He was pissed at us and at Global Hue because it was minority agency folks who ruined his plans.

Other events began to signal the coming conclusion of the Alliance. John Curtis, the president and owner of the Alliance's African American agency, died suddenly of a heart attack and his agency never recovered. The two principals of our LGBTQ agency split up. And Omnicom decided it was in love with our Hispanic agency, so they bought it. By 2004, it seemed that Marc Strachan and I were constantly patching holes in a leaky boat. The Alliance became more of a consultancy rather than a full-service agency operation. The original members of the Alliance all remain deeply loyal to each other. Cooperation and collaboration between former Alliance members continues to be commonplace.

Don't let it be forgot,
That once there was a spot,
For one brief shining moment . . .

◆ ◆ ◆

The Chrysler account became a major boost to the fortunes of GlobalHue. The company continued to grow and succeed, winning Agency of the Year twice. But over the years, rumors of mismanagement persisted. Size and success can conceal internal problems and vulnerabilities, but only for so long. Eventually, things break down.

There were numerous stories of operational and financial problems that began surfacing as early as 2004, including lawsuits and accusations from GlobalHue's business partners that Coleman had withheld financial records in order to avoid profit-sharing. In 2009, an auditor for the Government of Bermuda accused GlobalHue of extremely questionable accounting and billing practices (including media commissions of up to 181%) on their tourism account. This began to trigger some alarms. Current and former employee reviews on ratings websites such as Glassdoor began to suggest chronic unhappiness internally. Finally, in 2016, a series of employee and vendor lawsuits were filed, including a class action lawsuit by 10 employees, all seeking money that was owed due to missed payroll.

Don Coleman convened an agency-wide town hall meeting of his employees to explain that this was all a big misunderstanding caused by an error by the bank. A few weeks later, the agency closed its doors permanently.

It is a shame that an agency that was once as big and as successful as GlobalHue came to such an ignominious demise. It hurt the employees who lost their jobs and were owed money. It undercut whatever little respect Madison Avenue has for minority agencies and multicultural marketing. It left the rest of us to pick up the pieces and repair the damage.

CHAPTER TWENTY-FOUR

Chinese Food

In 2004, I was in Mainland China on business. I was working at the time with L3 Advertising, the oldest Asian advertising agency in America, and one of the original agencies in the Alliance. My very dear friend and professional colleague, Joe Lam was—quite literally—the father of Asian American advertising and marketing. In 1984, along with his partners Lawrence Lee and Wing Lee, Joe founded L3 Advertising and created the very first Asian American advertising for a Fortune 500 client. Since then, their agency has racked up a long and prestigious list of pioneering firsts and marketing successes.

Why was I working for an Asian ad agency? Well, as someone who had already spent over a decade in multicultural marketing at UniWorld, at Spike/DDB and with my own firm S/R Communications, it seemed like an obvious and natural way to learn more and stretch my skills. Turn left and see what's there. And, as I mentioned, Joe and Lawrence were (and are) good friends. Going to work every day with them was a rare pleasure. The older I have gotten, the more important it has become to work with people I like. (And the less tolerant I have become of working with people I don't.)

L3 always had a very interesting portfolio of clients; Fortune 500 corporate clients like JP Morgan Chase and Met Life and Diageo, premium liquor clients like Remy Martin and Hennessy, and casino clients like Mohegan Sun and Caesars Entertainment. Never a routine day at the office. Back in 2004, the government of China was a client of the agency, so Joe Lam and I were in China for meetings with various government officials. We weren't hired to help promote tourism. Nor was our job to promote business investment. We were hired to help teach the Chinese government western marketing and advertising strategies.

Teach a man to fish . . .

Specifically, we were hired to work with the Chinese Postal Authority. Post offices in China are similar to post offices here in the U.S., but they are much, much more. Throughout China, the post office does much more than ship letters and packages. They are also retailers of high-end merchandise; everything from the latest smartphones to name-brand fashion eyewear and expensive wristwatches. These are not discount store items. And of course, you can do all of your banking transactions at the postal teller.

But that's not the really interesting or unusual part.

In China, the Postal Service does not merely mail out your phone bill, cable TV bill, electric bill, etc. They aren't simply the delivery system. They produce and process those bills too. So when you get your phone bill, it is generated by a system at the Postal Service. They know who you've been calling. They know your favorite TV shows. And they know what you've been ordering from Alibaba.

And they want to use that knowledge to market other products to you.

That was their focus; how to become direct marketing giants. And they wanted to sell direct mail advertising to multinational advertisers. And, by the way, the Postal Service is by far the largest owner of outdoor billboards in China. We were there to help them do that.

This was 2004, at the height of the SARS outbreak in China which, understandably, made me more than just a little bit hesitant about making the trip. But this was an important opportunity, and they really wanted us to go, so Joe and I hopped on a Cathay Pacific flight and about 20 hours later we were there. Upon landing at Hong Kong Airport (our first stop), it became very clear just how seriously the government was taking the public health crisis. Before being allowed to disembark the plane, each passenger was greeted by a masked nurse flanked by two masked policemen with automatic rifles. The nurse had a thermometer gun which she pointed at your forehead. As long as you didn't have a fever, you were permitted to exit the plane. Looking back on those events, after living through more than a year of the Covid pandemic 17 years later, I realize the seriousness of the health crisis and the intensity and pervasiveness of the fear that gripped the country, even as people attempted to carry on normal lives.

Our clients were terrific hosts. They put a great deal of time and effort into sharing information with us and we definitely learned as much from them as they did from us. Work days were packed with meetings, activities and photo ops. When the workday was done, we socialized well into the night (every night) with dinner and drinking and karaoke and international bonding. In Chinese culture, relationships matter more than any other business criteria, and so we were engaged in important—and intense—relationship building.

On our first night at dinner—a small gathering of just 20 government officials—I learned the important social custom of toasting. At the start of dinner, waiters and waitresses poured a small amount of red wine in everyone's glass. At first, I thought that was so you could taste the wine and decide if you liked it. It was explained to me, however, that it is customary when someone makes a toast that you drink up all the wine that's in your glass. (It's good luck.) Of course, that's hard to do when your glass is full, so they give you just enough for the toast. Then the waitresses quickly run around the table and refill each glass with another splash of wine. Everyone at the table was expected to make a toast, so we toasted more than 20 times. Needless to say, I left dinner pretty toasted.

One evening while in Guangzhou, (China's 3rd most prosperous city after Hong Kong and Shanghai) our hosts treated us to an elaborate banquet in a private dining room at a restaurant that was a personal favorite of the local Postmaster. The restaurant was beautiful, with decorations that were both traditional and very modern, much like the city itself. The restaurant contained several private dining rooms tucked away behind the main dining room. Our room was the largest of all, with capacity for 30—40 guests, not including the restaurant staff, and there seemed to be an endless parade of staff attending to our every need. The one wrinkle, however, the one detail that seemed to be out of sync with the elaborate planning and arrangements for this evening's dinner was that this was a Szechuan restaurant and Guangzhou is a Cantonese city. Why does that matter? Why is that a big deal? The 20 Chinese government officials at the banquet were almost all Cantonese and were wholly unaccustomed to spicy Szechuan cuisine.

Now, this may seem totally ridiculous to the average American, especially to any New Yorker. A typical Chinese restaurant in an American city offers a menu that includes several different Chinese cuisines; Cantonese, Hunan, Fujian, Shandong, Taiwanese, . . . and Szechuan. We are accustomed to eating many different flavors and styles of Chinese food and probably don't even realize that they are actually different cuisines. To most of us, it's just "Chinese food." But in China, if you live in a particular region, you are accustomed to that specific region's cuisine and might be very unfamiliar with any other. Chinese government officials might like to think of themselves as being very worldly and cosmopolitan, but the reality is probably very different. They can be quite provincial, sometimes to their own considerable embarrassment.

As with many things in Chinese culture, ritual is an important part of the meal. Each item of food was served to us separately, as if it were its own course. That way, each item of food can be "presented" to you on a fresh plate. I'm sure I went through at least 10 plates, combining some, taking away others. It was quite an elaborate process. I ate a few things that I had no idea what they were, but everything I ate tasted incredibly good, and I didn't have any trouble finishing anything. And there wasn't one single thing that I had ever eaten in a Chinese restaurant before. There was nothing that even remotely resembled "standard fare."

Strangely enough, the dinner reminded me of an experience I had when I was just 13 years old. My mom took me to dinner at a very fancy restaurant and told me that I could order whatever I wanted from the very fancy menu. So, I ordered Steak Tartare, having absolutely no idea what it was. Of course my mother knew that, but decided to see how I would handle the situation. When my plate arrived, I was mortified. I was being served chopped raw steak with a raw egg yoke atop. Not only had I never eaten anything like that, I had never heard of anyone else eating anything like that. It stared back at me, daring me to eat it.

Recognizing my apprehension, my mother smiled at my dish and said, "I think they did an excellent job preparing your dish. I think you're going to love that." She winked at the waiter and politely suppressed a laugh.

After only a moment's hesitation, I thanked the waiter and began to eat my Steak Tartare. And I finished it. I can't say that it is my favorite dish, or even one that I eat regularly, but I have ordered it a few more times over the years, always remembering that night. My mom was extremely proud of the way that I handled the moment, not causing a fuss or a problem and being open to trying something unfamiliar and exotic. My mother traveled all over the world in her job for Time Magazine. She was there when Nixon made his trip to China in 1972 and later that year when Nixon went to Moscow. She often encountered situations—and meals—that were unfamiliar and exotic. And she knew that the ability to handle yourself gracefully and adventurously was the mark of a truly cosmopolitan person. And now, in Guangzhou, the lesson I learned as a 13-year-old boy was paying off and made this meal even more enjoyable.

But not all of my Chinese hosts shared my enthusiasm and appreciation for the meal.

Here I was, sitting at this enormous banquet table (a giant round beast almost 20 feet in diameter, hand-carved from Hongmu, a deep red Chinese wood, with a 12 foot glass lazy Susan resting atop the center) and watching all of these government officials stare at their food and whisper to each other. After a minute or two, they started calling over the waitresses and saying "What is that? I don't think that I can eat that. It's too spicy. Can you bring me something else?" Since I don't speak Cantonese, one of my colleagues needed to explain the situation and translated the bits of conversation.

To the uneasy surprise of my colleagues, I burst out laughing and exclaimed, "Oh come on! Stop being little girls and eat your dinner. I won't drink with you later if you don't eat what I'm eating."

The concept of "face" is extremely important in Chinese culture. Almost every social interaction—either directly or indirectly—is dictated by the principles of "face."

American culture focuses on the importance and preeminence of the individual. This shapes our perceptions of heroes and icons, as well as our system of laws and individual rights. It is also fundamental to how we market to consumers in America. Chinese culture focuses on the value and importance of community, familial cohesion and collective identity. I cannot stress enough just how important and significant these cultural differences are. As a result, Chinese sense of identity is not about how you stand out as an individual, but where you stand relative to the rest of the community.

This is the essence of the concept of "Face."

Losing "face" (sensing disrespect) in public is often considered one of the most egregious offenses. Causing someone to lose "face" by embarrassing or disrespecting them will not only offend the individual, but will likely offend their friends, family and peers as well, since they do not think primarily of that person as an individual, but as a member of their 'group.' The idea of a proud (vain perhaps) official of the Chinese People's Government "losing face" to a westerner over their own cuisine was totally unthinkable. My challenge was more than just a little bit reckless. If I embarrassed these men, it could have completely killed our business project.

Hell, it could have landed us in a Chinese prison.

Fortunately, we had bonded with them socially over excessive drinking during the previous nights (where my hosts taunted me mercilessly for my inability to keep up and for my truly pathetic karaoke attempt to sing Sinatra's "New York, New York"). Fortunately, we had already made a genuine and substantial investment in our relationship-building with our hosts. We had overcome our outsider status and become "connected" to them in ways that were meaningful and durable.

So, in just the same way that I ate my Steak Tartare back in the summer of '69, these government officials ate their dinner without any further complaint and agency-client relations survived dinner.

CHAPTER TWENTY-FIVE

This job is killing me

In the mid-2000s, after the Alliance, I did quite a bit of consulting work, everyone from AOL to Caesars Entertainment to the Department of Homeland Security. Some of the consulting work was marketing, some of it was leadership and management training, and some of it was diversity and inclusion training. All of it was interesting and fun, and I accumulated a nice portfolio of personal clients.

In late 2006, completely out of the blue, I received a phone call from a recruiter who had an interesting new assignment to discuss. The position was COO, Chief Operating Officer, reporting to the President. The client was a very large healthcare advertising agency in urgent need of a turn-around. The agency was losing clients and laying off staff faster than they could figure out what was happening.

Pharmaceutical advertising and healthcare ad agencies had ascended high and fast over the previous decade. In 1997, the FDA issued new regulations permitting DTC (Direct-To-Consumer) advertising of prescription drugs via broadcast media (TV commercials!) and the industry exploded with new spending. It didn't really matter if an agency was any good, everyone was riding the new pharma wave to riches and rapid growth.

Ten years later, there were a lot of healthcare ad agencies, a lot of them big and fat. Category growth was slowing down, while agency competition was becoming more serious. Being in the right place at the right time was no longer going to be enough to keep these agencies growing. Business Darwinism was casting an ominous shadow over a lot of fat, mediocre agencies.

When the recruiter on the phone said that word, "turn-around", she immediately got my attention. I had spent a lot of my career in new product development, and a lot of time in company start-ups, but I had no experience with turn-around situations. This job—if I got it—would be a tremendous challenge and a wonderful learning opportunity, a growth opportunity for me.

I couldn't resist.

I got the job and I started work at CommonHealth the last week of January 2007. I stepped immediately into the crucible. In my first week on the job, I was ordered to lay-off 32 employees. The job only got harder from there.

Flash-forward to a Monday afternoon in the middle of October, 2007. I arranged to have lunch with my boss in her office so that we could have time to discuss some changes I was desperately hoping to make at work. Piggy-backing our meeting over lunch was probably our only opportunity for an undisturbed one-on-one conversation. She was the President, and I was the COO of the largest healthcare ad agency in the country. Our day was scheduled in tightly packed half-hour or fifteen-minute increments that are usually double or triple-booked.

We sat across the desk from each other while she ate her salad, and I took bites from a delicious, sloppy Philly cheese-steak sub. My boss cast a disapproving look at my sandwich and admonished me to make better food choices.

My daily commute was roughly two hours each way by car in rush hour traffic. There was no other way to get there. I would get to the office before 9AM and usually not leave until 9PM. Frequently, I would just work until midnight and then check into the hotel down the street. My job description, which was two pages long when I started, was now four pages. My wife and I barely saw each other, except on weekends. I withdrew from all of the organizations and activities that I belonged to, whether professional or personal. I hadn't been free to have lunch with a friend in over six months.

I handed my boss a memo I had written entitled "Burn-Out" that chronicled how, since joining the company in January, my job description steadily seemed to grow and expand and led to an impossible daily 'To Do' list. Leaving the office at 9PM was now routine. My work/life balance had absolutely no balance.

I concluded my memo by saying that I love my job, but it's killing me. It was essential that we agree to make some changes. In typical fashion and without hesitation she fired off several suggestions for immediate changes. Her tone was brusque and authoritative, but her content was pure compassion. "You know all you have to do is ask for help and I will move heaven and earth for you," she said. "I can't afford for you to be sick or unhappy or burnt out, so let's make some changes."

When we were done I was surprised at how receptive my boss had been to addressing the subject. But I was also skeptical. We were in the midst of writing plans for the coming year, and it was hardly the time to begin taking things easier. I knew I would have to resist my own impulses to simply hunker down and work harder.

I left the office early (5:30) that day to attend a pharmaceutical industry awards dinner at a nearby country club. I had not planned on attending, but a late-afternoon call from the CEO's office suggested that it was important that the agency's senior executives needed to be visible at the event. Even though I don't regularly wear a tie to work, I keep a tie in the office for just such last-minute obligations. So, I put on my jacket and tie, grabbed directions to the country club and headed to the event. When I arrived, I mingled with colleagues at the cocktail reception, but couldn't shake the feeling that I had left behind a pile of unfinished work on my desk. The truth is, no matter what time I leave the office, I leave behind a pile of unfinished work. By 7:30 everyone had been ushered into the ballroom for dinner. As soon as I sat down, something felt very wrong.

I had this intense pain in the center of my chest that burned all the way through to my back between my shoulder blades. It wasn't something that I felt become progressively worse. It was simply—BAM— there and in a very big way. I started flexing my shoulders, wondering if it was some powerful muscle cramp. I drank lots of water, thinking it might be heartburn. I drank my glass and grabbed the glass of the person next to me. Nothing made a dent in the pain. I ate my salad but could no longer engage in small talk. At no point did I even consider the possibility that I was having a heart attack. The thought simply never entered my mind.

The pain literally made it impossible to eat, talk or even simply sit there and tough it out. I told my colleagues that I was going to make an early exit and excused myself from the table. I climbed in my car and made the 90-minute drive home, occasionally unsure that I could maintain the concentration to do so. The drive seemed to take forever. By the time the car pulled into my garage I was physically spent. I told my wife that I really didn't feel well and just wanted to go straight to bed. But the bed provided no rest as I lay there unable to sleep, hoping in vain that the pain would begin to ease. Finally, around 4AM I staggered to the bathroom medicine cabinet and grabbed 2 or 3 Tums thinking to myself, "this has got to help."

It didn't.

Morning came and nothing had changed. In the mildest, just-getting-started kind of way, the pain was beginning to frighten me. I wondered what was wrong with me, but still never made that association that perhaps I was having a heart attack. I went on the internet and began Googling my symptoms. Was there an exercise I could do that would make me feel better? There were too many different suggestions and too much information to figure out what to do.

I picked up the phone and left a voicemail message for my assistant saying that I was going to stop by the doctor's office on the way into work. Of course, the doctor's office didn't open until 9:00, so I had to wait before I could call to say I was coming by. My wife left for work at 8:30, and asked me to let her know how things went at the doctor when I was done.

Finally, it was 9:00, and I called my doctor. The receptionist cheerfully advised me that they could see me at 2:30. I said, "Oh no, you don't understand. I need to come in right now." Apparently, there was just enough panic in my voice that the receptionist handed the phone to a nearby nurse who said, "Mr. Robinson, tell me exactly what you're feeling."

I described the pain, and before I could finish, the nurse interrupted, "I'm sorry, you can't come here. You're having chest pains. You need to call 911 and have them take you to the hospital."

"No," I protested. "I just want to come in and see the doctor."

"Mr. Robinson, *do* as you're told." She commanded, raising her voice slightly. "Hang up this phone, call 911 and go to the hospital. Do it now."

And so, I did, feeling a little sheepish about the whole thing. I told the 911 dispatch operator that I didn't think I needed an ambulance, but the nurse made me call. "Do you have chest pains, Mr. Robinson?" He asked, sounding a bit impatient with my rambling explanation. I said yes. "Then we're sending an ambulance."

I called Veteran's Park Elementary School, where my wife worked, and left a message with the main office. "Hi, it's Mark Robinson," I said. "Would you mind giving Laura a message? Just tell her instead of going to the doctor, I decided to call 911 and go to the hospital. Okay, thanks."

I filled the dog's water dish, turned on the answering machine and walked out the front door to wait for the ambulance. By the time I locked the door behind me, the ambulance was already pulling into the driveway.

I'm not sure how many fire and EMS personnel showed up. They were on me like a swarm of bees and in the blink of an eye, I was on a gurney in the back of the ambulance. Most people probably think the ambulance immediately whisks you away and races to the hospital. Not so. The ambulance is like a mini ER on wheels. They can actually do a great deal more good by taking a few minutes to diagnose the situation and rendering some immediate treatment. I was hooked up to an EKG and blood pressure monitor, sending data back to the hospital while the EMT spoke on the phone with an ER doctor.

There was a second paramedic in the back of the ambulance that I hadn't noticed until he began sticking me and inserting an IV line into the back of my hand. I let out a loud **OW** in protest, turned to the first EMT, and said, "He's obviously not very good at this."

Ignoring my remark, the first EMT instructed me to open my mouth while he sprayed nitroglycerin under my tongue. "If you are having a heart attack, Mr. Robinson, this will open up those blood vessels and help your heart out a little."

The pace of events continued to accelerate beyond my ability to keep up. I was now in the Danbury Hospital Emergency Department in a "curtain area." Two or perhaps three nurses were swapping out the

EKG electrodes and IV lines from the ambulance with a set of their own. Blood was drawn and temperature and blood pressure taken with the efficiency of a NASCAR pit crew. A tall, middle-aged doctor with a clipboard pulled back the curtain and came toward my gurney. Trailing behind him was a young woman doctor roughly half his age and half his height.

"Mr. Robinson, I'm Doctor Chilappa." I remember his name only because it was printed on the prescriptions I received for various medications upon my discharge. Over the next 24 hours I would speak to or be treated by at least 20 different medical professionals. I probably remember the names of three of them, and that's only because they were written down. All the rest are a blur of white coats and cold stethoscopes. Perhaps that's a function of my advancing age. I'd like to believe that it was simply the result of the whirlwind of events.

"Mr. Robinson," the doctor continued. "You were brought in by ambulance because you were experiencing chest pains. That means there is a possibility you were having a heart attack. The most reliable way for us to determine if what you experienced was actually a heart attack is to test your blood for the presence of a specific enzyme that is released when the heart muscle is damaged." Without skipping a beat (no pun intended), the doctor matter-of-factly dropped the other shoe. "We have completed this test and the enzyme was present in your blood, so you did indeed have a heart attack."

After that, events just seemed to stream by like faster cars passing me on the highway. My brain needed several hours to process and comprehend each new thing that was happening, but each new thing that was happening came and went within minutes. My mind couldn't catch up. I was taken to the Cardiac Cath Lab where they performed an angioplasty and inserted a stent into one of my arteries. I was convinced that I was going to die. But I didn't. I came through all of it just fine, well, fine for a guy who just had a heart attack. And I spent the next two days recovering in the hospital before being sent home.

My recuperation at home gave me a lot of time to watch TV, but the experience was less than satisfying. My work schedule for the past year had been so intense that I had pretty much given up television. That was sacrilege. Not only did I love watching TV, I considered it a fundamental requirement of my business. You simply can't be a good advertising executive if you don't love television.

But since I hadn't watched anything in the past year, I didn't know the storylines for any of the shows. I wasn't invested in anything. You can't jump into the middle of the season on 24 or Lost.

After being home for a day, Laura permitted me to have my laptop back, but only because I whined and complained constantly. At the office, my boss had ordered everyone not to copy me on any emails or memos and not to call me. She had already begun dividing up my work among the other executives and demanding that the next level down in management start solving more of their own problems and stop bringing their problems to senior management. All smart decisions—long overdue—but it made checking my email very unsatisfying.

I have always been kind of a hyperactive personality, always pushing toward some objective. I love being by myself, because that's when I am the busiest, never idle. If I am not in the middle of completing a task, I'm at the start of planning a new one. I don't do "rest" well, especially if it takes longer than fifteen minutes. I was going to have to learn a new lifestyle. I was going to have to learn a new life.

I would like to say that my near-death experience opened my eyes and immediately changed my life. I'd like to say that almost dying forced me to re-evaluate my priorities and re-think all this relentless emphasis on work and accomplishment. I would like to say that, but the truth is that I am occasionally a slow-witted idiot. For me, brain-washing requires the occasional 'lather-rinse-repeat' regimen before having the necessary effect.

So, for me, recuperation was a bit like a boxer that gets knocked flat onto the canvas and, within a second or two, gamely rises back to his feet and bounces impatiently in place until the referee completes his standing eight count and permits him to rejoin the fight. His corner is yelling to him, "Stay down. Stay down." But he's not listening. The other boxer is looking at him from across the ring, thinking, "Don't make me have to knock you down again. Because I will."

God knew this, of course, because God knows everything. And He knew just what to do.

Every two years, my alma mater, Amherst College, hosts a Black Alumni Weekend in the spring. I really loved my time at Amherst and genuinely enjoy my visits back to campus, especially when I see old friends. As a student, the idea of being connected to the other Black students was never something I thought about consciously very much. You simply hung out with your friends, and some of them were Black. As an alumnus, however, maintaining that connection was something that I (and others) thought about and it had become important to me. Every two years, I would come for BAW. I don't think I missed one since I graduated.

Sidney Davis was class of 1973. He graduated the year before I arrived, so we never knew each other as students. Instead, we met and came to know each other pretty well as fellow alums attending BAW. Sidney was, in fact, one of the principal organizers of the reunion weekends and worked tirelessly for months in planning and preparation.

Thursday morning, as I opened and read the trickle of emails that I was receiving at home, I opened an email from Amherst College. The Alumni Office letter informed me that Sidney Davis had a heart attack a few days ago (the same day as me) and was pronounced dead at the hospital. Efforts to revive him were unsuccessful. Even though Sidney was five years older than me, he was a bachelor. But Sidney had met the love of his life and they were going to be married that weekend. Now Sidney was gone.

I closed my laptop and began to weep like a baby for a very long time. Laura was at work, and I was alone in my bed, crying. My friend Sidney, the good, kind, gentle bear of a man, was gone and I would never see him again. The marriage that would mark the beginning of a whole new chapter in his life would now never occur. All the great things that he could have done will not be done.

Until that moment, I had not really measured the full distance between dying and not dying. Nor had I thought that much about what is lost in death. Because I didn't die.

God did not take the life of my friend just to teach me a lesson. But God did spare my life, so that I might learn a lesson from the death of my friend. And this time the message took hold like embracing a rose bush. I still had something that Sidney had lost forever, life. It was as though I had just acquired a precious new possession and needed to learn immediately the proper way to care for that possession.

From that point forward, I stopped thinking about when I was going to return to work. I stopped thinking about what was happening at work in my absence. Sooner or later, I would be back at work and all of the other details would take care of themselves when that time came. I would be back at work in the blink of an eye, so try not to blink.

Instead, I began making plans for a special Thanksgiving holiday with my family. It was mid-October and I had only a month to plan, but now this was all I was thinking about. Ten years before, I had taken my family to Tortola in the British Virgin Islands, the idyllic place where my grandfather was born. Sadly, in the ten years since, we had taken only one other family vacation. That was almost unforgiveable and entirely my fault. We were going back to Tortola for a very special family Thanksgiving. My son and daughter, Sean and Lily, were both away at college. The logistics of coordinating flights from three different locations, all down to the Caribbean, was not easy. But at that moment, it was the most important thing I had to do. It was the only thing I had to do.

The trip was a wonderful idea. It was exactly what I needed—what we all needed—to be together, far away from the demands of our normal lives. We all wanted to be able to have some time just to be close to one another. And we had a lot to be thankful for this Thanksgiving.

On Tortola, we rented a gorgeous private villa called "Toa Toa" To get to Toa Toa, you take a sharp turn off the shoreline road and climb about 600 feet up a steep, winding drive to where the view changes from scenic to simply breath-taking. We walked onto the massive pool deck and took in the view that stretched 180 degrees. From Virgin Gorda in the east to St. John in the west, the vista was dotted with green islands and white sails. The seascape was not only lovely, but active and always changing as sun and sailboats slowly moved across the horizon.

On Thanksgiving Day, Lisa Mead arrived to take over the kitchen and begin preparing Thanksgiving dinner. Lisa was an executive chef for a luxury private yacht that sailed the Virgin Islands. Rather than take the holiday off, Lisa agreed to prepare a special dinner for our family. Lisa, who spoke with a thick Australian accent, was raised in Malaysia and Singapore. Although she would have been happy to prepare a traditional Thanksgiving meal, we decided to take her suggestion for an exotic Indonesian feast. Dinner was beyond spectacular.

The most spectacular thing about Thanksgiving dinner, however, was not the food. It was being with my family, being with Laura and Sean and Lily, in a place of beauty and serenity. Thanksgiving is traditionally a time to acknowledge all of one's blessings. That year, I learned to be thankful for each day, not just the good days, but every day, for each thing in my life, both great and small, and for the people that God had placed around me.

I cannot place all the blame for my heart attack on work. I am overweight. (Hell, I could lose 30 pounds and *still* be overweight.) I hate to exercise, and I used to eat all the wrong foods with reckless abandon. I was the poster child for at-risk behavior. But the job was a major contributing factor. The job was definitely the last brick in the load.

Work was like a cancer in my life, and yet I went back to work. I could have—*and should have*—just given notice from my hospital bed and never returned to work. But that's not what I did. I went back into the burning building.

When I went back to work, my boss had trimmed those two extra pages off my job description, so that I was back to just a normal full-time job. Those extra duties were either redirected to other senior executives, or pushed down to the next level of management. That seemed like a good idea in theory (like a great idea, actually), but in practice everyone felt they had a *better* idea. All the people who routinely came to me for approvals, decisions, explanations, resolutions, mentoring, confession and therapy all continued to do so. If a certain way of doing things was working for people in the past, they weren't going to give that up quite so easily.

Before long—by January 1—things were pretty much back to the way they had been before.

It wasn't until the summer of 2008, that I realized and fully accepted that I was someplace I really should not be. A job should not make you feel sick. A job should not fill you with regret. A job should not take more than it gives. I had to go—or die. So, finally, I left.

As far as that whole notion of life being "too short," I remember having to redefine my sense of time when I reached my 50th birthday. As you progress through early adulthood, you casually perceive age 50 as the mid-point of one's life. But on my 50th birthday, I came to the startling recognition that 50 was not the mid-point of my life. After all, how many people live to be 100? I realized that the true mid-point of my life had almost certainly come and gone unnoticed several years before. What's worse, I could not really be sure where I stood on my life's continuum. I had no way of knowing when that mid-point had actually passed.

And so, when I had my heart attack, instead of resetting the clocks, I threw them all away. The heart attack completely destroyed any expectation I might have had about how many years I may have left. All the mind games about my mid-point or my end-point became stupid and irrelevant. There is no such thing as how many years do I have left. I have today, only today. And every day that I finish is a good day.

I have days where bad things happen, but I don't have "bad days" anymore. Because when bad things happen, that's life. And life is a good thing.

CHAPTER TWENTY-SIX

Carol H. Williams

In the fall of 2015, while busy doing a handful of other things, yet nothing special in particular, I received a LinkedIn connection request from Carol Wyatt, the HR Director for Carol H. Williams Advertising, out in Oakland, California. I accepted the request and sent Carol a message, "Hi Carol, what's going on, out at Carol H. Williams?"

Carol responded by saying that they were looking for a Senior Vice President to run an important piece of business in New York. Did I know anyone I could recommend?

"Well . . .," I said, "Tell me more about it." I wasn't really looking for a job, but I was curious nevertheless. Carol Williams was an important figure in the history of Black professionals in advertising. She was an iconic figure, and the chance to work with someone like her was worth considering. In many respects, it reminded me of the circumstances that brought me together with Caroline Jones. I wasn't looking, but fate seemed to bring us together. Throughout my career, fate was often a lot smarter than I was, and when a door suddenly opened, it paid to step through it.

A few weeks later, I met Carol Williams at the Marriott Marquis in Times Square, her favorite hotel when visiting New York, although, ironically, she is not a fan of Times Square. We had lunch and hit it off right away. We were both products of an earlier time in the advertising business. We both had learned our craft at large, old-school, mainstream agencies. We both had found a way to convert mainstream skills into multicultural strengths. We understood and respected those traditions, yet we both understood the importance of being fresh and current and connected to a younger culture.

The other thing that impressed me about Carol, something I found quite rare in celebrities and people with iconic public images, was her very grounded sense of self-awareness. I have met too many people who believe this idealized and artificial image of themselves. Not Carol. She is quite comfortable seeing and acknowledging her flaws and imperfections alongside her strengths. I found that very refreshing.

Carol also has a wicked sense of humor. Most of the jokes or comic asides that she has shared with me over the past few years, I cannot print in this book. She told me how she recently ran into an old friend at a women's organization meeting where they are both members. The friend gushed over seeing her. "Carol, you look amazing. What is your secret? How do you stay so young looking?"

Carol smiled a Mona Lisa smile and tilted her head toward her friend. "I get laid a lot."

Carol was a product of the Midwest advertising agency experience, which I believe was a very different world from my own in New York. Most of the giant household brands that tapped into the wholesome values and ethos of America's heartland chose the middle-American, middle-class messaging created by Chicago-based agencies.

Carol was a native of Chicago, but her family's roots were in the South. And those roots were evident in both her personality and in the cultural perspective that influenced her creative work. Her family had come north to Chicago as part of the Great Migration and the pursuit of opportunity and a better, more ambitious life for their children. Carol attended Northwestern University and was a biology major, hoping to become a doctor someday. Although her career took a sharp turn in a very different direction, her love of medicine has never been far away. Later in life, Carol married a prominent orthopedic surgeon, and she now sits as a member of the board of trustees of Meharry Medical College.

While Carol was a student at Northwestern, however, she was recruited by Bill Sharp to participate in the Basic Advertising Course (BAC), a career training program sponsored by the 4A's. The program was created and run by Bill Sharp and Bob Ross, who was chairman of the Chicago chapter of the 4A's. Bill Sharp, a Black man, was a copy supervisor at J. Walter Thompson in Chicago at the time. He later went on to become VP of Advertising at Coca-Cola, and launched his own Atlanta-based ad agency. Bill Sharp was one of the pioneers among African Americans in the advertising business.

Created by these two men in 1967, the Basic Advertising Course was the forerunner to the 4A's MAIP program, which began six years later, in 1973. The BAC grew out of 1960s civil rights efforts in various business sectors, and was part of the 4A's nascent commitment to promoting greater diversity within advertising agencies. And so, both Carol and I entered the advertising business through a 4A's internship program created specifically for minorities.

Carol met Bill Sharp in 1968, when he attended a play on the Northwestern campus. He was so impressed with the work that he decided to meet the playwright, Carol Williams. Sharp told her about the BAC program and encouraged her to apply, even though the application deadline had passed. (*It seems that both Carol and I faced deadline challenges when it came to applying for 4A's internships.*) And in spite of the fact that there were only eight openings and 165 applicants, Carol got in. That summer, Carol began learning and perfecting the craft that would become a lifelong career.

Carol was still a student, however, and at the end of the summer, she returned to Northwestern. The following summer, in 1969, Carol looked to get back into advertising and obtained an internship at the prestigious Chicago agency, Leo Burnett. At the end of the internship, Carol received two job offers; one from J. Walter Thompson, where Bill Sharp was working, and one from Leo Burnett. She chose Burnett.

While most of her classmates from the BAC lasted only a few years in advertising before leaving the profession, Carol's career thrived. Within just a couple of years, Carol became a copy supervisor, and by 1976, Carol was promoted to Vice President, Creative Director. The following year, the Women's Advertising Club of Chicago named her the Advertising Woman of the Year. At a time when neither Blacks nor women held much power or status in the advertising business, Carol Williams had both.

Carol's big break at Burnett had come on the Pillsbury account, which, initially, was not her account. Carol overheard a bunch of men talking and working in Jim Gilmore's office, so she came and stood in the doorway. Gilmore was the Associate Creative Director who had initially interviewed Carol and hired her. He invited Carol in to see what they were working on. It was an assignment for Pillsbury biscuits, which the client wished to promote as a breakfast treat. To all of these white men working on the project, biscuits belonged on the dinner table. They couldn't relate to biscuits as a breakfast item.

Carol went back to her cubicle and started to work. Even though she was a native Chicagoan, her family's southern roots brought many important traditions, including Sunday morning biscuits before church. It was a potent memory that made it easy to come up with just the right words. The next day, Carol went back to Jim Gilmore and showed him the tagline, "It's Pillsbury's best time of day." He took her line and presented it. The client loved it. That was all it took to put her on the Pillsbury account. And putting Carol on the Pillsbury account was all it took to get her noticed, including by Mr. Leo Burnett himself.

On the night that Carol Williams was inducted into the Advertising Hall of Fame in 2017, she told the story of the night many years before, when she left the office feeling anxious, insecure and blue because her Hungry Jack TV script, called "Uncle Henry", had been rejected by the client. As she rode down in the elevator, the legendary Leo Burnett, smoking a big cigar, stepped onto the elevator to join her. With just a few short words, he let the young copywriter know that not only did he know her name and who she was, but he had read her TV script and said, "Anybody who can write 'Uncle Henry' can write anything they want."

Carol went on to create "Say hello to Poppin Fresh Dough" (the actual name of the Pillsbury Doughboy), and "Frosting so smooth and creamy, you can spread it with a paper knife."

Carol was creating great advertising campaigns and winning awards for them. She was also helping her clients sell an awful lot of products. Just like Caroline Jones, Carol Williams believed that all good advertising was built upon a solid foundation of smart strategy. In Carol's career, perhaps the most famous example of this was her work for Secret Anti-Perspirant, which became a literal case study in smart marketing.

At the time, the leading anti-perspirant brands were Right Guard and Ban, and both were targeted to men. But the early 1970s were a time when women were entering the workforce in rapidly growing numbers. These new working women were very focused on how they presented themselves and being at their best. This wasn't about feeling dainty and pretty, but about avoiding sweaty armpits at the office. They needed a strong anti-perspirant.

Here again, Carol was able to draw upon a perspective that her white, male counterparts could not relate to. For Black women, being part of the workforce was nothing new. Black women have always worked, and rarely were the jobs ever glamorous. And so, Carol understood perfectly that what women wanted was an anti-perspirant that was "*Strong enough for a man, but made for a woman.*" The line, and the campaign, made advertising history. And Secret became the number one anti-perspirant brand in America.

Carol was now a big name in the advertising business nationally, and agencies across the country came calling. Among those, FCB offered Carol a Senior Vice Presidency and the top job running the creative department for their San Francisco office. Although San Francisco was a long way from her family in Chicago, in 1980, she took the job, only to discover that it was also a very long way from the world she knew at Leo Burnett.

Leo Burnett was known as a place where the only thing that mattered was whether you were any good and could do the work. If you were a good creative, all the other nonsense tended to fall away. Although Burnett was hardly a beacon of diversity, Carol's abilities tended to insulate her from having to deal with the discrimination and mistreatment that most Black ad professionals experienced. Burnett had been a nurturing cocoon for Carol.

Not so at FCB.

After just two years, Carol Williams decided that she had enough of FCB and enough of the advertising business. The toxic, racist environment that had driven so many other Black professionals out of the business, was finally more than she could take. Carol walked away, choosing instead to spend the time with her new husband, Dr. Tipkins Hood, her new family, and travel the world for a bit.

But when Carol left the business, her former clients went looking for her. They offered her freelance creative consulting projects. At first, she resisted, but the inquiries and offers kept coming. Eventually, Carol said yes, and a steady stream of independent project engagements followed. Carol conducted her own focus group research, developed strategies and brand positioning, and created the campaigns.

In 1985, Carol was contacted by someone from Pacific Bell who wanted to engage her services. But this time the assignment was different. The client asked her, "Do you know how to do targeted advertising?"

Carol understood that "targeted advertising" meant advertising targeted to African Americans. To herself, Carol thought, "I'm Black and I sure know advertising," so she told him, chuckling, "Yeah! I can do it!"

At the time, there were no other west coast Black ad agencies. There was no one else. This gave Carol the opportunity for an important new beginning in her career, a reset as the first major Black-owned advertising agency on the west coast. In 1986, Carol launched Carol H. Williams Advertising (CHWA), operating at first from Carol's living room. But Carol's career reset wasn't quite so easy.

> *"I found out it was a lot harder than I thought it was, because when you really want to dig deep and understand the cultural insights, it's bigger than just functioning on the executional level or casting a person of color. There were certain issues in the marketplace and a lot of times mass market agencies don't realize that it's much deeper."* (Excerpted from an interview with Carol Williams by Judy Foster Davis in 2014.)

Carol was learning what many, many mainstream agency professionals were learning; this stuff is not so easy! The difference, however, was that Carol understood how to leverage her own experience and perspective to access and understand the perspectives of other Black consumers. And Carol was prepared to make the commitment to put all her chips on the table and make this her new professional calling.

This became the credo of her new agency: "*Whose eyes are you looking through when you view the world?*" This credo served Carol and her agency well. Throughout the 1990s, her agency grew steadily, acquiring blue-chip clients, from Coca-Cola to General Mills, from AARP to Cingular Wireless and Wells Fargo. By the late 90s, CHWA was consistently listed among the top 10 Black advertising agencies in the country.

In 2002, Carol's agency won the African American business for the General Motors account. Overnight, this huge new assignment transformed the agency from "Top 10" to #2, just behind Global Hue. The sudden growth spurt became a massive organizational challenge for Carol, as the agency doubled its personnel roster and took on the logistics of a client this size. Not all of those challenges were met fully or optimally, but Carol held the agency together.

And then, in the fall of 2008, on the eve of an historic presidency, the nation's economy collapsed. And nowhere was the impact of the collapsing economy more devastating than on the automobile industry. There was genuine danger that the entire American car industry might implode. Suddenly, the client that had transformed Carol H. Williams Advertising into an all-star giant, had turned off the spigot. The targeted advertising stopped almost completely. Most of the agency's other clients also cut their budgets.

As has always been the case, corporate America perceives multicultural marketing as a luxury that is affordable only in good times, not as a business essential. There will always be "next year" for multicultural marketing budgets. Practically overnight, CHWA went from several hundred employees to 60 or 70. Many agencies would have simply folded up their tents and called it a day. But through grit, savvy and her father's advice that only quitters leave the game before it's over, Carol stuck it out. She survived.

When Carol and I met in the winter of 2015, she had endured a few long, hard years of "survival mode." That was, in fact, part of what shaped my interest in talking to Carol. I told her that I always wanted to meet her, and I would be thrilled to work with her. And I told her that I wanted to be part of the team that put Carol H. Williams Advertising back on top once again.

I joined the agency in January 2016. Carol asked me to run the agency's New York office, which included the U.S. Army account and a handful of other businesses. CHWA was headquartered in Oakland, California, with offices in Chicago and New York.

The U.S. Army account was the agency's 800-pound gorilla, a huge account and revenue source for CHWA. Even so, the account had shrunk considerably over the past decade of the relationship. This was not because the Army had decreased its advertising budget. The U.S. government and the Department of Defense don't decrease budgets. Ever. The revenue shrinkage was due entirely to the controlling hand of the prime contractor agency, McCann Worldgroup. And money that disappeared from our agency's bottom line always managed to reappear in McCann's pockets.

There were ten agencies that worked on the Army account, all under the management and control of the prime contractor agency, McCann. Most of those ten agencies were owned by McCann, or by McCann's parent company, Interpublic. One was not; Carol H. Williams Advertising, one of the very few privately held large minority agencies in the country. When all of those other agencies did well, it meant that McCann did well. When CHWA did well, it meant that money was going someplace other than McCann.

I think you can see the problem with that.

In the beginning, Carol H. Williams Advertising was paid directly by the Army client. But the government (always) pays its bills too slow, usually around 120 days. That's a major cash-flow hardship for a minority-owned business. So, Carol's CFO complained to McCann and asked for their help getting paid faster. And McCann was eager to help.

They said, "Let us pay you instead of the Army. We'll pay you net 30 days." And they smiled.

And so, Carol's CFO convinced her that it would be so much better to be paid in 30 days instead of 120 days. Lots and lots of legal papers were signed and voila! McCann Worldgroup was now in control of every nickel that would—or would not—be paid to CHWA on the Army account. Almost overnight, CHWA's role on the account began to shrink. We used to do PR. That was taken away. We used to do events. That was taken away. And then McCann came for the big one. They told Carol that she would need to relinquish the African American media buying. That core responsibility and revenue lode would be turned over to a small, minority-owned media company that no one had ever heard of before. They were hand-picked by Universal McCann, the media buying unit of McCann Worldgroup. Carol recommended that she be allowed to vet this obscure new company, but the request was denied.

CHWA would continue to handle planning the print and broadcast media targeted to African Americans, but PennGood, this other obscure company, would handle the financial transaction. And PennGood would be responsible for paying the media. The only problem was that they didn't pay the media. The Army paid McCann. McCann paid PennGood. But PennGood never paid the media companies. At least that is what the media companies claimed when lawsuits began appearing left and right. The media attempted to sue PennGood. Unfortunately, PennGood's attorney said he had no idea where his clients were, or even if they were still in the country. That's right. The attorney for PennGood had no idea where the agency's owners were. They had disappeared. So the media sued Carol H. Williams Advertising. After all, they didn't get their money from PennGood and they had to sue **somebody**.

Defending her agency against this lawsuit cost Carol literally hundreds of thousands of dollars, while McCann, who set all of this in motion, told Carol, "Isn't this awful that this happened to you? We feel terrible."

All of this was already in motion when I came on board in January of 2016. So, a key part of my objective in my new role was to begin pushing back against McCann, and pushing back hard. Carol H. Williams Advertising was going to continue to deliver outstanding work to the U.S. Army client, but the agency had been pushed around and abused by McCann, and that needed to stop right away.

One of the chronic problems with McCann was communication. When it came to the dissemination of vital (and often time-sensitive) task information to the multicultural subcontractor agencies, McCann routinely treated it as an afterthought. Simply not that important.

"Oh, yeah, that happened last week. We didn't get a chance to tell you. We were busy."

It's no fun walking into a meeting without having read the briefing materials because you never received them. Information is power.

Willfully withholding information is a reliable way of maintaining an iron grip on that power.

The account managers on the U.S. Army account at McCann often seemed to resemble a brigade of "Karens", hired for their ability to dish out micro-aggressions and passive-aggressive behavior. Their specialty was handing out assignments to the multicultural agencies with the instruction that "I need this by the end of the day today."

This would send the relevant multicultural agency into a frenzied fire drill, scrambling to meet the impossible deadline. So it came as quite a shock to the McCann account managers the first time that I replied to them, "No. I'll let you know when I can get this back to you."

Predictably, this produced a gob-smacked, "Excuse me??!!"

For the first few times that this happened, I would point out that Army guidelines were quite explicit in stating that the multicultural agencies are "subject matter experts" who are the only ones with the authority to determine how long it will take to complete and deliver an assignment.

"But I need this today!"

"Then you should have given us the assignment a lot sooner."

"Well, when will I get it?"

"We'll let you know."

The account manager would storm off in a huff to complain to her management. McCann management would be unhappy, but knew there was nothing they could do. On the U.S. Army account, you follow Army guidelines or there will be hell to pay, even for McCann.

The Army was unlike any account I ever worked on. There were roughly 500 people, spread across the ten agencies, who worked on the account. Keeping track of who-did-what sometimes seemed impossible. The orientation and onboarding process for new staff members took weeks, and still it only scratched the surface. There was a 134-page glossary of abbreviations and acronyms that you had to learn. God forbid you were in a meeting and the client used an acronym and you did not know what it meant. And everything had to be documented. Your paper trail needed a paper trail. Your days were spent reading paperwork, generating paperwork or sitting in meetings. And with ten agencies and 500 people, there was always a meeting you were supposed to be sitting in.

Because so much of the work on the account was bureaucratic, most of the agencies staffed the account with competent bureaucrats, skilled paper-pushers, believing that this met the Army client in their comfort zone and would impress them. It did not. First, no one was ever going to out-clerk the Army. They were in a league all their own. Second, that simply was not why they hired us. They hired us for the things they couldn't do; be smart marketers.

We dealt with many different departments and divisions within the Army, but mostly we dealt with a department called AMRG (Army Marketing & Research Group). They were our day-to-day clients. One day, during a bathroom break in the middle of a very long client meeting, I found myself standing at a men's room urinal next to the head of AMRG. The client was not a particularly big man, but he had the physical presence of R. Lee Ermey in Full Metal Jacket (Yes, I know, that's a Marine movie.)

He said to me, "You know, you're the smartest person in the room."

"Thanks," I said, preferring not to make eye contact.

"And the rest of the people in that conference room know it, but they'll never fucking tell you." And then he pointed over his shoulder. "And so does that guy in the stall, listening to our conversation." He grinned as we both heard a toilet flush.

On the Army account, "Mission" was the technical term for the Army's annual recruitment quota. Literally everything we did in Army marketing was about "making Mission." Everything else was irrelevant. And that was what made our agency bullet-proof on the Army account. Because nobody—and I mean fucking nobody—was as good as Carol H. Williams Advertising at helping the Army to "make Mission."

Let's say, for example, that Army Command has set a target of 65,000 successful recruitment contracts for the coming year. That 65,000 becomes "Mission" and it is the mission of AMRG and the agency teams to deliver that Mission. That mission then gets divided up proportionately among the various ethnic groups and the various agencies must deliver their share.

Okay, I'm going to get a little bit technical here. Sorry.

USAREC (U.S. Army Recruiting) is the department of the Army responsible for recruiting. They use a metric called P2P. P2P stands for "Production-2-Population." P2P is a measure of the percentage of successful enlistment contracts compared to the percentage of population of 17-24 year-olds (the target audience) for each of the various ethnic groups.

Ideal P2P is 100.0, which indicates the percentage of production for a given racial group is equal to the population percentage for that racial group. 100 means you hit your target. Above 100 means you outperformed your target, and under 100 means you underperformed. For example, if African Americans represent 14.2% of the population in that age range, then 14.2% of that year's new recruits should be African American. That would be a P2P of 100. And that would mean that the Army's African American ad agency is doing its job well.

Since 2012, white P2P stats have underperformed, with performance numbers getting lower each successive year, declining from 95.1 to 89.1. Over this same period, Hispanic P2P stats have been abysmal, ranging from 72.1 to 68.2. Fortunately for the Army, over this same period, Black P2P stats have ranged from 137.0 to 161.4. The net result is that Black over-performance effectively picked up the slack for the other ethnic groups, helping to ensure that the Army met its overall Mission target.

So . . . maybe the Black agency just got lucky. Maybe Blacks were going to enlist at disproportionately higher rates no matter which agency was handling the advertising.

That might be so, except the statistics say otherwise. After 9/11/2001, Black P2P dropped precipitously as the "War on Terror" (i.e., the war on Muslims) alienated a sizable segment of African Americans. African American recruitment remained at or below 100 for a full decade. The numbers did not turn upward until 2011/2012, when the first advertising campaign from Carol H. Williams Advertising launched. The slump immediately halted and a new decade of robust performance began.

The CHWA campaign for the Army was built on a foundation of meaningful consumer insight and smart strategy. Both McCann and the Army had conducted a tremendous amount of market research on millennial attitudes and mindset. They found that this new generation, which came of age in the aftermath of 9/11, was very focused on being the agent of positive social change. This target audience wanted to change the world. However, not surprisingly, McCann's research under-sampled African Americans and under-represented the young, African American perspective.

White millennials wanted to change the world. Black millennials wanted to change *their* world. That subtle difference meant everything. It meant a completely different strategic direction. Young Black men and women were focused on lifting up their own communities, and they understood the first step to accomplishing this objective would be to lift themselves up. White millennials saw military service as a calling, a call of duty, a noble service. Black millennials saw the Army as a transaction; pay for my college and train me in a sought-after vocation skill so that I can go back to my community and make things better.

Carol H. Williams Advertising conducted its own research. It understood the target audience and what motivated them, and the agency built a compelling campaign around those insights. That's what delivered those amazing P2P numbers.

Not only was the Black agency doing a great job, it was preventing AMRG and USAREC from being embarrassed by McCann's underperformance.

And so, when the time came for McCann, et al. to compete in an open RFP for renewal of their contract with the Army, the McCann executives were eager (and in fact quite anxious) for Carol Williams to sign a "Teaming Agreement" formalizing a pledge that her agency would continue to be part of the "McCann Worldgroup team" on the Army account. McCann pressured me daily to get Carol's signature on the agreement. They were extremely worried that another big agency would woo us away, and together we would poach the Army account.

But Carol was a shrewd negotiator. She told McCann that if they wanted her to stay on the team, McCann would have to indemnify her and her agency completely from the ridiculous PennGood lawsuit that McCann caused in the first place. McCann's lawyers balked and Carol dug in her heels. McCann offered to cover Carol's legal expenses. She told them that was only half a loaf. She needed full indemnification, and she needed it in writing. McCann's lawyer called Carol's lawyer. He was irate. He instructed her attorney to tell Carol to stop playing games and sign the damned teaming agreement, and once he had it, he would work on what she asked for.

At the time, Carol was flying back to Oakland from Washington, where she had just come from giving a deposition in the lawsuit. As she boarded the plane, she called me from her cell phone and shared these last few details with me.

"Mark, there's a lot of money on the line here. A whole lot of money. What do you think we should do?" She asked me.

"Only you can make this decision, Carol, but I'll tell you what I think."

"That's all I want, darling. I'll make the decision." I think Carol had already made up her mind, but she wanted to hear what I would say.

I took a moment to think before I spoke. "Carol, in all the years that McCann has worked with us, they have never treated the agency with respect. They have never treated us as an equal partner. It was their reckless decision-making that got us in this lawsuit, then they turned their back on you." I paused again for a moment. "Now they want you to just shut up and sign the damned teaming agreement before they get around to their half of the bargain." One last pause. "Carol, tell them to kiss your ass."

"Mark, you got that right." I could hear her smile through the phone. "But my flight is about to take off and I have to turn off this phone. So, you're going to have to call McCann and deliver the good news."

"If that's what you want me to do, I'll take care of it." And the two of us hung up.

It never occurred to McCann that Carol might stand her ground. No one at McCann was prepared for this outcome. Subcontractor agencies are supposed to be subservient. McCann was left completely flat-footed. Not only would they have to scramble to find another free-agent African American agency willing to partner with them on the contract renewal pitch, but they would also have to explain to the client why Carol H. Williams Advertising, the agency highly regarded by the Army client, the agency that had partnered with McCann for several years, had now chosen to walk away.

The news caused a ripple effect of disruptions throughout the 10-agency team on the account. Unfortunately, there was another nine months remaining on the current contract. Another nine months of working together. It was as awkward and uncomfortable as you could imagine, perhaps more. After seven months, McCann decided to write Carol a check so that we would just go away.

It was not a good time for McCann. Perhaps karma had caught up with them. Their bid for the Army contract renewal was disqualified in the first round due to multiple technical errors. This was an almost unheard-of loss for an incumbent, and of course, McCann would appeal. At the same time, two separate scandals broke in the trade press regarding the relationship between McCann and the Army. The first story involved a marriage-wrecking affair between one of the Army clients and a senior account person at McCann. The second story involved alleged payoffs and bribes by McCann to certain Army clients, including "duffle bags full of cash", as one reporter alleged. The outcome of these stories was quietly and discreetly handled outside of media purview, but it was pretty clear to all observers that McCann's relationship with the Army would never recover.

And it never did.

Meanwhile, Carol and her agency moved on. CHWA had just won the 2020 U.S. Census account. This was again part of a mega 10-agency team, this time led by VMLY&R. (Formerly Y&R, formerly Young & Rubicam. VML was some Kansas City digital agency no one ever heard of before.) The 2020 U.S. Census account, just like the Army account, would be another episode of minority agency sharecropping.

If I gave the impression that McCann is somehow unique in their treatment of, and attitudes toward, minority agencies, they most definitely are not. They are probably no worse, or better, than most other major mainstream agencies that routinely "partner" with minority-owned agencies as a marriage of convenience in order to qualify to pitch major accounts, especially large, lucrative government accounts. Whether it is McCann or VMLY&R, FCB or any other advertising mega-player, it's all sharecropping on Madison Avenue.

CHAPTER TWENTY-SEVEN

"We're so glad you're here"

In New York State, Governor Cuomo and the state legislature made it a requirement that all state contracts in all state agencies and departments must include a set-aside of 30% for minority-owned businesses. A set-aside means that, no matter what happens with the rest of the contract, 30% of the contract must be awarded to one or more minority-owned businesses. This is very progressive. It's good for the state and it's good for minority businesses.

Win-win.

It's a little less straight-forward in actual practice, however, because government transparency isn't always what it should be. Despite the rules and regulations, and the very best of intentions, government RFPs (Requests for Proposals) are not promoted in a way that makes them known to all potential bidders and vendors. The only people who typically know when a new RFP is being issued are the same companies that already do business with the government again and again and again.

There is nothing to prevent a newcomer from submitting a contract proposal, but that assumes, of course, that they know about the RFP in the first place.

Still, the 30% minority business set-aside is a very good thing. I know it's a good thing because Campbell Ewald, a New York mainstream advertising agency called up Carol H. Williams Advertising to say, "We'd like to give you some business. Can you help us?"

To which Carol happily replied, "Why yes, I think we can."

Campbell Ewald is the ad agency handling the Empire State Development account for the State of New York. Empire State Development is the business development counterpart to New York's tourism marketing. Their job is to attract businesses to the state. And because of the contract set-aside legislation, Campbell Ewald was required to find a minority-owned business partner that could handle 30% of the contract. Carol's agency is not owned by a big advertising holding company, it is independent and 100% minority-owned. Carol's agency is also 100% woman-owned, so her agency is able to check two boxes on the contract.

Even though Campbell Ewald reached out to us and invited us to join them on the account, the arrangement between the two agencies always felt more like a shotgun wedding than a relationship. C-E was quite content for our agency to do absolutely as little as possible on the account. In fact, they preferred it that way. It was like being invited to someone's home and being told not to touch anything. CHWA was not to have any involvement in the creation or production of any advertising. Our role would be strictly media. Even there, CHWA would not have any involvement in the development of media plans for where the advertising should run. C-E would do that too. All of the areas where our agency brought unique expertise were not of any interest to them. Our only role would be to purchase media that C-E had planned. We would purchase 30% of all the media and earn commissions from that share of the plan. That would satisfy the legislative requirement of the set-aside without interfering with what C-E wanted to do on the account. It was, literally, the least we could do. The two agencies barely had to talk to each other. But we earned our money, and we were happy to cash the checks.

But circumstances changed in January of 2016, right around the time that I joined CHWA. (The timing was purely coincidental, I swear.) Campbell Ewald suddenly found themselves stepping on a landmine of their own planting, and the agency found itself splashed across the front pages of not just the industry trade publications, but the general media as well.

The Creative Director of C-E's San Antonio office had written and sent out an agency-wide email announcing that . . ., well, I'll just quote from his email.

> *"Please share with the teams that today is officially Ghetto Day in the SA, and we're inviting our Big D home-bitches to cycle in and pop a freak with us. Ghetto music, Malt 45s at lunch, and of course, drugs and prostitution are legal all day until close of business. Word, my cerebral gangsters."*

That was bad. But what made it worse was the fact that the email had been written and circulated in October. It was now January. And someone at the agency had now leaked the email to the media. Of course, the first question that reporters were asking was, "What action did the agency take to discipline the Creative Director who wrote the email?"

At first, the response was, "Well, uh . . ." But then, the agency's PR department stepped in and informed the press that the agency has zero tolerance for this sort of thing, and they released the following statement from the agency CEO.

> *"This email is in no way reflective of who we are as an agency and what we stand for. We addressed this matter very seriously when it happened back in October. To those that were hurt and offended by this language, we sincerely apologize."*

Campbell Ewald proudly announced that they had fired the Creative Director. But that didn't happen back in October when the email was circulated. It happened, uh . . . yesterday, four months after the email was sent. That did not go over well with the agency's clients, who began firing Campbell Ewald, one after another. Within just a couple of weeks, Campbell Ewald was cut to half its size. So, Interpublic, C-E's parent company, fired the CEO and prayed that they could stop the client exodus.

After that, Campbell Ewald started acting very nice to us at Carol H. Williams Advertising, at least on the surface.

A year later, Campbell Ewald called us again to say that they had a new piece of New York State business where they would need our help. The new account was the Port Authority of New York & New Jersey. Apparently, our original arrangement was working well enough that Campbell Ewald did not hesitate to call on us again. This time, however, was different, and we were only just beginning to understand how different. Right at the start, C-E told us that the client wanted to meet us, and they wanted Carol to fly out from California for the meeting. After several years on Empire State Development, we had never met the client. Never. The request from the Port Authority client seemed like a very good sign.

Little bits of additional information began to trickle in from C-E. The client would like us to present our agency credentials and capabilities when we meet. A few days later we heard that the client might want us to work on creating advertising as well as media. We were game. We were eager.

On the day of the meeting, Carol and I went to Port Authority headquarters at 4 World Trade Center, directly across the street from where the twin towers once stood, and now the site of the World Trade Center Memorial and Museum. There is no building on that ground, nor will there ever be. The new World Trade Tower stands one block north. Just looking across the street at the site makes your body move more slowly, with an unconscious and involuntary solemnity. There is a stillness about the space that has its own energy, like a force that slows the rotation of the earth. It was a weird feeling, and it had the effect of slightly dampening our enthusiasm and anticipation as we entered the Port Authority building for our meeting. In the building lobby, more than a dozen Campbell Ewald people were waiting for us with a look of slight agitation. We were on time, but we were not early. They wanted us to be early so that they could "prepare us" for the meeting. Even though they already had the Port Authority account, they planned to present their agency credentials to the client as well. They did not wish to be upstaged by anything that Carol and I might do. They were going to put on a whole show with a small army of their senior people.

When we all stepped off the elevator on the 21st floor, we had a bit of an odd reception. Actually, it was no reception at all. This was a floor without a receptionist and without any reception area at all, just the area where you come and go from the elevators. There was a phone on the wall alongside a locked glass door, but there was no directory or listing, so we had no idea what to do with the phone. When we were in the lobby downstairs, building security called and definitely alerted someone to our arrival, and that person said to send us up. So, someone definitely knew we were here. But no one came to the door. As we had begun to debate whether to simply go back downstairs, a security guard happened to wander by, and we shouted for him to let us in, which he did.

But then he asked us a question we were unable to answer. "Do you know what conference room your meeting is in?"

We had no idea.

One of us asked, "There's more than one?"

"Oh yes." The guard nodded. "There's quite a few."

"It's a large meeting," I said. "With quite a few people."

"Then you probably want 21-C." The guard answered, as he pointed to the left.

So we all marched as a group down the long narrow corridor to 21-C, and someone opened the door to look inside. "Is this the marketing meeting?"

"No. It's not." Came the curt reply. "Try the other end of the floor."

We did, and this time we got lucky. Someone opened the door and we were greeted by multiple calls of "Hi. Hello. Don't be shy. Come on in." The greetings were genuinely warm and friendly, but there was absolutely no acknowledgment that we expected someone to meet us at the elevators. There were about a dozen people seated around an enormous 20-foot long boardroom table, with another three or four who wandered in after we arrived. Every spot at the extra long table was filled.

And then someone began handing out this 11 x 17 sheet with the Port Authority logo. On this sheet were close to two dozen color photographs—head shots—of all the members of the Port Authority Marketing Department, from the Chief Communications Officer to the junior staff members. Under each head shot was the name, title, email address and phone number of each person. It was extremely thorough and tremendously helpful. And, in 40+ years in this business, I have only seen a client do this once or twice before. Everyone then went around the room and introduced him or herself. This was clearly an extremely important ritual for the client.

After introductions were completed and someone briefly summarized the meeting agenda, the Campbell Ewald team began their credentials presentation. C-E had given me an advance copy of their deck the night before (encouraging me to reciprocate by sending them my deck) and I saw that their presentation contained 135 slides. My suspicion was that C-E intended to filibuster the meeting with their presentation, so that the clock would run out before we got to our credentials.

Fortunately, after about 40 or 50 slides in, the client spoke up. Jawauna Greene, the Director of Brand and Customer Partnerships, seemed to be the point person from the client side. She led the meeting, and she was the one speaking up now. "You know, we've already seen this presentation. That's how Campbell Ewald won our business." The client smiled. "Why don't we take a quick bathroom break and when we come back, Carol can present her credentials." Jawauna looked slowly around the room to see if anyone was going to challenge her.

Jawauna had only recently relocated to New York and joined the Port Authority. Previously, she was Director of Advertising and Marketing for the Washington, DC Metropolitan Transit Authority, and prior to that, she held a similar position with the Maryland Transit Authority. She was the de facto leader of her team and very comfortable in that position.

Carol got up from the table and Jawauna quickly came around and said, "Let me show you where the ladies' room is." And the two ladies left the conference room.

I got up to go to the men's room, but no one rushed to show me where it was. I followed behind Carol and Jawauna, assuming that the men's room would probably be next to the ladies' room. It wasn't. In fact, it wasn't anywhere near the ladies' room. At that moment, I began thinking to myself, "Yeah, this building floor plan must have been laid out by the Port Authority." I think that at one point I crossed paths with that security guard who let us in an hour earlier. By the time I found my way to the men's room and back, everyone else was in his seat and the meeting was ready to reconvene.

As I sat down, Carol pulled at my sleeve. "I need to talk to you later."

"Is everything okay?" I asked, half puzzled, and half concerned.

"I think so." Carol replied.

Now I was just perplexed. But Carol smiled a knowing smile and said, "Just give the presentation and show them what we do. Just do your thing." So, I did. Carol and I have presented together so many times that we have a rhythm. We finish each other's sentences. We ask each other questions to unspool stories. We give a good show and make it look casual and impromptu.

At the end, Jawauna announced that the Port Authority had a serious image problem, both among consumers and among businesses. They were going to need smart marketing and advertising to help them address those challenges and there was going to be a great deal of work— for both agencies in the weeks and months ahead. Jawauna then turned and spoke directly to Carol. "I'm going to need you to do some of that great advertising work for us."

"We are honored to be asked and happy to help." Carol replied.

As the meeting concluded and Carol and I left the building together, her car service drove us back up to midtown. In the car, we had that talk Carol wanted to have.

Carol leaned toward me as though confiding a secret. "I think this is going to be a very interesting client."

"Oh?" I had nothing more to volunteer.

"When I came out of the ladies' room, the client was standing there by the door, waiting for me to come out." Carol began.

"That's nice."

"That woman grabbed my arm and said, 'We're so glad you're here.' So, I said, "Thank you."" Carol grabbed my arm to demonstrate what happened. "She said, 'You don't understand. We made them go get you and bring you to the meeting. They didn't want to do that.' So, I said, what was that all about?"

Okay, this story was getting interesting.

Jawauna Greene told Carol that when Campbell Ewald came for their first big meeting at the Port Authority, she called them out for their conspicuous lack of diversity. She said, "You brought 13 people to this meeting and not one of them is a person of color. Don't you have ANY people of color back at your agency?"

Carol started to laugh. "Mark, I was trying my best to keep a straight face while she was telling me this. And then she told the Campbell Ewald folks, 'Wasn't your agency in trouble last year for not having any diversity? Didn't you fix that?'"

Now I started to laugh. "She told them that?"

"She told them that the Port Authority's biggest advertising project in the coming year was around diversity and inclusion, and she could not have an all-white agency working on diversity for the Port Authority." Carol shook her head. "Campbell Ewald probably thinks this client is crazy." And then Carol smiled. "But she's my kind of crazy."

The car service driver must have thought that his two passengers were crazy, because Carol and I were cracking up in the back of the car.

Carol stopped laughing and composed herself. After a pause, she looked at me seriously and asked, "Don't you just love it when a client has some goddamn sense?"

CHAPTER TWENTY-EIGHT

Sharecropping on Madison Avenue

Sharecropping is a system where the landlord/planter allows a tenant (usually a poor, Black family) to farm the land in exchange for a share of the crops they harvest. This encouraged the poor tenants to work hard to produce the biggest harvest that they could, and it ensured they would remain tied to the land and unlikely to leave for other opportunities. In many cases, the landlords would lease equipment to the tenants, and offer seed, fertilizer, food, and other items on credit until the harvest season. At that time, the tenant and landlord would settle up, figuring out who owed whom and how much.

High interest rates, unpredictable harvests, and unscrupulous landlords kept tenant families severely indebted, requiring the debt to be carried over until the next year or the year after that. Laws favoring landowners made it difficult, or even illegal, for sharecroppers to sell their crops to others besides their landlord. Or they prevented sharecroppers from moving if they were indebted to their landlord.

In rural America, not just in the old South, sharecropping replaced the antebellum plantation system. It was a new form of bondage and stolen labor.

Sharecropping exists on Madison Avenue as well. It looks very different, but feels very much the same.

The majority of accounts held by multicultural agencies are with clients they share with a mainstream agency. The multicultural agency works on a particular ethnic segment, while the mainstream agency works on the general market. (*If I have not said so before, terms like "mainstream" and "general market" are used here because they are the common vernacular of our business, not because they are technically accurate.*) It isn't necessarily a bad arrangement. Often it works fairly well, especially when the clients are smart, and they care about the success of their marketing programs. When it is done right and done well, inter-agency collaboration is a thing of beauty and a marvel to behold. Sometimes, however, a client will insist that the multicultural agency follow the creative and strategic lead of the mainstream agency, even when it makes absolutely no marketing sense to do so. The client is focused entirely on ensuring that nothing detracts from the mainstream campaign and directs their multicultural agency to carry out an "ethnic version" of the mainstream campaign.

Why bother hiring a multicultural agency when all you really want is an ethnic casting director? At multicultural agencies, we call this "man-tanning."

These are clients who hired their minority agencies strictly because their management told them to, strictly for political cover and to keep the activists and picket signs out of their parking lot. They hired their minority agency because it's good optics. Multicultural agencies accept these "stay in the kitchen" relationships, even at the cost to their self-respect, because it is still better than not having the business at all. Sometimes, being Black on Madison Avenue means that pride is expendable. Sometimes survival is the only rule in the game.

But this is not what I meant by sharecropping on Madison Avenue. This is not the bad stuff. This is just the everyday reality. This stuff is so commonplace, no one loses any sleep over it.

Every agency wants to win the really big accounts, accounts with the ability to actually change the size of the agency, accounts that enable agencies to weather the really tough days in agency life, accounts that offer the opportunity to deliver your very best work, work you can show off for years afterward. These are the whales that we all go after. And just like Captain Ahab, sometimes we hunt that whale to our own peril.

When a whale goes up for review, it takes a team of agencies to catch it. Ad agencies today have become so highly specialized in their positioning and their offering that no single agency possesses the portfolio of capabilities and resources to meet the comprehensive marketing needs of a whale client. Not even a team of two or three agencies is enough. Typically, answering the RFP of a whale requires assembling a team of at least five agencies, and sometimes (especially on big government contracts) as many as ten agencies. This gaggle of agencies ("team" seems too generous a label) is led by the big alpha agency in the bunch, the agency that declares themselves to be the "prime" agency for the engagement. All of the other agencies are "sub" or "subcontractor" agencies. Ninety per cent of the time, all of these sub agencies are all owned by the same parent company as the prime agency. They are all family. They operate separately, but they play like family.

That is, of course, except for the multicultural agencies. More often than not, multicultural agencies are not part of the family. Instead, they are whichever multicultural agency happens to be available when the prime agency is ready to pitch. It is likely that the minority agency pitched with the prime agency previously, but their only actual connection is familiarity.

Why not work with a multicultural agency that is part of your parent company family? After all, every advertising holding company owns one. Good question. The answer is basic math. Advertising holding companies like Omnicom or WPP or Interpublic all have 50-100 agencies in their network, including at least a half-dozen or more that would present as prime agencies. But they will only have one African American agency, one Hispanic agency, and one Asian agency in their entire network. Those three little agencies can't possibly be available for every new business opportunity in their network. So, the prime agencies have to shop outside their own networks. That means doing business with somebody who is "not family." If that conjures up images of the extremely insular operations of The Godfather, you are not entirely wrong.

But there is also another dynamic, and I would be remiss not to mention it. More often than you might guess, the prime agency simply does not like working with the multicultural agency that is part of their parent company network. No one ever offers an official explanation, but they just refuse to work with them. One explanation is that as soon as one of the giant financial holding companies buys up a small, entrepreneurial, independent-minded multicultural shop, the small agency starts to suck. Badly. These holding companies try to run something that they don't really understand and everything about the collaboration quickly goes off course. The giant holding company assumes that they are the best thing that ever happened to this insignificant little multicultural agency, but in reality, they probably have accidentally smothered it to death.

And now these prime agencies look outside the family for minority-owned agencies they can team with.

To be part of the "team" that will work on one of these great big accounts, the minority agency must sign a contract with the prime agency, not with the client. Legally, the minority agency signs away the right to have any relationship with the client. The minority agency must deal only with the prime agency. And that contract comes with a handful of serious restrictions.

- The minority agency agrees not to place its agency name on any of its work product, but must instead refer to itself and its work as coming from "Team _____."
- The minority agency is not permitted to have any contact or communication with the client unless the prime agency is present. This includes telephone conversations and email communications.
- The minority agency is not permitted to disparage the prime agency in any way. This includes any statements that are critical of the prime agency, its operations, its personnel, its work or recommendations. Not in internal communications, inter-agency (within the team) communications, or communications with the client.
- The minority agency is not permitted to speak to the press about its work on the account, unless cleared to do so by the prime agency.
- The marketing budget for the minority agency will be set at the discretion of the prime agency.

- The agency retainer fee for the minority agency will be set at the discretion of the prime agency.
- Roles and responsibilities will be set at the discretion of the prime agency.

If the minority agency doesn't like it, the agency can take its complaints to the prime agency.

Sharecropping on Madison Avenue.

This incredibly oppressive and discriminatory system is responsible for the majority of income at many minority agencies. Their economic survival depends upon a system that oppresses and abuses them. And yet, I doubt you will find any minority agency willing to speak out against these practices. They can't take the risk that they won't be black-balled and shut out from future team agreements. You don't dare bite the hand that feeds you, even when the food is stale crumbs.

Clients love the convenience of having to enter into only one contract with one agency and managing one relationship. It's a very cost-efficient way of doing business. Managing multiple agency relationships can be a full-time job, and a lot like herding kittens. But that convenience and efficiency come at a very high cost. There is no way that the sub agencies (whether "family members" or not) can consistently deliver their best work under these operating conditions. There is no way that the best work survives getting processed through the filter of whatever makes the prime agency look good. So, the best work never reaches the client. And if the client is not getting the best work, why bother with any of this?

Where has any of this gotten us? Where has any of this gotten our clients? There has to be a better way.

The truth is that the "better way" is not all that complicated. It is not that difficult to achieve, if that is our choice. Agencies say that they want to do their best work. We are happiest and most prosperous when we do our best work. Clients say they want our best work. They hope that is what their money is buying. They would be pretty unhappy if it were not.

And we say that we want the system to be fair and equitable for everyone, and that diversity plays an important role in making it fair and equitable. Our clients say they expect this. They even go so far as to make it a mandatory provision of the RFP. A requirement.

And yet, does anyone really think that any of the mainstream agencies would bother including minority or multicultural agencies in their pitch team if it were not a requirement of the RFP? Does anyone really think they would give it five minutes of thought? Any agency that tells you that they would is lying.

There is nothing inherently wrong with a group of agencies "teaming up" to pitch a large piece of business together. In fact, it is a demonstration—and a promise—for collaboration and synergy if they are fortunate enough to win the business. And it is possible to work well together as equals. But the "prime agency" paradigm is an inherently unequal, discriminatory practice that inevitably leads to inside-the-box thinking and handcuffed creativity, at best. And millions in stolen and cheated money at worst.

The time is long overdue to abolish the prime agency system completely.

And all we have to do to change would be for clients—most especially the large, government clients—to agree to contract with each of their agencies separately and individually, so that each agency has the same rights and the same rules of engagement, so that one ad agency does not control the fortunes of another. A little extra paperwork and a little extra project management is an insignificant price to pay for the tremendous dividends that it would yield. And it would—at last—live up to the diversity, equity and inclusion objectives that so many of these clients have set.

Think of the PR bonanza that awaits the first major client to announce this. Think of the PR bonanza, the industry goodwill, and the regulatory and political support that the 4A's and the ANA (Association of National Advertisers) would receive by publicly supporting this practice. Think of the economic impact on small, independent and minority-owned agencies. That's a lot to think about.

An end to sharecropping on Madison Avenue.

Afterword

Madison Avenue Excuses
& Other Baloney

The excuses that advertising agency executives give to justify their own poor minority representation numbers are only believable if you know very little about the advertising agency business, or if your desire to believe is so strong that you are willing to swallow just about anything.

1. "We Can't Find Any Minority Professionals"

Mainstream agencies say, "*We're looking, but we just can't find any talented minority professionals to hire.*"

If that is true, why don't any of their Fortune 500 clients have the same trouble finding and hiring minority professionals? Minorities make up 10.3% *(2.9% for Blacks)* of officers and managers at New York ad agencies. Minorities make up 24% of officers and managers at DiversityInc's ranking of the top 50 corporations. That's two and a half times the representation at advertising agencies.

If mainstream agencies can't find any minority professionals, why is it that minority agencies—with *less* glamour, *less* money and *less* resources—don't have any trouble finding and hiring minority talent?

Mainstream agencies can't find any minority professionals, and yet, if they need a copywriter with six or more years of light beer experience, they can find him and hire him in less than a week, if the client is big enough. Mainstream agencies have no trouble finding what they **want** to find.

And there is one incredibly obvious truth that is being overlooked and ignored. Minority advertising professionals—in their hearts—are no different from white ad execs. We love this business. We're not sitting back waiting for you to call or find the magic key to knock on our door with a job offer. We're out there every day, knocking on **your** doors, calling **your** offices, emailing our resumes, trying to get interviews, trying to get jobs. **We're not hiding. We're standing right here, waiting for you to let us in.**

2. "They Lack the Necessary Training"

Mainstream ad agencies argue that they no longer have the time, the money or the resources for training programs. They say they simply can't afford to hire someone who isn't prepared to hit the ground running. That all seems reasonable. I can't argue with that. But then they say that the reason they haven't hired more minorities is that they lack this necessary training.

What does that mean, really?

- o Are these agencies saying that minorities in general receive less of a college education than their white counterparts?
- o Are these agencies saying that minorities in general are less willing or less able to engage in the same career preparations as their white counterparts?

On what basis do they make these sweeping generalizations and condemnations? In fact, the opposite is true. Overall, minority candidates for entry-level ad agency jobs are more likely to be significantly better trained and better prepared than their white counterparts.

How is this possible? Because the advertising industry's major trade organizations have gone to considerable lengths to make it possible.

4A's—MAIP

Since 1973, the 4A's has conducted the **Multicultural Advertising Internship Program** to encourage college students of color to consider advertising as a career.

Each year, over 100 qualified undergraduate and graduate students are selected to spend a 10-week paid summer internship at member agencies nationwide.

The program offers Ad agencies a ***cost-effective way*** to identify, observe and recruit highly qualified student talent. The program offers serious students of advertising the chance to gain real-world work experience, establish industry contacts and acquire valuable professional credit.

Since its inception, MAIP has graduated more than **4,000** interns. I am one of them. I am, in fact, one of the earliest alumni of this program.

AAF's Most Promising Minority Students Program

Since 1997, AAF (American Advertising Federation) has assisted in connecting the advertising industry with hundreds of outstanding minority career candidates. These are students who are deemed exceptional by their college professors/advisers and specially selected to participate in the program.

The program enables students to:

- ○ Meet recruiters from major ad agencies, media companies and client organizations
- ○ Participate in professional development workshops
- ○ Get exposure to the inner workings of major industry companies.

3. "We can't attract good people"

Mainstream ad agency executives claim that they aren't able to hire more minority professionals because multicultural agencies have swallowed up the entire talent pool.

- o Is this the answer from the people who are supposed to be masters at communicating persuasive selling messages?
- o Is this the answer from the people who spend billions of dollars every year to help their clients steal market share from the competition?
- o Is this the answer from the people who can offer better salaries, better benefits, and bigger, more glamorous assignments?

If it weren't so insulting, it would be laughable.

4. "We Can't Hold Onto People"

Mainstream ad agency executives claim that once they hire minority professionals, they don't stick around very long and they leave. This may be true. Anecdotal evidence suggests a higher-than-normal attrition rate for minority advertising professionals.

Let's say it is true. Why is that? Advertising agencies have perfected the art of "Golden Handcuffs" that make it almost impossible for their favorite employees to leave. What efforts have these agencies made to increase retention?

If it is true that minority employees are not staying, have these agencies conducted exit interviews or any other effort to learn why? To see if there is a pattern? To attempt to address the problem? If this is a real problem for you, why aren't you trying to fix it?

5. **"We Have a Diversity Program in Place" or "We've Hired a Chief Diversity Officer"**

This is perhaps the smarmiest of the excuses. *"Don't pick on us, we're the good guys. We have a diversity program in place. We're doing everything we can."*

Perhaps I am being overly cynical, but I think that many mainstream agencies believe that they never actually have to produce any results as long as they can show that they are "trying." It seems that saying that you have a diversity program or that you have hired a Chief Diversity Officer is the practical equivalent of a "get out of jail free card."

I believe we must do more than allow these agencies to get an "E" for effort. We must hold these agencies accountable to a higher action standard. Specifically:

- Does the program include measurable goals or merely feel-good mission statements?
- Have benchmarks been established so that progress can be measured?
- Does the program have a strategy for employee development and retention?
- Does the diversity program include meaningful incentives for senior management to deliver against program goals? If not, why not?
- Has the program and its goals been communicated and promoted to employees internally?
- Has management support for the program been conspicuously and unconditionally communicated to all employees?

6. **The Industry Smokescreen**

Thus far, the public discourse has been primarily about "industry statistics" for ad agency minority representation. Although industry statistics are important and do provide an overall context to the issue, they are also a diversionary veil that conceals and obscures the minority representation performance of individual agencies. The price that these individual ad agencies should pay for the incredibly regressive condition of their industry is that their individual agency statistics should be made public. Their business should be "in the street."

This public dialog on this issue can and should push past the "industry spokesperson" role played by the 4A's and make this discussion about the specific individual agencies. As long as the statistics and the responses are industry-wide, they will never be about what a specific agency is or is not doing. This prevents individual agencies from ever being vulnerable to scrutiny or to attack. This prevents individual agencies from ever being compelled to change.

7. The 4A's—Asking More From Their Members

The 4A's, the American Association of Advertising Agencies, is an outstanding organization that has been absolutely vital to the health and prosperity of the advertising industry. Historically, the accomplishments of the 4A's have demonstrated time and again its value and importance to our business.

Jock Elliott was a plain-spoken ex-Marine who went into advertising after serving in WWII. He tried his hand at copywriting at BBDO, but soon switched to account management, explaining that he was good, but not that good. He also switched from BBDO to Ogilvy & Mather and came under the mentorship of advertising legend David Ogilvy. The tutelage paid off and Jock Elliott became chairman of Ogilvy's U.S. operations in 1965 and global chairman in 1975.

Jock Elliott also served a tenure as chairman of the 4A's during the late 1960s. On April 25, 1968, while keynoting the 4A's Annual Meeting, Chairman Jock Elliot addressed the assembled advertising executives on the topic of diversity on Madison Avenue. The speech was just three weeks after the assassination of Dr. Martin Luther King Jr. This is a brief excerpt from that speech.

> "**It's up to us**. The buck stops with agency management—*with us*. Nothing will happen in the use of minority group talent unless we set the policy,

unless we make that policy known to all our staff, unless we set up procedures to make it work, unless we cope with the occasional client who drags his heels. We can't expect the copywriters or producers or the casting department to take the initiative in getting this job done. It is up to us."

It would be easy to assume that with the progress of time, the 4A's became even more forceful and forthright in its advocacy of diversity within advertising. But that assumption would be a mistake. Occasionally, the leadership of the 4A's has taken one step forward and two steps back. In the December 1991 issue of Black Enterprise magazine, former 4A's president John O'Toole was quoted as saying, "It is hard to conceive of advertising's role as depicting the ethnic diversity of American society. Advertising, in general, not only has no obligation, but it has no business trying to depict national diversity."

Of course, I sent a response, which ran in Black Enterprise and Adweek. I said that John O'Toole undoubtedly spoke accurately on behalf of the industry and most of the major agencies. I said that advertising agencies were "the Shoal Creek of the corporate world." I wasn't very popular at the 4A's for a while after that. After John O'Toole, the 4A's was led by Burtch Drake until 2008. Burtch liked me even less. The feeling was mutual. Burtch was "Mr. Status Quo", and when he retired in 2008, many in the advertising industry felt that the 4A's was long overdue for fresh leadership that reflected a more welcoming posture toward diversity. Drake's successor, Nancy Hill, represented that change and that more welcoming posture. Today, Marla Kaplowitz is at the helm of the 4A's, bringing a more progressive perspective to the association's priorities. The organization has not always moved forward with the momentum and progress that was needed, but at least it was moving in the right direction. This was (and is) probably equally true of the advertising industry that the 4A's represents.

◆ ◆ ◆

ONE FINAL RECOMMENDATION

One could easily fill an entire library with all of the recommendations and proposals that have been written about how to bring greater diversity to the advertising business. People much smarter than me have been trying to accomplish this for decades. And yet, in spite of all those words and all that effort, Madison Avenue is only slightly more diverse today than it was when I entered the business 44 years ago, or when Jock Elliott gave his speech to the 4A's 54 years ago. So, there is absolutely no reason to think that my suggestions will do anything to advance the conversation or improve the landscape. And yet, like those before me, I am compelled to try.

Instead of asking for more promises and more programs from the advertising industry, however, I propose asking for **more transparency and more accountability**. Let's harness the power of sunlight.

An Annual Report Card—
Publish the Data for Each Agency Every Year

- The 4A's doesn't actually have much power, but there are some things it may be able to do. I think that the 4A's can—and should—ask each member agency to disclose their diversity numbers—like a simple EEO-1 report, once a year for the next 10 years.
- The 4A's would take the data and create a report, not aggregating data, but showing each individual agency, and issue that report to the industry's major trade publications; Advertising Age and Adweek. These publications already publish annual agency report cards on other criteria. If they published an annual agency diversity report card, those issues would be sell-outs. I'll bet that those agencies with good records will buy pages of advertising in those issues to trumpet their performance.
- Let the numbers speak for themselves and let their clients, their prospective clients and their shareholders form their own judgments and react accordingly.

Use Salaries, Not Titles, in the Diversity Surveys

- ○ If we create an ad agency diversity report card, we have to be sure that each agency is evaluated equally. What can we use as a fair and objective method of measurement? Titles mean different things at different agencies. And at advertising agencies, some titles don't mean anything at all.

- ○ How do we measure? With money. **The golden common denominator.** Ask each agency to divide their staff into quintiles based on compensation (salary *and* bonus). Then, simply report the percentage of minorities in each compensation quintile. Specific dollar amounts are not necessary and the quintiles are completely anonymous. From this, it will be easy to tell who the valued employees are, and who are not. It will also be easy to tell if progress has been achieved year-to-year.

As I stated in the opening of this book, I have given my entire adult professional life to the advertising business. Advertising is not just what I do. It is a part of who I am. And if I wish to take some pride in what I do and who I am, I must take responsibility for addressing what's wrong with the advertising agency business and try to be a part of the solution. And so, I conclude this book not with another anecdote about me or my career, but with these observations about what is wrong and my modest suggestion for how to make it better.

Madison Avenue was not part of the original street grid of Manhattan, however, a wealthy real estate developer, Samuel Ruggles, paid to have the street added later. From its inception, money talks on Madison Avenue. The street begins in the lush, green oasis of Madison Park on East 23rd Street and runs north to the Madison Avenue Bridge at 138th Street. Some of the most exclusive and expensive shops in New York (Hermes, Prada, Baccarat, Rolex, Cartier and Jimmy Choo, to name a few) reside on Madison Avenue. These are places where you cannot even walk through the front door without an appointment. But eventually the street continues its journey north, until it finds its way across 110th Street and into Harlem, so that sooner or later, there is Black on Madison Avenue.

About the Author

Mark Robinson has spent the past 40+ years in advertising at some of the industry's most prestigious agencies. Mark has been featured in <u>Fortune</u> magazine, <u>The New York Times</u>, <u>The Wall Street Journal</u> and <u>Advertising Age</u>.

Mark is a past member of the American Advertising Federation's Multicultural Marketing Leadership Council, a national touring lecturer for the American Educational Foundation, and an ongoing mentor for MAIP (Minority Advertising Internship Program) for the American Association of Advertising Agencies.

Mark was chosen by filmmaker Spike Lee to co-found and manage his new agency, Spike/DDB. In 1998, Mark launched Heritage Apparel, an internet-based clothing company that celebrated African American history and heroes. In 2001, he was recognized as the Entrepreneur of the Year for the successful launch of his next company, S/R Communications Alliance; the first 100% minority-owned network of 10 multicultural advertising companies, with combined business of $225 million.

Mark was nominated for the 1994 Connecticut Human Rights Award for his community service and work in multicultural education. In 2000, Mark was appointed by the Governor to serve on the State's Martin Luther King Commission. And in 2009, he was chosen by the State of Connecticut to receive the Martin Luther King Leadership Award.

Mark lives in Connecticut and is a highly sought-after strategist and advisor to various clients, including political campaigns and community organizations. He also serves on the board of directors of The Connecticut Mirror newspaper.

CPSIA information can be obtained
at www.ICGtesting.com
Printed in the USA
LVHW051418210723
752765LV00015B/714